NEW DIRECTION

BIBLE READING GUIDE
with David Mainse

Crossroads Christian Communications Inc.
100 Huntley Street, Toronto, Ont. M4Y 2L1

ISBN-0-919463-11-8

Published by CROSSROADS CHRISTIAN COMMUNICATIONS INC.
100 Huntley Street, Toronto, Ontario

Copyright © 1985 Mainroads Productions

Printed in Canada by Harmony Printing Limited, Toronto, Ontario.

NEW DIRECTION

BIBLE READING GUIDE
with David Mainse

VOLUME 1

With David Mainse

Edited by Paul Knowles

Photography by David Helsdon
Graphics and layout by
Christine Campbell
Front cover by Anno Domini

FOREWORD

The Word of God is the believer's weapon. It's the "Sword of the Spirit". In fact, it's sharper than any two edged sword. With this weapon you can cut down the "strongholds of the enemy" (II Corinthians 10:4). The scripture declares:

"Then they cried out to the Lord in their trouble,
And He saved them out of their distresses.
He sent His word and healed them,
And delivered them from their destructions."

Psalm 107:19,20

Something or someone will bring you distress. God saves you out of distress by sending His Word. This book is like a daily mail delivery service which will keep the Word of God regularly as a part of your day.

For many years, we have been publishing a daily devotional guide here at Crossroads Christian Communications, Inc. I have received tremendous inspiration and input from many of our team members. I want to thank God, with all my heart, for the wonderful gift of the following loving and faithful people who had direct written input into these commentaries through the years: Rev. Bill Absolom, Rev. Cal Bombay, Richard Bowman, Rev. Ralph Bradley, Rev. Rob Brouwer, Douglas Burke, Rev. Jack Chamberlain, Geoffrey Corbett, Rev. George Elsasser, Rev. Walter Gamble, Rev. Stan Grant, Rev. Paul Hope, Paul Knowles, John Jefkins, Rev. Bob MacDougall, Rev. Onofrio Miccolis, Rev. Don Osborne, Rev. Allan Perks, Rev. James Poynter, Marion Poynter, Rev. Art Rader, Rev. Al Reimers, Rev. Geoffrey Shaw, Lorne Shepherd, Bob Wells, Rev. Gordon Williams, Rev. Tom Wright, and other members of our staff.

There are others who have given tremendous assistance in editing and general preparation. I want to make special mention of Douglas Burke, Paul Knowles, Halina Cleland, and Karen Shepherd, all of whom have worked long hours in editing. Special thanks also to Irene Forbes who typed manuscripts again and again.

My sincere prayer is that the Holy Spirit, the only one who can truly throw the light of understanding upon the Word of God, will bring great insight, with a fuller understanding of your eternal salvation, along with healing of spirit, soul, mind, and body, and deliverance from everything that would hurt you either from within or from the circumstances outside yourself.

In Christ's Love and Service

David Mainse
President & Host of 100 Huntley Street

Please Talk To Me

I've come a long way since Jesus touched me,
But sometimes I still get downhearted,
And sometimes am troubled and dismayed,
And others looking on don't know the reason . . .
Don't understand what makes me this way.
They don't know the scars caused by rejection,
Or pain of memories that won't go away.
"Where is he at?" they wonder,
"Why does he behave that way?"
It's a long story - and it hurts with the telling,
But I need to tell it to someone,
Someone who'll listen . . . and pray.
I know I haven't asked for help or guidance
And perhaps seem unfriendly and far away,
*But, **please**,*
Don't just shake your head, and wonder, and say,
"I love him in Jesus, but keep him out of my way."
I need you, though I don't show it,
And the reason I don't show it is that I am scared;
Scared that you'd react with horror
If you knew of some of my deeds;
Scared that you'd be too busy
To bother with someone like me.
Yes, I need you, please believe me.
To the Father, I am precious
He sent His Son to save me,
His Spirit to guide me
And YOU to befriend me
So . . .
Talk to me.
PLEASE TALK TO ME,
PLEASE.

– Doug Burke

1

Ephesians

The Apostle Paul wrote this letter to the Ephesians, a people that he dearly loved. We learn from the Book of Acts that Paul spent approximately two years there in pioneering this church and later, when he passed nearby the coasts of Ephesus, he met with the elders of the church, and they wept on each other's shoulders.

As you read this epistle, allow the Holy Spirit to teach you the magnificent scope of God's purpose for the human race. Sometimes in school we are asked to summarize a book. I think that this is Paul's summary of the entire Bible. The great themes of God's dealing with man are underlined here.

Firstly, we have been chosen by God, and this choice is based on the fact that we, by faith, have come into Christ. Secondly, the barriers are broken down between God and man and between man and his fellowman. This has been done by Jesus Christ. All barriers between races and between masters and slaves have also been broken down. Jesus Christ broke down the system where man dominated the woman and now male and female are equal before God. Thirdly, the church is to function as the Body of Christ. In other words, Christ lives in this world through the church just as our individual personalities live in this world through our physical bodies. Paul points out that every member of this Body of Christ is tremendously important.

Memory Verse

"So God created man in His own image; in the image of God He created him; male and female He created them." Genesis 1:27 NKJV

January 1: Read Ephesians 1

Key verse: "I keep asking that the God of our Lord Jesus Christ, the glorious Father, may give you the Spirit of wisdom and revelation, so that you may know Him better" (Ephesians 1:17 NIV).

The book of James tells us that, if anyone lacks wisdom, he should ask God to give it to him, and God will do so. We are given wisdom through the Holy Spirit!

As the Spirit is allowed control of our lives, and as we seek all of the good things that He brings to us, we will have wisdom and revelation to know the path which we should take. But, most importantly, the wisdom and revelation that come through the Holy Spirit help us to know God better!

Jesus told us that there is nothing more important than knowing and loving God. And praise God, He knows us perfectly, and wants us to come to know Him more and more. As we walk in the Spirit, we will know God.

Direction for today: Allow the Holy Spirit free reign to bring you closer to God.

Prayer for today: Father, grant me the fullness of the Spirit of wisdom and revelation.

January 2: Read Ephesians 2

Key verse: *"Now therefore ye are no more strangers and foreigners, but are fellow citizens with the saints, and of the household of God" (Ephesians 2:19 KJV).*

Christians, awake! Take note of your position through Jesus Christ. We who were not only strangers, but enemies of God, are now citizens of the greatest kingdom in all eternity: the kingdom of God! In Christ, we are members of the family of God and of His household, brothers and sisters with all who have ever found life in Christ.

Have you realized the glorious position prepared by the Lord for you? Are you walking in the victory He has already won for you? Let it thrill your heart as you realize that you are a child of God, a member of His family and an heir of the Creator of the Universe!

Direction for today: Because I am no longer a stranger to Christ, I can go forth in His power.

Prayer for today: Father, give me an increased love for my brothers and sisters in Your family.

January 3: Read Ephesians 3

Key verse: *"And I pray that you, being rooted and established in love, may have power, together with all the saints, to grasp how wide and long and high and deep is the love of Christ, and to know this love that surpasses knowledge — that you may be filled to the measure of all the fullness of God" (Ephesians 3:17-19 NIV).*

Every Christian is called, commissioned and commanded to become more like Christ. It has been suggested that if you are not becoming more like Him, you are probably becoming more like the devil, for there is no standing still when it comes to your spiritual state! To be more like Christ is to "be filled to the measure of all the fullness of God". In Ephesians 3:16-19, Paul outlines a three-step plan for Christ-likeness.

First, Paul prays that "He may strengthen you with power through His Spirit in your inner being." We grow to be like Christ from the inside out, as the Holy Spirit strengthens our inner being. We start with attitude, not actions.

3

Second, Paul asks Christ to dwell in our hearts by faith. As we allow Christ to rule our lives, our faith — which might be called spiritual sight — will grow.

Finally, the apostle writes, we will "grasp the love of Christ". Nothing will spur us onward to Christ-likeness more than realizing His great love for us!

Direction for today: Allow the Spirit to help you grow into Christ-likeness.

Prayer for today: "Father, may my life reflect my Saviour".

January 4: Read Ephesians 4

Key verse: "You were taught, with regard to your former way of life, to put off your old self, which is being corrupted by its deceitful desires; to be made new in the attitude of your minds; and to put on the new self, created to be like God in true righteousness and holiness" (Ephesians 4:22,23 NIV).

Being a Christian should make a difference! It is very sad that public opinion polls in North America continue to show a majority of people who say they believe in God, while morality continues to plunge downward! It is not enough just to believe. James says that even the demons believe in God! Our faith is to make a very practical difference, as we put off our old way of life, like we would a dirty set of clothing, and put on our new suit of Spirit-filled righteousness.

Remember: God did not save you merely to assure you of heaven; He saved you to be like Him, in true righteousness and holiness.

Direction for today: Allow the Holy Spirit to show you areas of your life which need to be "put off".

Prayer for today: "Reveal any held-over sin, Lord, that I may repent."

Memory Verse

"Now therefore, if you will indeed obey My voice and keep My covenant, then you shall be a special treasure to Me above all people; for all the earth is Mine." Exodus 19:5 NKJV

January 5: Read Ephesians 5,6

Key verse: "Put on the full armour of God, that you may be able to stand firm against the schemes of the devil" (Ephesians 6:11 NAS).

What a great statement: God has provided for us everything that we need to stand against the attacks of the enemy! A Christian can never claim, "The devil made me do it", because the devil cannot force a believer to do anything — we have the strength and the power in Christ to stand against him.

But remember, it is Christ's power and the armour of God that is our sure defence. Anyone who tries to stand alone against the devil, without the protection of God, may face defeat. It is only as we claim God's provisions that victory is assured.

Direction for today: Put on the full armour of God.

Prayer for today: "Praise You, Lord, that in You, the victory is assured."

I and II Chronicles

God often repeats His important lessons to us; thus, we have four gospels, which often tell the same stories – He doesn't want us to miss these key truths!

The same is true in the history of His people. The books which we are about to read tell virtually the same stories we have already encountered in the books of Samuel and the Kings. Ask God to show you the key truths of these repeated stories – He has much to teach us from the examples of His people of Israel, in both their obedience and their disobedience.

January 6: Read I Chronicles 1

Key verse: "Adam, Seth, Enosh . . . The sons of Abraham: Isaac and Ishmael" (I Chronicles 1:1, 28 NIV).

It is hard to approach with enthusiasm any chapter that seems simply to be a list of names. But this is more than a meaningless chronicle; this is a genealogical map of God's plan.

Remember: God, who knows all things, always knows the best path for His people to take. And interwoven in this list are the names of those who would carry out the plan of God, chosen before the world was created: Adam, Noah, Abraham, Isaac, Israel and others.

We can always trust God to know the way we should go, as well.

But remember, too: God doesn't only list the "important" names. In these chronicles appear the names of many who are mentioned nowhere else.

We can be assured that God loves each of us as much as He does someone who seems to be very important in His plans. He knows each of us by name, and He calls to each of us by our name.

Direction for today: Believe that God knows the direction you should take.

Prayer for today: "Father, show me Your plan for me.

January 7: Read Chronicles 2

Key verse: "And Jesse begat his firstborn Eliab, and Abinadab the second, and Shimma the third" (I Chronicles 2:13 KJV).

The names in these chapters are like treasures in a field. The study of proper names sheds a bright light on Hebrew faith, history and literature. (You can learn much more in G.B. Gray's *Studies in Hebrew Proper Names*, from A. and C. Black, publishers, London).

For example, the meaning of Eliab is "God my Father". All Hebrew names which include the syllable "El": Elijah, Elisha, Eli and many more, remind us of the early Hebrews' dependence on God. Perhaps the most significant "El" name is "Emmanuel", which means "God with us", and is one of the names ascribed to Jesus.

We can see that the relationship between the Israelites and their God was much different than that of the other nations around. The original Canaanites and people in neighbouring lands worshipped their gods in fear or terror, and through terribly corrupt ceremonies. But the Israelites knew their God personally; they could call Him "Father".

Direction for today: Realize that you, too, can know God as your loving Father.

Prayer for today: "Thank you, Father, that this Old Testament name is true for me: You are God my Father".

January 8: Read I Chronicles 3,4

Key verse: "And Jabez was more honourable than his brothers . . . now Jabez called on the God of Israel, saying, 'Oh, that Thou wouldst bless me indeed, and enlarge my border, and that Thou wouldst keep me from harm . . .' and God granted him what he requested" (I Chronicles 4:9-10 NAS).

We know very little about Jabez. But we do know that he prayed for something besides worldly fame and acclaim. He was "more honourable that his brethren . . . and God granted him that which he requested". Jabez found the joy that comes as one gives oneself to God for His pleasure alone, seeking to be led in the path of His choice.

Accomplishments that bring eternal results are those that God initiates. Therefore, when we are faithfully serving Christ, we shall neither murmur about anything nor be proud of our accomplishments. Furthermore, we should never be jealous of the advantages which other people have. If our supreme desire is to gain His blessing, there is no need to fear that we are being cheated. Our main goal in life should be to do the best we can, each day, with what we have (Philippians 4:11).

6

The only really important thing is what we are in the eyes of God. Anything God wants us to do, He will help us do, so long as we are yielded to His will for our lives.

Direction for today: Those who give their all receive God's best.

Prayer for today: "Father, I yield myself completely to You."

January 9: Read Chronicles 5

Key verse: "But they were unfaithful to the God of their fathers" (I Chronicles 5:25 NIV).

Never take your relationship with God for granted. The people of Israel did just that. Although they knew that God had brought them to the land they now occupied, they were easily swept away by the religions of their neighbours.

This pattern is repeated throughout the Old Testament, and it is repeated among Christians today, as we allow the things of the world to draw us from our faith in God.

Even as the unfaithful Israelites were taken into exile (vs. 26), they might have proclaimed their faith in God, for many people continue to confess God with their lips while denying Him with their lives. May we never be seduced into the error of these Israelites, ignoring God for more immediate pleasures.

Direction for today: Is God still on the throne of your life?

Prayer for today: "Lord, I proclaim that You are King of my life."

January 10: Read I Chronicles 6

Key verse: "Now these are those whom David appointed over the service of song in the house of the Lord, after the ark rested there" (I Chronicles 6:31 NAS).

The ministry of song in God's house is given such great importance here. This should be true in our churches today, as well. Song is a key part of a worship service, along with prayer, the reading of the Bible, and anointed preaching.

The Scriptures have much to say about the wonderful ministry of song. In Psalm 100:2, we are told to "serve the Lord with gladness; come before Him with joyful singing". In Ephesians 5:18-19, Paul instructs us to "be filled with the Spirit, speaking to one another with psalms and hymns and spiritual songs, singing and making melody with our hearts to the Lord."

These are just two of numerous passages throughout the Bible which instruct the people of God to sing, especially to sing to God. The Lord has put a new song in our mouths, to proclaim His love, His power and His majesty.

Direction for today: I will sing unto the Lord, for He has done great things!

Prayer for today: "Father, may I joyfully sing Your new song of salvation."

January 11: Read I Chronicles 7

Key verse: ". . . they were valiant men of might in their generations; whose number was in the days of David two and twenty thousand and six hundred" (I Chronicles 7:2 NAS).

Throughout these chapters, we are presented with lists of fighting men, and the total number of soldiers in each tribe and sub-tribal division.

When they are all added together, they form an army of many thousands. These armies, and others like them, were able to conquer the Canaanites, capture the land of Israel, and then extend its territories until, during Solomon's reign, it was a genuine empire.

As we reflect on this, it might be appropriate to realize that these numbers are small compared to the number of Christians attending church each week in Canada, let alone in North America, or around the world. Yet the army of God today is having a minimal impact in many parts of the world.

The Old Testament is full of stories of how God can win great victories with few people. If we were as valiant in the battle for souls as these men were in the battle for their king, the impact for Jesus would be enormous!

Direction for today: Take your place in the army of God.

Prayer for today: "Father, may I be valiant in the fight against the powers of the enemy."

Memory Verse

"You shall observe My statutes and keep My judgements, and perform them; and you will dwell in the land in safety." Leviticus 25:18 NKJV

January 12: Read I Chronicles 8,9

Key verse: "And they spent the night around the house of God, because the watch was committed to them, and they were in charge of opening it morning by morning. Now some of them had charge of the utensils for service, for they counted them when they brought them in and when they took them out" (I Chronicles 9:27-28 NAS).

In chapter nine, we have an account of those who first took possession of Jerusalem after their return from Babylon. Their goal was to rebuild the city upon its old foundation, and it is to their credit that the priests are also listed among them (verses 10-12). The priests were considered "very able men for the work of the service of the house of God" (vs. 13). Service in the house of God was an important task. For this reason, the priests were held in great respect. Their responsibilities were varied: some were gatekeepers, some cared for the vessels, some prepared meat offerings and some were singers, but all were involved in establishing a place of worship.

The Kingdom of God has room for many people with diverse talents. It is not so much our ability, but rather our *availability* that matters to God. Times have changed, but service to God in any capacity still requires people with courage and commitment to a cause: spreading the Gospel!

Direction for today: Let us work so that others may say of us, "they were able for the service of God."

Prayer for today: "Father, use me in Your service."

January 13: Read I Chronicles 10,11

Key verse: "Therefore, Saul took his own sword, and fell upon it" (I Chronicles 10:4 RSV).

Suicide! What a tragedy for one of God's men: Saul, the king of Israel.

Through his unfaithfulness to the Lord, this proud, once faithful man of God had reduced himself to a defeated, unhappy human being. The same warning is true for anyone who gives his or her life to God. It is important to seek guidance from the Lord, and Him only, and not consult with mediums, horoscopes or anything of the occult. Anyone who does so is in danger of the same tragic end that befell Saul.

Saul had not learned to don God's weapons for warfare (Ephesians 6), and he had forgotten a key rule in battle: maintain contact with the commander.

Every person who serves Jesus must consult Him about everything that affects his or her life, or that life will quickly flounder upon bad decisions and lost hope. Don't let this happen — take everything to Jesus in prayer.

Direction for today: Take it to the Lord in prayer!

Prayer for today: "Lord, teach me to 'pray without ceasing'."

January 14: Read I Chronicles 12,13

Key verse: "Then the Spirit came upon Amasai, who was chief of the captains, and he said, Thine are we, David, and on thy side, thou son of Jesse: peace, peace be unto thee. Then David received them, and made them captains of the band" (I Chronicles 12:18 KJV).

To read of David's life is to be wonderfully refreshed by his life's attitude: his unselfishness, his godliness, his humility, his devotion, his

9

faith. God could use him, and did so mightily, to the strengthening of His people of Israel.

In rallying to his side, therefore, the great men recorded in our reading today simply showed their own good sense and judgment. In wisely choosing this leader, they shared in his triumphs.

Thank God that today, as Christians, we rally to the cause of the Son of David, Jesus Christ our Lord. As we serve with the King of kings and Lord of lords, accepting His cause as our own, we also share in His triumph — and therefore, in eternal life! All glory to Him!

Direction for today: Let your whole life be focused on the cause of Christ.

Prayer for today: "Thank You, Jesus, that I can share in Your triumph!" triumph!"

January 15: Read I Chronicles 14,15

Key verse: "And David inquired of God, saying, Shall I go up against the Philistines? And wilt Thou deliver them into mine hand? And the Lord said unto him, Go up, for I will deliver them into thine hand" (I Chronicles 14:10 KJV).

There is more recorded praise about David in the Scriptures than there is concerning any other king. This account may indicate an important reason for that: he kept in touch with God.

In this story, David is under attack from the Philistines. Most military strategists would immediately begin to formulate plans for defence, but David began to pray! Before he did anything in retaliation, David inquired of the Lord, and God gave him the victorious battle plan!

Because David honoured God, God honoured him. Because David spoke to God, God spoke to him. David's fame spread to the lands around. Even so, God has promised to honour us if we honour Him.

We also realize that on occasion David failed to inquire of the Lord. In those cases, he invariably fell into sin and terrible trouble. Whenever we are under attack from the enemy, we should immediately turn to God, seeking His defence. If we use attacks from Satan as reminders to pray, we need never fall!

Direction for today: We should be "praying always with all prayer and supplication in the Spirit" (Ephesians 6:18).

Prayer for today: "Father, as I take time to listen, speak to me."

January 16: Read I Chronicles 16

Key verse: "O give thanks to the Lord, for He is good; for His lovingkindness is everlasting" (I Chronicles 16:34 NAS).

The great King was a great songwriter. He lifted his voice in praise to God in this wonderful psalm. Praise and worship are the most exalting parts of our service to the Lord!

David proclaims that God's lovingkindness, or mercy, is everlasting. The same God who did marvellous works in the time of David is still watching over us today. The protection He afforded to Israel is still ours.

At the end of verse 31, we are reminded that "the Lord reigns". He reigns still! He reigns over all things, and He reigns in great peace and joy in the hearts of all who will receive Him. As we accept God's forgiveness in Christ, and allow Him to reign, we truly know that "His lovingkindness is everlasting".

Direction for today: Allow Jesus to have full reign in your life.

Prayer for today: "Thank You, Lord, for You are good; Your lovingkindness is everlasting."

January 17: Read I Chronicles 17,18

Key verse: "Go and tell David My servant, 'Thus says the Lord, You shall not build a house for Me to dwell in'" (I Chronicles 17:4 NIV).

Sometimes, we have a good idea. We know exactly what we would like to do and, because it sounds so right, we believe that God must approve of it, as well.

But this is not always the case. It was a good idea for a king to build a temple, and David's efforts were approved by the Lord. But God had not chosen him for that particular task.

Imagine what chaos could have resulted if David had gone ahead with his good idea anyway. A great many Christians do just that — they don't

11

bother to confirm anything with the Lord, but just follow their own dream, and then come to grief, because the vision was not from Him!

No matter how much we desire to follow a certain path, we must listen to the voice of the Lord. And we must follow David's example: he immediately set his own plans and desires aside, and obeyed the Lord.

Direction for today: Do not follow every good idea; follow only God's ideas.

Prayer for today: "Father, are all the things I am doing part of Your plan for me?"

January 18: Read I Chronicles 19,20

Key verse: *"When the vassals fo Hadadezer saw that they had been defeated by Israel, they made peace with David and became subject to him" (I Chronicles 19:19 NIV).*

What a parallel to our spiritual lives we find here in this chapter. Like these people, we have been offered peace (vs. 1) but, like them, we so often choose to rebel, and to fight against God.

The basic truth is: God is going to win! His is the victory. Jesus has triumphed over sin, death and hell, and all things have been placed under His feet.

There can only be two results from our rebellion, the same that befell those who rejected David's offer of peace: misery, and death. Many enemy soldiers died because of the rebellion of those nations. And many people in our world will die because of rebellion against God.

But praise the Lord for those in our key verse who repented, and made peace. God's mercy endures, and there is still time to accept His offer of peace.

If you have never made peace with God, come to Him now. And if you are a Christian, but in rebellion in some area of your life, realize that you will never win through rebellion!

Direction for today: Accept God's offer of peace.

Prayer for today: "Thank You, Jesus, that You are the Prince of Peace."

Memory Verse

"If the Lord delights in us, then He will bring us into this land and give it to us, 'a land which flows with milk and honey'."

January 19: Read I Chronicles 21,22

Key verse: *"Is it not I that commanded? . . . even I it is that have sinned and done evil indeed" (I Chronicles 21:17 NAS).*

Rarely does anyone find it east to admit one's own wrong-doing. And yet David does so, for he finds that his sin is going to bring the judgment of God upon a vast nation, numbering in the millions.

Never conclude that your sins affect only you. None of us lives unto himself or herself.

David set about to rectify the problem, but it was not without cost. And although Oman offered (21:23) to give all that David needed, David wisely refused the offer and paid the costs himself. Would any of us do the same? It is plain that David's repentance was sincere.

When God, by His Spirit, makes us aware of our own sin, may we be as ready as David to recognize it, admit it and do something about it for, as surely as night follows day, judgment awaits even God's own children who are disobedient.

Direction for today: The blessing of God awaits every truly repentant heart.

Prayer for today: "Father, show me any areas of sin in my life, that I might repent from them."

January 20: Read I Chronicles 23,24

Key verse: "He gathered together all the leaders of Israel with the priests and the Levites" (I Chronicles 23:2 NAS).

David was preparing to hand over the leadership of the nation of Israel to his son, Solomon. He was not only passing on the crown, but also entrusting Solomon with his beloved dream: the building of a house for the Lord. David was not permitted to build the temple, but he never lost the vision for the project.

Among his first instructions to Solomon, and the leaders of Israel, were details concerning the construction of the temple.

There was no doubt that this building was to be something very special. Every detail was carefully planned, and the workers were charged with enormous responsibility.

Today, the church is the temple of God. May we care as much as did the aged King David about the state of God's temple, the church of Jesus Christ.

Direction for today: Accept your responsibility for maintaining the unity and strength of the temple of Jesus Christ.

Prayer for today: "Lord Jesus, use me to help build Your church."

January 21: Read I Chronicles 25,26

Key verse: "Under Jeduthun, who led in giving thanks and praising the Lord were his six sons . . ." (I Chronicles 25:3 LB).

Giving thanks and praising the Lord were very important elements of Hebrew worship. We might wonder whether they always had much for which to thank and praise the Lord. After all the trials they had been through, why would they incorporate praise and thanksgiving into their worship?

Giving praise to God is not something people do because He has performed according to their expectations, but rather because He is God, the Creator of the universe, the Great Physician, the Provider. He is worthy to receive honour and glory because of Who He is. The Israelites had a concept of the awesomeness of God and worshipped Him in His majesty and glory.

Thanksgiving was an expression of appreciation to God for what He had done for them, because they realized that God had done great things in the past, and that He promised to continue to bless them.

Praise and thanksgiving went hand in hand in the corporate worship of the Israelites. They were, however, distinct from one another: praise was offered to God for Who He was, and thanksgiving was given for His blessings given to His people.

Direction for today: Make praise and thanksgiving an important part of your daily worship.

Prayer for today: "Lord, I praise You because You are holy and righteous, and I thank You for the gift of Jesus."

January 22: Read I Chronicles 27

Key verse: *"David did not take the number of the men twenty years old or less, because the Lord had promised to make Israel as numerous as the stars in the sky" (I Chronicles 27:23 NIV).*

There is a familiar saying: "God said it; I believe it; that settles it".

David might have said it more poetically, but he clearly believed this truth. God had promised Israel that their numbers would be uncountable. And although David certainly knew that he could count the young men of his time, his action expressed a sure faith that God's promise would come to pass.

His action was in a sense prophetic, an affirmation that he believed God, perhaps even in spite of immediate appearances. And God's prophecy came true beyond doubt: the people of God in our day are absolutely uncountable, for each of us who is a descendant of Abraham through faith is included in that heavenly census.

God may at times call us to believe, in spite of appearances. If you ever have to choose between what is apparently true, and what God says, you can be sure that God's promise will come to pass.

Direction for today: Believe God!

Prayer for today: "Lord, give me the faith to trust You in every situation."

January 23: Read I Chronicles 28

Key verse: *". . . be strong and of good courage, and do it. Fear not, nor be dismayed, for the Lord God, even my God, will be with thee; He will not fail thee, nor forsake thee . . ." (I Chronicles 28:20 KJV).*

There are times in our lives when we are overwhelmed by the circumstances, and we wonder how we will ever be able to do that which we are called to do. Solomon must have felt that way when David called him aside and told him of the work God wanted him to do. It must have been overwhelming to think that God had chosen him to oversee the building of the Temple. But, with his calling, God gave him instructions and a promise.

The first instruction was to know the God of his father, and to serve Him (vs. 9). To know the power of God, we must first have Christ in our hearts as Saviour and Lord. He was also instructed to take heed. When God calls, we must listen attentively. Finally, Solomon was exhorted to be strong and of good courage, and to do it. When God calls us to do something, we must do it, in spite of any opposition.

Perhaps even today you are facing something that God has called you to do, but which seems to be impossible. The enemy wants you to abandon it, but do not listen to the enemies. Instead, go forward in Christ, confident in His promise to never leave or forsake you!

Direction for today: "I can do all things through Christ which stengtheneth me" (Philippians 4:13).

Prayer for today: "Lord, give me the courage to obey."

January 24: Read I Chronicle 29

Key verse: *"But who am I and who are my people that we should be able to offer as generously as this? For all things have come from Thee and from Thy hand we have given Thee" (I Chronicles 29:14 NAS).*

If ever the people of Israel and their leaders had cause for pride, it was at this time in their history. Under David, the land had been completely subdued, and the nation had come to a time of peace and of political importance in the world of that day. David was about to be succeeded by Solomon, who would build on this base to make Israel a power some have called an empire.

The country had a well-developed governmental and military system; the nation knew unprecedented prosperity; great buildings were being constructed in the land, and the greatest of all was now planned — the Temple in Jerusalem.

And yet, as King David stood before his people, there was no trace of pride. Rather, he was humble and thankful before the Lord. "All things come from Thee," he prayed.

Direction for today: "It is better to be of a humble spirit with the lowly, than to divide the spoil with the proud" (Proverbs 16:19).

Prayer for today: "Father, help me always to examine myself and never to be ruled by pride."

January 25: Read II Chronicles 1,2

Key verse: "Give me now wisdom and knowledge, that I may go out and come in before this people; for who can judge this Thy people, that is so great?" (II Chronicles 1:10 KJV).

How important it is to choose wisely! The choice made by Solomon received the commendation of Almighty God. There was an awareness of both privilege and responsibility in his request. To give leadership to the people under him, Solomon recognized his need for divine wisdom and understanding.

Putting God first, the people next and himself last, constituted a good beginning. God honoured this and gave to Solomon wisdom and understanding that allowed him to bring the nation of Israel to even greater prominence and prosperity. The completion of the Temple and other building projects brought international acclaim and respect, as evidenced by the visit of the Queen of Sheba.

Had this initial recognition of his need for God's guidance continued, the future would have been different for Solomon's descendants. But forsaking spiritual purity for expediency led Solomon along a path that led to spiritual poverty and national disintegration.

Direction for today: Be certain to remain true to your original commitment to the Lord.

Prayer for today: "Lord Jesus, help me to be constant and consistent in my love for You."

Memory Verse

"Therefore you shall keep the commandments of the Lord your God, to walk in His ways and to fear Him." Deuteronomy 8:6 NKJV

January 26: Read II Chronicles 3-5

Key verse: "So the priests could not stand to minister because of the cloud; for the glory of the Lord filled the house of God" (II Chronicles 5:14 NAS).

God does not keep His people guessing. When the Temple was completed, there was no question about the blessing of the Lord upon the project. His glory filled the Temple in a cloud, and the priests could not go to their assigned places.

We can expect the Lord to demonstrate His approval upon the things we have been called by Him to do in His name. That is the heart of the promises in the New Testament that declare that signs will follow the proclamation of the gospel: healings and miracles, tongues and prophecies and many other demonstrations of the presence of the Lord.

Direction for today: Expect the Lord to confirm His work with miracles!

Prayer for today: "Father, give me the faith to see You at work in power."

January 27: Read II Chronicles 6

Key verse: "The Lord therefore hath performed His word that He hath spoken: for I am risen up in the room of David, my father, and am set on the throne of Israel, as the Lord promised, and have built the house for the name of the Lord God of Israel" (II Chronicles 6:10 KJV).

The construction of a house for the Lord was a strong desire of David's heart. This did not arise from any desire to bring glory to himself, but from his desire to please God.

God promised that David's son would build this house of God and that the son's kingdom would be firmly established.

Many years were spent in the planning, preparation, organizing and construction of the Temple. It was no easy task, and hundreds of thousands of work-hours, with sweat and tears, were poured into the project. But during Solomon's reign, the glorious Temple was completed; innumerable sacrifices were offered and Solomon dedicated the completed Temple to the glory of God. God was pleased, and revealed His glory to all Israel.

When God makes a promise, He keeps it. When He charges one of His people with a task, He provides the strength and the means to complete it. He told Solomon that he would build a Temple to His glory, and he did. He told the apostles to carry the gospel throughout the world, and they did. He has told us that we will do miraculous works, even as Christ id — and we do them in the power of the Holy Spirit!

All of this is part of the construction of Christ's temple now on earth: His church! Le us be dedicated workers in this eternal project.

Direction for today: Be busy in the temple.

Prayer for today: "Lord, help me to be an effective worker in Your kingdom."

January 28: Read II Chronicles 7,8

Key verse: "When all the Israelites saw the fire coming down and the glory of the Lord above the temple, they knelt on the pavement with their faces on the ground and they worshipped and gave

thanks to the Lord, saying 'He is good; His love endures forever'" (II Chronicles 7:3 NIV).

Our God is a God of surprises! He has a habit of giving more than we ask. In his long prayer (II Chronicles 6), Solomon had repeatedly asked God to forgive His people; he had invited God to rest in the temple; and he had asked God's blessings on both the priests and the people. Solomon had not asked for any supernatural manifestations of God's presence, but that is what God gave. It was His declaration that "I have heard your prayer and I am with you!".

The fire and bright cloud were signs that spoke more powerfully than any prophet could, because everyone knew that it was by fire and cloud that God has shown His presence with the Israelites during the forty years of wilderness wandering. The people received the signs as evidence of God's eternal and unchanging love, and sang the familiar words: "He is good and His love endures forever".

Many years later, on a certain feast of Pentecost, and again unexpectedly, fire came down upon 120 disciples of Jesus who were becoming a living temple. Again, God gave more than had been requested, giving not only a sense of His presence but also the gift of tongues and a power to witness.

Direction for today: Pray, wait upon God, and be prepared for dynamic evidences of His love.

Prayer for today: "Father, may I know Your presence today."

January 29: Read II Chronicles 9,10

Key verse: *"And all the kings of the earth sought the presence of Solomon to hear his wisdom, which God had put in his heart" (II Chronicles 9:23 NKJV).*

Solomon was a great and mighty king. But we must rmemeber that it was the wisdom God gave to him that made him so attractive and so powerful.

In the book of Proverbs, Solomon encourages us to "incline our ear to wisdom and to apply our hearts to understanding" (Proverbs 2:2 NKJV). In doing so, we will "understand the fear of the Lord and find the knowledge of God" (Proverbs 2:5 NKJV). But this is only given to those who seek out the Lord in His word and who totally surrender their lives to the lordship of Jesus Christ.

God wants us to walk uprightly before Him. As we do this, we gain the wisdom that He wants to give to those who walk close to Him.

God delights in displaying His character through our yielded lives.

Direction for today: A wise person will hear God and increase in wisdom.

Prayer for today: "Lord, give me Your wisdom."

18

January 30: Read II Chronicles 11,12

Key verse: *"And he did evil because he prepared not his heart to seek the Lord" (II Chronicles 12:14 KJV).*

There is always a cause for any effect. At times, Rehoboam would listen to the voice of the Lord, and the nation would prosper. But when things went well he forsook the law of the Lord. Immediately, Shishak, King of Egypt, came up against him. When we withdraw from God, God will withdraw His blessing from us!

Shemiah the prophet reminded Rehoboam of his sinfulness, and the king and the priests humbled themselves. God's wrath was turned from Rehoboam, and he escaped destruction.

Like Rehoboam, we will inevitably get into trouble when we fail to seek the Lord. The minute we begin to live our lives by our own wisdom, we are in trouble! Let us return to the Lord before He finds it necessary to allow an enemy army to camp on our front lawn!

Direction for today: Seek the Lord continually; return to Him immediately if you discover you have strayed.

Prayer for today: "Lord, by Your Spirit, draw me ever closer to You."

January 31: Read II Chronicles 13,14

Key verse: *". . . the children of Judah prevailed, because they relied upon the God of their fathers" (II Chronicles 13:18 KJV).*

Solomon's son, Rehoboam, had forsaken his father's counsel, and the nation of Israel was split in two. Jeroboam had been appointed by the Lord to rule in the north, and Rehoboam continued to reign in the smaller southern kingdom of Judah.

When Rehoboam humbled himself, things would go well, but then, he would forsake the law of the Lord. Like many of us, he sought the Lord only when he was in trouble.

Jeroboam also forsook the Lord who had anointed him. He appointed false priests and initiated pagan worship, erecting golden calf-gods for the people to worship. Both nations were in inner turmoil, and at war with each other.

But Rehoboam's son, Abijah, obeyed the Lord. When at war with Jeroboam's Israel, Judah's defeat seemed inevitable, but the people took the wise course — "They cried unto the Lord, and God smote Jeroboam and all Israel" (II Chronicles 13:14).

When we seek the Lord, and rely on Him to overcome the enemy, we can truly say "The battle is the Lord's and the victory is ours" (I Samuel 17:47).

Direction for today: Call unto the Lord; He hears and helps.

Prayer for today: "Father, help me to communicate with You always, not only when I am in trouble."

2

Surrender

Lord I come to you . . .
Not because of what you can do for me;
Or because when we sing
I feel good all over,
Or because I am deep in sin
And desperate.
But because of who you are,
Very God, the Anointed One,
And you've bid me come.
I seek no favours,
Ask no thrill,
Make no demands.
I simply come
In obedience to your command.
Do with me what you will.
I'm not looking for gimmicks, Lord,
For quick answers
Or easy ways out, or in.
I seek no power,
No instant panacea,
Just you, Lord,
And Your will.
And so I come,
Unconditionally,
Because of who you are,
Very God, the Anointed One,
And my Lord.

February 1: Read II Chronicles 15

Key verse: *"Be strong and do not give up, for your work will be rewarded" (II Chronicles 15:7 NIV).*

We live in an "instant" age. We have come to expect immediate results, whatever we do. Cars are sold on the basis of the fastest pick-up; foods are ever more "instant"; we can communicate immediately with almost anyone in the world.

Some things about the Christian faith are immediate, as well — we are saved the instant we call on Jesus; we see miraculous healings and life-changing deliverances that happen on the spot.

But the overall job of the church, winning the lost world to Jesus, is not an "instant" job. It has been going on for almost 2,000 years, and will continue until Christ returns. And the individual responsibility of each Christian, to be more like Christ, is also not an "instant" project. Christian maturity develops slowly, and with effort.

Let us not abandon our tasks as Christians because we see no immediate results. Instead, "be strong and do not give up".

Direction for today: Allow the Holy Spirit to develop in you the fruit of patience.

Prayer for today: "Father, help me to be strong and not to give up."

Memory Verse

"This Book of the Law shall not depart from your mouth, but you shall meditate in it day and night, that you may observe to do according to all that is written in it. For then you will make your way prosperous, and then you will have good success." Joshua 1:8 NKJV

February 2: Read II Chronicles 16,17

Key verse: *"The eyes of the Lord range throughout the earth to strengthen those whose hearts as fully committed to Him" (II Chronicles 16:9a NIV).*

Through the mouth of His prophet, God had promised to be with Asa as long as he sought after the Lord. Asa led the people in a declaration of covenant before the Lord.

However, in chapter 16, we discover Asa sending silver and gold to Ben-Hadad, King of Aram. He made a treaty with Ben-Hadad to insure that the Aramic king would break his treaty with the king of Israel, who was attacking Judah. Ben-Hadad had agreed, and in fact sent his forces to attack and vanquish several cities in northern Israel. This caused the Israelite armies to cease their onslaught against Judah. It seemed as though Asa had done the right thing.

However, Hanani pointed out that Asa had relied on the King of Aram and not on the Lord. He reminded Asa that reliance on the Lord had guaranteed earlier victories, and reminded him that the Lord strengthens those who are fully committed to Him. The prophet then announced that Asa's faithlessness would result in continual war.

Asa's reaction was typical of those with a guilty conscience: he put Hanai in prison and became a stubborn and rebellious leader, removed from the blessings of God.

Direction for today: Rebellion against the Lord is a cancer that will destroy.

Prayer for today: "Lord, help me to rely solely on You."

February 3: Read II Chronicles 18

Key verse: "And Jehoshaphat said to the king of Israel, 'Inquire, I pray thee, at the word of the Lord today'" (II Chronicles 18:4 KJV).

Jehoshaphat, king of Judah, was a man of God. He felt it would be beneficial to establish a friendship with Ahab, king of Israel. That alliance brought him into war alongside Ahab against Ramoth-gilead. Ahab believed that, if Jehoshaphat was with him, the blessing of God would be with him also.

Jehoshaphat understood the seriousness of the war that Ahab was about to wage, and asked, "Have you inquired of the Lord?" Ahab immediately sought his 500 prophets of Baal, but Jehoshaphat, a man of God, was not satisfied and asked, "Do you not have a prophet of God?" The prophet of the Lord was approached, and his announcement was of judgment. For this, he was imprisoned.

Jehoshaphat learned a lesson that many Christians must learn. He came to the place where he rejected God's counsel and accepted the counsel of the ungodly, and it brought defeat. The Bible says, "Blessed is the man that walketh not in the counsel of the ungodly, nor standeth in the way of sinners, nor sitteth in the seat of the scornful. But his delight is in the law of the Lord; and in His law doth he meditate day and night" (Psalm 1:1-2 KJV).

Direction for today: Ignoring God's plan usually lands us in the middle of a battle we cannot win.

Prayer for today: "Father, keep me in the centre of Your will."

February 4: Read II Chronicles 19,20

Key verse: "And Jehoshaphat was afraid, and turned his attention to seek the Lord; and proclaimed a fast throughout all Judah" (II Chronicles 20:3 NAS).

Jehoshaphat obviously learned his lesson. When another crisis came, he did not seek the counsel of men, but "turned his attention to seek the Lord". And victory came through his obedience.

Jehoshaphat knew and worshipped the Lord. After his bad experience with Ahab, the attack of the Moabites and Ammonites sent him straight to his God.

There is a powerful declaration of faith in verse 20:19: "Should evil come upon us, the sword, or judgment, or pestilence or famine, we will stand before this house and before Thee and cry to Thee and Thou wilt hear and deliver us."

God's response to such faith was dramatic: "Do not fear or be dismayed . . . for the battle is not yours but God's". This led to the apparently absurd tactic of the singers and praisers going against the enemy army, ahead of the soldiers! But God is faithful, and the enemy was routed without one sword-thrust by the armies of Judah.

How good it is to know that we serve the same God today. As we put our full trust in Him, and obey Him fully, He will strengthen us and meet our needs.

Direction for today: Meet attacks of the enemy with praise, and watch the Lord win the battle.

Prayer for today: "Father, in trouble, I will stand before You, and I know You will deliver me."

February 5: Read II Chronicles 21,22

Key verse: "And he [Joash] was with them hid in the house of God six years: and Athaliah reigned over the land" (II Chronicles 22:12 KJV).

Jehu was carrying out judgment upon the land. Ahaziah was caught and killed "because, said they, he is the son of Jehoshaphat, who sought the Lord with all his heart" (II Chronicles 22:9). It seemed as if the godly decendants of Jehoshaphat were all to be slain, but into the picture stepped Jehoshabeath, the king's daughter. She rescued Joash, then about one year old, and hid him in the temple. After six years Joash was anointed king.

God's provision is always complete. It was not God's will for the righteous influence in the royal family to cease. God knew what would happen, and He had prepared Jehoshabeath and Jehoiada, the high priest, to intervene.

Joash was hidden in the temple for six years. What a beautiful image this provides us of God's love and His power to provide for His people. Sometimes we, in our own wisdom, wonder how God could possibly make a way through a certain situation. But in our reading today is one of hundreds of Bible examples of God's provision in impossible circumstances.

Direction for today: Place your life totally in God's hands, and trust Him to provide for your needs in His own creative way.

Prayer for today: "Father, as you protected Joash, please protect Your people facing persecution in dangerous parts of the world."

February 6: Read II Chronicles 23

Key verse: *"Then Jehoiada made a covenant between himself and all the people and the king, that they should be the Lord's people" (II Chronicles 23:16 NAS).*

In the midst of a record of the ungodliness and self-seeking lives of the Israelites, this verse stands out like a jewel. In one of the darkest periods of Israel's history, it is encouraging to find that faith in God was still alive. The actions of Jehoiada the priest, along with Jehoshabeath, reveal a bedrock confidence in the faithfulness of God.

They had not rescued Joash for selfish purposes; instead, they had a deep desire to see their people brought back to a relationship with God. The influence exerted by this God-fearing couple raised the spiritual level of the nation from the depths to which it had fallen.

How clearly this illustrates what can happen when people begin looking with eyes of faith beyond their circumstances to the living God. In our day, spiritual renewal can become a reality when individuals are willing to risk their all in personal covenant relationship with the Lord Jesus Christ.

Direction for today: In the most trying hours of your life, coming into a covenant relationship with Jesus Christ can change the direction of all your circumstances.

Prayer for today: "Lord, may I be willing to risk all for You."

February 7: Read II Chronicles 24

Key verse: *"And Joash did that which was right in the sight of the Lord all the days of Jehoiada the priest" (II Chronicles 24:2 KJV).*

Joash was the king. His was the power and influence. He had the fame, and the authority in the land. All of the attention came to him while he ruled.

And yet another man, Jehoiada, and his wife Jehoshabeath, played a role just as important in the great story of faith and restoration which we have read in the last few days.

It is not only those who receive the attention, that are important in the kingdom of God. The apostle Paul was used to spread the gospel throughout many nations — but Ananias ministered the Lord to Paul. Billy Graham has brought countless thousands to faith in Jesus — but someone led Billy Graham to Jesus, and that person is vitally important in the kingdom of God.

In your life, there are people who have gone unnoticed, and yet who have contributed much to your Christian walk. Take a moment today, and thank the Lord for them. If possible, talk to those people, as well, and thank them for the part they have played in your Christian life.

Direction for today: If possible, contact the one who led you to Jesus; and say thanks. If you can't, thank the Lord for that one.

Prayer for today: "Father, thank You for the faithful saints who serve You without the recognition of man. May I be willing to do the same."

February 8: Read II Chronicles 25

Key verse: *"He did what was right in the eyes of the Lord, but not wholeheartedly" (II Chronicles 25:2 NIV).*

Amaziah was a lot like many of us who claim to be Christians. This verse, written centuries ago about this king of Judah, could apply to many of us also.

Unfortunately, the results of his "lukewarm" heart may also be applied to us. The Lord gave Amaziah a number of opportunities to turn completely to Him but, when he failed to make that total commitment, the king suffered the terrible consequences of his own hypocrisy.

Even after his initial disobedience, God gave Amaziah other chances. He sent a prophet, and Amaziah listened to him. But soon he had turned away again, even falling so far as to worship other gods. When he refused yet again to repent, he heard the terrible words, "God has determined to destroy you."

The Lord is merciful, and His grace extends far. Perhaps even as you read this, you are realizing that God is once again calling you to repentance and a complete commitment to Him. If you hear His voice, obey!

Direction for today: Serve the Lord with all your heart!

Prayer for today: "Father, if my commitment to You has been lukewarm, I hear Your warning. I repent and turn wholly to You."

Memory Verse

"I will call upon the Lord, who is worthy to be praised; so shall I be saved from my enemies." 2 Samuel 22:4 NKJV

February 9: Read II Chronicles 26-28

Key verse: *"And he continued to seek God in the days of Zechariah, who had understanding through the vision of God; and as long as he sought the Lord, God prospered him" (II Chronicles 26:5 NAS).*

The history of Judah during this period is like a roller-coaster. Because King Uzziah and his son, Jotham, did that which was right in the sight of the Lord and sought to be obedient to Him, God blessed them as well as all of Judah. The nation became secure, powerful and respected.

However, when Jotham's son Ahaz took the throne, a dramatic change began to occur. Ahaz did not honour the Lord but began to sacrifice to the idols of the surrounding heathen nations. God's judgment fell, and many people of Judah were slain by enemy forces, while many more were taken into captivity. Judah was eventually impoverished and broken.

God desires to abundantly bless His children. However, His blessing is directly proportionate to our submission and obedience to Him. God's promises of blessing are to those who love and obey Him.

Direction for today: Let us learn that it pays to "do that which is right in the sight of God" (II Chronicles 26:4).

Prayer for today: "Father, may our children continue strong in faith in Jesus Christ."

February 10: Read II Chronicles 29

Key verse: "Now I intend to make a covenant with the Lord, the God of Israel, so that His fierce anger will turn away from us" (II Chronicles 29:10 NIV).

Hezekiah understood a principle that is vitally important to all of the people of God: that of repentance. The fickle nation had once again abandoned God; their new king, who served the Lord, brought his people back to obedience.

He realized that no matter how far the people had fallen into sin, true repentance would once again restore them to a right relationship with their God.

Satan would love to convince Christians that, once they have fallen away from the Lord, their chance of a loving relationship with God is ended. But nothing could be further from the truth. John wrote, "If we confess our sins, He is faithful and just and will forgive us our sins and purify us from all unrighteousness" (I John 1:9).

And the psalmist Asaph proclaimed the possibility of revival, even in sinful times, saying that if we teach our children about God, "then they would put their trust in God and . . . would keep His commands. They would not be like their forefathers — a stubborn and rebellious generation" (Psalm 78:7,8). Let us believe God for a true revival of repentance in our day.

Direction for today: Repent of sin, personally, and pray for repentance by our people and in our land.

Prayer for today: "Lord, bring the people of our nation to a place of repentance before You."

February 11: Read II Chronicles 30

Key verse: "And the Lord heard Hezekiah, and healed the people" (II Chronicles 30:20 NIV).

Throughout the history of the people of God, there are wonderful examples of intercession. Frequently, a man or woman stood before the Lord on behalf of needy people, and brought their need to God in prayer.

Hezekiah called the people to repentance, and then called upon the Lord for healing. God heard, and healed. This reminds us of the prayers of Moses for the people; the intercession of David and, above all, the prayers and sacrifice of Jesus for us.

God also calls each one of us to be an intercessor. How often do our prayers concern only ourselves and our needs? Yet the apostle Paul frequently tells us to pray for one another.

There are many warriors on the battlefield for Jesus who depend on the prayer support of God's people. Neither 100 Huntley Street nor any other Christian ministry will survive without the prayers of Christian supporters. And there are many struggling Christians who need the power of the Spirit in their lives, power that comes as believers pray.

Direction for today: Pray for one another, and for any ministry God lays on your heart.

Prayer for today: "Father, please bless and prosper all ministries that are bringing glory to You."

February 12: Read II Chronicles 31

Key verse: *"In everything that he undertook in the service of God's temple and in obedience to the law and the commands, he sought his God and worked wholeheartedly. And so he prospered" (II Chronicles 31:21 NIV).*

What a wonderful recipe for successful living! Hezekiah prospered because of three key elements of his life: he sought God, he obeyed God, and he worked wholeheartedly.

These are vital principles to follow if we genuinely desire to live successful lives as Christians. Remember "success" can mean many things; it does not necessarily imply financial prosperity. But these principles are a sure road to peace, contentment, and a joyful heart.

Too many Christians are eager to work wholeheartedly for the Kingdom, without first seeking God and finding out what His work schedule is. Others seek God until His will is in conflict with theirs, and then they turn away from obedience.

Hezekiah never wavered: he sought the Lord until he heard from Him; he then obeyed unquestioningly, and poured his whole heart into the work to which he was called. His is an excellent example for us to follow.

Direction for today: Seek the Lord. Obey Him and work wholeheartedly at whatever is given to you to do.

Prayer for today: "Father, show me Your will, and I will do it!"

February 13: Read II Chronicles 32

Key verse: *"But King Hezekiah and Isaiah the prophet, the son of Amoz, prayed about this and cried out to heaven. And the Lord sent an angel who destroyed every mighty warrior, commander and officer in the camp of the King of Assyria" (II Chronicles 32:20,21 NAS).*

This consistent message runs through the Bible: if you choose to stand with the Lord, you cannot lose. This may not always mean victory and success as those terms are understood by the world. Hebrews 11 tells us of those who found victory in faith by suffering or dying for the cause of the Lord. Their triumph is eternal! But, throughout history, a person standing with God has been found to be truly unbeatable.

Here we have another example of this principle: the shrunken kingdom of Judah had no chance in pitched battle with the armies of the Assyrian Empire. Sennacherib spoke the truth when he proclaimed that his armies had triumphed everywhere!

He was right — neither the gods of those lands nor their armies could save them. But he did not know the true God of Israel. And Sennacherib was attacking not only God's people, but God Himself, and the Assyrian monarch soon felt the full force of his adversary. Hezekiah and Isaiah found more power in prayer than in weaponry, and more strength in faith than in armies!

Direction for today: Prayer is the true defence against all kinds of attack.

Prayer for today: "Father, may I always stand with You in victory".

February 14: Read II Chronicles 33

Key verse: *"He rebuilt the high places his father Hezekiah had demolished; he also erected altars to the Baals and made Asherah poles. He bowed down to all the starry hosts and worshipped them" (II Chronicles 33:3 NIV).*

The more times change, the more they stay the same. This chapter tells of the sins of Manasseh, and many of those sins sound as though they could be lifted from the pages of today's newspapers and magazines.

Not only are unbelievers today caught in the same kind of sin as was Manasseh, but Christians participate in some of these things as well. Notice some of the practices for which God severely punished the king.

He made "Asherah poles". These were places where sexual sins were practiced. This is certainly rampant in our world.

He worshipped the "starry host". An incredible number of Christians turn eagerly to the horoscope column in the daily paper, seeking to learn from the stars. This is an abomination before the Lord!

He practiced divination and witchcraft. This is exactly what anyone is doing by using a ouija board, or having a fortune told by cards, tea leaves or palm reading.

If you have fallen into any of these or related sins, repent immediately. Turn from them. Manasseh repented, but only after he paid a terrible price. God can deliver you, now!

Direction for today: Turn from temptation in any areas involving the occult.

Prayer for today: "Father, deliver me from any bonds that any involvement in the occult may have caused."

February 15: Read II Chronicles 34

Key verse: *"And it came about when the king heard the words of the law that he tore his clothes" (II Chronicles 34:19 NAS).*

In the eighteenth year of his reign, Josiah gathered a host of workmen to repair the temple of God. The workmen discovered a priceless book of the Law, probably a portion of the book of Deuteronomy, teaching belief in the grace of the living God, illustrating how His people should worship Him and how they should interact one with another.

Has it occurred to you that the assembling of that book, many years before the workmen discovered it, required a great deal of labour? There were no modern-day print shops to run off a copy of the Law. It was patiently and carefully hand-written. And all of that effort was rewarded, perhaps centuries later, just when the kingdom was threatened and God's people so desperately needed His word.

How often we lose heart when we fail to see the fruit of our labours but, according to the teaching of Jesus, we can rejoice in our sowing, and leave the reaping to the Lord! As we work for Him, we can trust Him with the results.

Direction for today: Serve God, and leave the results to Him.

Prayer for today: "Father, thank You for opportunities to sow seed for You".

Memory Verse

"Blessed be the Lord, who has given rest to His people Israel, according to all that He promised. There has not failed one word of all His promise, which He promised through His servant Moses." I Kings 8:56 NKJV

February 16: Read II Chronicles 35

Key verse: *"Josiah provided for all the lay people who were there a total of thirty thousand sheep and goats for the Passover offerings, and also three thousand cattle — all from the king's own possession" (II Chronicles 35:7 NIV).*

Let's think, for just a minute, about the tremendous slaughter necessitated by this important feast. Thirty three thousand animals died that day so that the people of Israel could celebrate the Passover, and be reminded of God's deliverance from Egypt.

And although all of these animals were killed, it was not enough. Each year, thousands and thousands of animals were killed, and it was still not enough. The book of Hebrews tells us, in fact, that the blood of bulls and goats will <u>never</u> remove sin.

These deaths were a picture of that one death to come which would remove sin. The death of Jesus was the ultimate sacrifice, the only death worthy to remove the terrible stain of sin from our lives. Praise God that we can claim that sacrifice on our behalf, that we no longer need to slaughter sheep or goats, for Jesus has defeated sin and death once and for all.

Direction for today: Be sure that you have claimed Jesus' sacrifice to cleanse you from the stain of sin.

Prayer for today: "Cleanse me from all sin, Lord Jesus."

February 17: Read II Chronicles 36

Key verse: *"But they mocked God's messengers, despised His words and scoffed at His prophets until the wrath of the Lord was aroused against his people and there was no remedy" (II Chronicles 36:16 NIV).*

This is a sobering verse, in a sobering chapter. This last chapter of II Chronicles tells of the final days of the nation of Judah, and of the exile of the people of God, an exile that lasted for many decades.

It is even more sobering when we realize tht it never need have happened. God had repeatedly called His people to repentance. He had spoken to them through the prophets and through His word. He had warned them again and again, but they would not listen.

And they went too far in their rebellion.

We must pay close attention to this. Even we, the people of God, can ignore Him, turn from Him, and fall into rebellion, as well. Do not do so lightly, for eventually God will allow you to receive the fruit of your rebellion. The Jews of that day saw their land destroyed, their families killed or split up, and everything they valued lost.

Direction for today: Remember the consequences of sin and rebellion.

Prayer for today: "Father, I will always listen to Your voice."

Philippians

This epistle of Paul's is very different from his letter to the Ephesians. There is very little formal doctrine here. The main theme of this letter is Joy. The Apostle Paul is writing from prison and it shows that he has a radiant experience in Christ.

There were several reasons why Paul wrote this letter. Firstly, the church at Philippi had sent a generous gift and there was a very deep sense of thankfulness in Paul's heart for their financial support of his ministry. Secondly, he tried to constantly encourage the churches which he had pioneered.

Thirdly, there were minor problems which Paul wished to correct, such as some disunity that was appearing within the church and the threat from the Judaizers who would come there also, as they had come to Galatia.

February 18: Read Philippians 1

Key verse: *"I thank my God every time I remember you" (Philippians 1:3 NIV).*

This succinct statement by Paul stands in marked contrast to the attitudes of many Christians in our day. Too often, also to quote Paul, we "keep on biting and devouring each other" (Galations 5:15 NIV).

It is the will of Jesus that the world will see a great example of God's love in the love that Christians show to one another. And in the Bible, love is never an emotional feeling — love is always portrayed in action.

One of the most effective loving actions is shown in our key verse: consciously, and frequently, thanking the Lord for one another. It is very hard to fight with a brother or sister about the colour of hymnals in our church sancturary if I have spent time thanking God for the good things he or she has done in the church. Similarly, it is hard to be critical of a prominent Christian teacher or evangelist is I have consciously thanked the Lord for the many people in the kingdom because of his or her ministry.

Paul is actually showing us the best antidote against that terminal disease among Christians — bitterness. The way of joy and peace lies in following his example.

Direction for today: Thank God every time you think of a Christian brother or sister.

Prayer for today: "Father, thank You for the Christians You have brought into my life to build me up".

February 19: Read Philippians 2

Key verse: *"Do nothing from selfishness or empty conceit, but with humility of mind let each of you regard one another as more than himself" (Philippians 2:3 NAS).*

Such a glorious ideal means that we will live without regard for self-interest, and that we would do nothing that would intentionally bring glory to ourselves. This command means instead that everything we do is done

32

to enhance and elevate the other person. At first glance, this seems to be an impossible goal, given our weak and often carnal nature.

However, Jesus points the way in Philippians 2:5-8. We are told to have the same attitude in us that was also in Christ Jesus. He was willing to give up all glory to bring us into glory! He said "no" to the lures of the world, just as we are to stand against temptations to seek our own glory or the fulfillment of our selfish desires. To take up our cross and to follow Him is to empty ourselves of the pride of the flesh and to come alive, born again of His Spirit.

Direction for today: With the guidance of the Spirit, live to build up your brothers and sisters in Christ.

Prayer for today: "Father, cleanse me of selfishness."

Memory Verse

"Call to Me, and I will answer you, and show you great and mighty things, which you do not know." Jeremiah 33:3 NKJV

February 20: Read Philippians 3

Key verse: "That I may know Him, and the power of His resurrection and the fellowship of His sufferings, being conformed to His death" (Philippians 3:10 NAS).

Paul exhorts the believer to rejoice in the Lord. He then speaks against a danger that will rob believers of joy: in the church of Philippi there were legalists who urged the Christians to keep the law of Moses as part of the means to salvation. Paul strongly cautions against such teaching.

Paul had been the chief of legalists, and he "boasts" of his former standing as a Pharisee, but he quickly adds that none of his accomplishments were worth anything in comparison to his relationship with Jesus.

What was his greatest desire? That he might know Christ, the power of His resurrection, and the fellowship of His suffering. These are three important ambitions for a believer. We can spend a lifetime of effort and still not fully comprehend Christ, but the more we know Him, the more we will consecrate our lives to Him. To know the power of His resurrection is to know Him victorious, the conqueror of sin and evil. In this knowledge there is great spiritual courage.

Direction for today: Allow the Holy Spirit to conform you to be like Christ.

Prayer for today: "Father, may I desire, always, to know more of Jesus."

February 21: Read Philippians 4

Key verse: "But my God shall supply all your need according to His riches in glory by Christ Jesus" (Philippians 4:19 KJV).

The epistle, written from a Roman jail, is a monument of faith in real life. When Paul encouraged the Philippian Christians to trust Christ completely, they knew he was not making idle statements. He was putting his experience where his mouth was, and it was not for the first time: the Philippians could also remember what Paul had gone through in their city!

The assurance that God would meet them at every point of their need was a declaration of truth proven in life. And the man who urged them to rejoice in the Lord was the same man who had sang harmony with Silas in the Philippian jail!

The Philippians knew that Paul's words about Jesus were backed up by his consistently faithful life. May the same be true of each of us.

Direction for today: Seek the Lord, trusting Him to supply all your need.

Prayer for today: "Father, thank You that I can always depend on You."

The exiles return!

The next two books that we will read, Ezra and Nehemiah, are closely related. They happen during the same time period, and each is part of the story of the return of the exiled people of God to the land of Israel.

The land has remained empty for seventy years, since the conquering armies of Babylon carried virtually the entire nation of Israel away into exile in Babylon (II Chronicles 36:20,21). But, in Babylon, His people returned to true worship of the Lord God (See Psalm 137:1-6), and God responded in faithfulness to His promise of II Chronicles 7:14: "If My people who are called by My name shall humble themselves and pray, and seek My face and turn from their wicked ways, then I will hear from heaven, will forgive their sin, and will heal their land."

In Ezra, we see the healing process begun. Cyrus, king of Persia, who had conquered Babylon, ordered the return of the exiles to their homeland. This is clearly the act of God – in Isaiah, Cyrus is prophetically named "My shepherd" by the Lord; God had chosen him to allow the resettlement of Israel long before Cyrus ascended any throne!

Ezra, both the main character and the probable writer of this book, is called a "scribe", a learned interpreter of the law. The book begins with the account of the initial return (in 538 B.C.), and the beginnings of work to rebuild the temple in Jerusalem. This work was delayed, then finally completed, but the people quickly began to backslide.

Eighty years after the initial return of the exiles, Ezra travelled from Babylon to initiate a much-needed revival. His stern and unbending call to true worship brought results. The final portion of the book details the deep concern of the scribe for his people, and the response of God to one man's intercessory prayers.

February 22: Read Ezra 1,2

Key verse: "Whoever is among you of all His people, may his God be with them, and let him go up to Jerusalem, which is in Judah, and rebuild the house of the Lord, the God of Israel — He is the God who is in Jerusalem" (Ezra 1:33 RSV).

It was a dream come true! The prophet Jeremiah had spoken God's promise, that the Jews would be allowed to return to their land. And now it had come to pass.

After 70 years in exile, the people could return home to rebuild the house of the Lord. But permission to go does not always mean courage to go. There were those who stayed behind and who gave an offering to help rebuild the temple. There were the doers, and there were the supporters, and together they formed a team.

The same is true today, as we work to build the temple of God: the living temple that is the church of Jesus Christ. There are some who are gifted to bring many building blocks — new believers — to this growing temple. And there are others who are part of the support team, working in less noticed ways. But, as long as we are faithful to the job God has given to us, we are doing exactly what we should on this eternal construction site.

Direction for today: Instead of seeking more "important" jobs, be faithful in the work God has given to you.

Prayer for today: "Thank you, Father, that You have a specific job for me to do. Help me to be faithful to You in all things."

February 23: Read Ezra 3,4

Key verse: *"Yet many of the priests and Levites and heads of the father's households, the old men who had seen the first temple, wept with a loud voice when the foundation of this house was laid before their eyes, while many shouted aloud for joy" (Ezra 3:12 NAS).*

These chapters tell a story of trials and triumphs. The people had followed a two-year plan of worship and work; now the foundation of the house of the Lord had been built. It was a time of rejoicing, reminiscence, hope for the future and acknowledgement of the faithfulness of God. They expressed their deep emotion with weeping and shouting, displaying their individuality. Truly the blessings of the past give hope for the future.

We note, as well, that the destruction of the Temple had not hindered worship in the hearts of God's people, for when they returned to Jerusalem they immediately set up an altar to express the reverence for God that lived in their spirits.

Let us thank God for the many places of worship in our contry where people are free to meet together in His presence. And let us be sure to take advantage of that privilege ourselves.

Direction for today: Be sure that you worship the Lord with His people.

Prayer for today: "Lord, bless my brothers and sisters in countries where there are no church buildings, and where they face persecution for worshipping You."

February 24: Read Ezra 5,6

Key verse: "Leave the work on the house of God alone; let the governor of the Jews and the elders of the Jews build this house of God on its site" (Ezra 6:7 NAS).

Even though Darius was not a godly king, God used him to command all the enemies of Israel to leave the Israelites alone, that they might work and rebuild the temple.

We live in a world today where secular humanism, atheism, the occult and other anti-God forces aim to destroy God's church. However, just as God established Darius, so He still sets up and puts down national leaders. God will have His rulers who will command His enemies to leave Christians alone and let them go about their Father's business to build the church.

Jesus said, "I will build My church and the gates of Hades shall not overpower it" (Matthew 16:18). We are living in a time of reconciliation, when the backslider, the unsaved loved one and those who have been rebellious are coming back to God. It is a time of revival, in which the Holy Spirit is being poured out on all flesh. It is a time of building the church of God before Jesus comes again. God will find a way to hold back every evil force until all be fulfilled and His church built completely.

Then shall the end come.

Direction for today: Pray for our leaders, that the church will have the freedom to speak for Christ.

Prayer for today: "Father, bless the leaders of this country and lead them into Your truth."

February 25: Read Ezra 7,8

Key verse: "The hand of our God is upon all of them for good that seek Him; but His power and His wrath is against all them that forsake Him" (Ezra 8:22 KJV).

We must be prepared to practice what we preach. The writer here had proclaimed to the king that the hand of God was upon those who seek Him, but His power and wrath was against all who forsook Him. Now he was ashamed to ask the king for help.

Where then could he go? There was only once choice, and he took it: he went to God. With fasting he sought God, and his prayers were answered.

Isn't that just like our loving God? He is truly interested in our every need, but He will never force Himself upon us. Matthew 7:7 tells us, "Ask and it shall be given to you; seek and ye shall find; knock and it shall be opened unto you."

God enjoys it when we are in the same position as Ezra, when we know that all else has failed and we have no other place to go but to Him. Then, when He answers, we fully realize His greatness. Reach out to Jesus!

Direction for today: Remember that nothing is impossible with God!

Prayer for today: "Thank you, Lord, that You are the answer in every situation."

February 26: Read Ezra 9,10

Key verse: "Now while Ezra was praying and making confession, weeping and prostrating himself before the house of God, a very large assembly, men, women and children, gathered to him from Israel; for the people wept bitterly" (Ezra 10:1 NAS).

The people of God, newly returned to their land, were once again falling into the same sins that had brought corruption and eventual destruction in earlier centuries. They were disobeying the command of God regarding the heathen peoples of the land: "You shall not intermarry with them . . . for they will turn your sons away from following Me to serve other gods" (Deuteronomy 7:3,4).

What is beautiful about today's reading is the intercessary action of Ezra. We see how deeply felt the need for reconciliation between the people and the Lord. Christians are called to the same ministry. "If anyone sees his brother committing a sin not leading to death, he shall ask and God will for him give life to those who commit sin not leading to death" (I John 5:16). Both in Ezra and in I John we see a believer standing before God on behalf of other believers, asking God to forgive them.

And notice the reaction: the entire nation, touched by Ezra's intercession, returned to the Lord! Similarly, out intercession on behalf of others will bring results!

Direction for today: Remember your intercessory ministry!

Prayer for today: "Father, may I be right before You so that I can be a true intercessor."

Nehemiah

The way to reconstruction of the land of Israel was a long and hard one. The temple was rebuilt (although a mere shadow of that constructed by Solomon), but the city of Jerusalem remained unwalled – a dangerous situation in those days (Nehemiah 1:3).

Nehemiah, cup-bearer to the king of Persia, Artaxerxes, carried a deep burden for the land of his fathers, the land of Israel. He asked the king if he might be allowed to return to Israel, to rebuild the walls of the holy city.

This book, probably written by the main character, Nehemiah, details the rebuilding of the walls by the people of Israel, despite considerable opposition. The book spans the period of 445 B.C. to about 420 B.C.

Nehemiah tells us both of the rebuilding of the walls, and of the rebuilding of the faith of the people. When the walls were complete, the spiritual leaders (including Ezra, the scribe, and Nehemiah), assembled the people and read the law of Moses to them. Confrontation with the Word of God first brought tears of repentance, and then a celebration of joy (Nehemiah 8-10).

Once again, at the conclusion of the book, a final cleansing is needed, and is carried out, as foreigners actually living in the temple are expelled.

February 27: Read Nehemiah 1,2

Key verse: "Then I told them of the hand of my God which was good upon me; as also the king's words that he had spoken unto me. And they said, Let us rise up and build. So they strengthened their hands for this good work" (Nehemiah 2:18 KJV).

God gave Nehemiah a dream of what He wanted done in Jerusalem. It is exciting to see how the Lord will lay a burden on someone's heart to stir him or her into action. As Nehemiah humbled himself before God with fasting and prayer, the direction of the Lord became more evident. God showed Nehemiah the precise steps to take.

With the king's letter in hand, Nehemiah investigated the situation in Jerusalem. He challenged the Jews to rise up and build to remove their reproach. Despite bitter opposition, each man and his family built the walls side by side until God's command was obeyed.

As we seek the Lord, He will make plain what He wants us to do. The important thing is to know God's will, and to do it. It may be a big task, or something apparently small, but it is never unimportant to obey God.

Direction for today: Whatever God gives to you to do, do it!

Prayer for today: "Lord, give me clear direction concerning Your will for me."

February 28: Read Nehemiah 3,4

Key verse: "So built we the wall; and all the wall was joined together unto the half thereof; for the people had a mind to work" (Nehemiah 4:6 KJV).

God had called Nehemiah to organize the people of Israel to build the wall around Jerusalem. God has called us to build the church of Christ. It requires a mind to work and a determination not to turn back, because the devil strives to prevent the building.

The first attack of the enemy came through ridicule. People mocked the efforts of those building the walls. It is amazing how often Christians have abandoned their efforts to build the church because of ridicule. Perhaps a friend mocks their faith, or a neighbour challenges them for being "holier-than-thou".

It is sad that so often only a few mocking words are enough to cause us to hide our faith, and to stop our work.

That isn't what the people of Israel did. Under Nehemiah's leadership, they strengthened their defences and carried on.

Remember, Jesus said that if we are ashamed of Him, He will be ashamed of us!

Direction for today: Expect persecution and ridicule, and remember that Jesus suffered these more than we will ever encounter!

Prayer for today: "Father, may I stand faithful in the face of ridicule."

3

Jerusalem

Jerusalem. . .
Jerusalem . . .

How oft have I watched you,
And in watching have wept.

How much I have loved you,
Though your children have slept
So steeped in tradition;
They mock the Lord's goals
And, drowning in darkness,
They barter their souls.

You have murdered the prophets
commissioned by God.

You have broken the tablets,
and trampled the rod.
And now I am come,
As a hen to her nest,
To gather my children
and give you my rest.

But you would not. . .
You would not. . .
Jerusalem.

— Bonnie Knowles

March 1: Read Nehemiah 5,6

Key verse: *"I am doing a great work and I cannot come down. Why should the work stop while I leave and come down to you?" (Nehemiah 6:3b NAS).*

Nehemiah was busy rebuilding the walls of Jerusalem. The enemies of Israel did not like it. They tried to lure him away, to harm him, and thus to stop the reconstruction. They also tried to damage his reputation with the people, accusing him of seeking to be king. The final attempt to stop the construction involved the threat of his life. They hoped he would run and hide, and thus abort the project.

But Nehemiah had received his instructions straight from God. His reverence for God was greater than his fear of men. He had learned a truth that Jesus later taught: "do not fear those who kill the body but cannot kill the soul; rather fear Him who can destroy both body and soul in hell" (Matthew 10:28).

When Jesus calls you to do something, do it regardless of what others say. You are accountable only to the Lord. "Not everyone who says to me, 'Lord, Lord', shall enter the kingdom of heaven, but he who does the will of My Father who is in heaven" (Matthew 7:21). Do what Jesus tells you to do.

Direction for today: Instead of being afraid of men, develop a reverent fear of God, and you will accomplish great things.

Prayer for today: "Lord, give me a spirit of power, love, and self-discipline, instead of timidity."

Memory Verse

"We fasted and entreated our God for this, and He answered our prayer." Ezra 8:23 NKJV

March 2: Read Nehemiah 7,8

Key verse: *"And all the people went away to eat, to drink, to send portions and to celebrate a great festival, because they understood the words which had been made known to them" (Nehemiah 8:12 NAS).*

Does this sound like what happens in your church after a service, when the word of God has been read and preached? Do you feel like celebrating when you read your Bible?

The people of Israel certainly did! First, the word of God brought them to repentance and weeping as they realized their faithlessness. But then they burst into rejoicing, because they "understood" that God's faithfulness was far greater than their weakness, and that they could return to Him. When they heard the word of the Lord, it exploded in joy in their hearts.

As we read these chapters today, let us ask God to bring the joy of His presence in our spirits. Let us ask Him to give us a love for His word. Let us pray that our Christian gatherings will be celebrations.

Direction for today: Rejoice!

Prayer for today: "Father, as I read Your word, bring the joy of Your presence to my spirit, and give me a growing love for the Bible."

March 3: Read Nehemiah 9

Key verse: "And the seed of Israel separated themselves from all strangers, and stood and confessed their sins and the iniquities of their fathers" (Nehemiah 9:2 KJV).

Repentance and confession are essential steps in establishing a right relationship with God. In Luke 13:3, Jesus said, "I tell you, Nay: but except ye repent, ye shall all likewise perish". Repentance is not a popular subject in these days. Many people want to do everything the easy way. It seems that everywhere we turn we see shortcuts to success, fame and wealth. People are looking for the "express lane" to heaven without wanting to pay the price.

It has been said that salvation is a free gift — it only costs you your whole life. Salvation is free. But the condition is, "if we confess our sins". To confess something as sin, we must first recognize that it is sin. When we recognize sin, we as believers must then repent (turn away). We cannot be totally committed to Jesus and yet entertain known sin.

Repentance is necessary for the believer to come to know Jesus; it is also necessary for the believer to maintain a right relationship with God.

Direction for today: Recognize that repentance is a continuing necessity for a growing Christian life.

Prayer for today: "Lord, show me those areas of my life from which I must turn away, because they are displeasing to you."

March 4: Read Nehemiah 10,11

Key verse: "All these now join their brothers the nobles, and bind themselves with a curse and an oath to follow the law of God given through Moses the servant of God and to obey carefully all the commands, regulations and decrees of the Lord our God" (Nehemiah 10:29 NIV).

This is true commitment. These people, through oath, bound themselves to God. They gave themselves fully to follow God's laws and to carefully obey all direction given by Him. The need for us to obey is just as real today.

There are times when we may be tempted to consider the directions given in the Scriptures to be old-fashioned or outdated. But we must remember that they are God's principles. His ways and His requirements do not change, for they are eternal as He is eternal. God does not give regulations to stifle us, but to mould our characters and make us more like His Son. His commands are for our good. As we carefully obey them, His blessing will be ours.

Direction for today: The only way to truly please God is to obey Him.

Prayer for today: "Lord I commit myself to obedience to You."

March 5: Read Nehemiah 12

Key verse: *"For in the days of David and Asaph, in ancient times, there were leaders of the singers, songs of praise and hymns of thanksgiving to God" (Nehemiah 12:46 NAS).*

David was an enthusiast for singing psalms, praises and thanksgivings unto God. In fact, he set aside large groups of people to this specific ministry, and scheduled all kinds of praises and thanksgiving as part of the nation's daily worship.

As David knew, there is great power, joy and victory in praising God. He lived a life of victory and joy, with God's blessing on his life. Compare this record to that of the Israelites, whose complaints led to 40 years of wandering in the wilderness.

Let us follow David's example. Compile a list of all the good things God has done for you: count your blessings. Each day, review the list, praise God for each item, and add any new blessing that occurs to you. Contentment will grow in your heart as you learn to praise God continually. "And having food and raiment, let us be therewith content" (I Timothy 6:8 KJV).

Praise and thanksgiving unto the Lord is the key that will release the blessing of God in your life.

Direction for today: All good things come from God. Only He deserves our praise for them.

Prayer for today: "Thank You, Father, for every good gift."

March 6: Read Nehemiah 13

Key verse: *"Our God turned the curse into a blessing" (Nehemiah 13:2b KJV).*

Our God is a good God. He wills the best for our lives. Many people think God sends sickness and trouble to "purify" us, but God said, "I am the Lord that healeth thee" (Exodus 15:26b). God can take any bad situation and turn it into our good if we trust Him and submit to His will. He can even turn curses into blessings. He can turn bitter friends and relatives into loving, caring individuals, as we minister His grace and mercy to them. God ministered grace and mercy to us even before we became His children, and He expects us to share that grace and mercy with others.

If we trust Him, we can see all of our problems transformed into victories.

"There hath no temptation taken you but such as is common to man: but God is faithful, who will not suffer you to be tempted above that you are able; but will with the temptation also make a way to escape, that ye may be able to bear it" (I Corinthians 10:13).

Direction for today: Let go of your problems, and let God turn them into victories.

Prayer for today: "Thank You Father, that You can even turn curses to blessings."

Colossians

The church at Ephesus, which was near Colosse, had been founded by Paul, and it seems fairly certain that he sent Epaphras to be the founder of this particular church. This church did not have the benefit of Paul's direct teaching in those early days and, perhaps for this reason, we find serious error in the church which the Apostle is trying to correct.

First of all, there was an over-emphasis on the observance of sacred days and seasons and upon obedience to religious regulations and forms. Secondly, there were severe regulations imposed concerning food and drink. The implication of this teaching was that one would become more spiritual when extreme denial of the needs of the body was practised. Thirdly, some of the congregation's mystical visions and revelations, which only the inner circle could receive, led them to the worship of angels. Paul takes the sword of the Spirit which is the Word of God, and cuts away these false doctrines.

Obviously the people were very much influenced by the practice of the denomination of the Pharisees within the Jewish religion, and also they were influenced by the current thinking of the Greeks.

Paul very clearly teaches that in Christ there is the only mediator, and in Him dwells all wisdom and knowledge.

March 7: Read Colossians 1

Key verse: "We give thanks to the God and Father of our Lord Jesus Christ, praying always for you, since we heard of your faith in Christ Jesus and of your love for all the saints" (Colossians 1:3,4 NKJV).

Does your love for Jesus result in love toward all the people of God? Too often, we profess love for Christ in one breath, and criticize or complain about our fellow Christians in the next.

In these verses, Paul shows us how unChristian this is. If we really love Jesus, we will also live in active love toward our brothers and sisters.

Of course, it is sometimes difficult to love our fellow believers; and undoubtedly, they find it equally difficult to love us! In verse 3, Paul offers two helpful tips. It is always easier to act in love toward someone for whom you are consistently praying, and for whom you are thanking God.

If there are brothers and sisters towards whom you feel no love, act in love, anyway. Thank God for them. Pray for them. The love you are showing in your actions will soon seep into your emotions.

And remember: Jesus said that the world will judge the truth of the Christian message by the love Christians have one for the other. If we claim to love Christ, and do not love our fellow believers, we are showing ourselves to be liars, and holding the gospel up to disrepute.

Direction for today: People will only believe that Jesus loves them when they see love in the people of Jesus.

Prayer for today: "Lord Jesus, may I follow in Your footsteps of love."

March 8: Read Colossians 2

Key verse: "For in Him dwelleth all the fulness of the Godhead bodily. And ye are complete in Him, which is the head of all principality and power" (Colossians 2:9,10 KJV).

The concern that Paul expresses in this epistle is a very practical one. Surrounded by a heathen culture and ideas, these newly converted Christians needed a firm grounding in spiritual understanding. Misplaced faith can be as dangerous as the failure to exercise that faith which is imparted to each person.

The central theme of this letter is the person and ministry of Jesus Christ. He is presented as the head of all power and authority. The final answers are to be found in Him, not in man's philosophies and traditions. As Head of the Church, He has the right to govern and direct its activities. Having all the fulness of the Godhead, He cannot be impressed by anything that man can offer.

Centuries of learning, and the compiling of man's acquired knowledge, have confirmed the validity of this epistle. The solution to mankind's problems is not in the realm of intellectual pursuit but in an understanding of who Jesus Christ really is. When we come to know Him, we find that the search for reality has ended.

Direction for today: The ultimate answer is only found in Jesus. Do not look anywhere else.

Prayer for today: "Father, may my faith be anchored in You."

Memory Verse

"Do not sorrow, for the joy of the Lord is your strength." Nehemiah 8:10b NKJV

March 9: Read Colossians 3,4

Key verse: "And whatsoever ye do in word or deed, do all in the name of the Lord Jesus Christ, giving thanks to God and the Father by Him" (Colossians 3:17 KJV).

We are told to set our affections on things above and not on things of this world. When Christ comes into our lives, He changes us and our whole outlook.

After they have had an experience with Jesus, some people try to hang on to the old nature. They still look on "things on the earth", but Jesus Christ has drawn us up, releasing us from the bondage of sin. Our lives have been made new, but the old sin nature ever seeks to make a come-back. Don't let it!

The Bible tells us that faith without works is dead. With Christ in our hearts, God expects that our lives will glorify Him. In the natural, we seek to please those whom we love. If we're in love with Jesus, as we should be, we should seek to please Him.

Direction for today: Whether talking or working, let your words and actions glorify Christ.

Prayer for today: "Father, may my eyes and my heart be set only on You."

Esther

"Esther" is a Persian word meaning "star". And Esther is certainly a star, a shining example of courage and faithfulness.

This exciting narrative took place in Persia in the period following the exile, when thousands of Jews remained living in the various countries of their displacement, even after some, such as Ezra, had returned to the land of Israel. The author of this book is unknown, but is obviously a Jew living in Persia at the time of Esther and Mordecai.

The book is a clear example of the triumph of righteousness over evil; even more (although God is not specifically mentioned in the book), Esther is a beautiful picture of God's deliverance for His people.

March 10: Read Esther 1,2

Key verse: "He had brought up Hadassah, that is, Esther, his uncle's daughter: for she had neither father nor mother and the maid was fair and beautiful; whom Mordecai, when her father and mother were dead, took for his own daughter" (Esther 2:7 NAS).

The central figure of this book is, of course, Esther. She was beautiful and courageous, cunning and resourceful. Mordecai, a patriot devoted to his people, made the necessary arrangements for Esther to be brought before the King. She may have been reluctant to become the bride of a Gentile, but once Esther accepted her mission she played her role heroically. She was to be the instrument by which her people would be delivered. She had no foreknowledge of what would be required of her, but she met each demand as it came.

Christians, too, are called to trust in God's providence one day at at time.

Esther became queen just as Haman was plotting to exterminate the Jews. Mordecai pleaded with his niece to intercede with the king. Esther loved her people, but feared death for entering the king's inner court without his permission. But she realized that she must take the risk; she saw her duty, and she did it.

In our everyday life, we often look for easy ways out of opportunities which God presents to us. But, after reflection, a mature Christian will obey God, trusting Him with the outcome.

Direction for today: Whatever happens, and whatever the result, I will keep my eyes on Jesus, and my faith in Him.

Prayer for today: "Lord, I declare my trust in You."

March 11: Read Esther 3,4

Key verse: ". . . but Mordecai bowed not, nor did him reverence" (Esther 3:2b NAS).

The whole book of Esther is an account of the traumatic pressure on the Jews, and how Esther the Queen intervened on behalf of the Jewish people to save their very lives.

It all hinged on the disobedience of one man, Mordecai, who refused to reverence a man because it contravened the law of God. The story written in this book would never have taken place had Mordecai bowed to Haman. But because of this one man's loyalty to God, there was precipitiated one of the greatest turn-arounds in the history of Israel.

We are not suggesting that every act of civil disobedience is blessed of God, nor are we suggesting that we should make a great public show of our dedication to the word and purposes of God. But we do suggest that everyone must learn to relate personally to God in such obedience and dedication that we care little about the consequences which may follow. As it turned out, Mordecai was not only exonerated, but exalted to become the second-in-command in the nation.

The often-quoted words of Mordecai to Esther, "Who knows but that you were brought to the kingdom for such an hour as this", could apply to every one of us in our daily obedience to God and our witness for Christ.

Direction for today: Obedience to the word of God inevitably brings blessing to His obedient child.

Prayer for today: "Lord, help me to know to obey You, regardless of the cost."

March 12: Read Esther 5,6

Key verse: *"On that night could not the King sleep, and he commanded to bring the book of the records of the Chronicles; and they were read before the King" (Esther 6:1 KJV).*

You cannot help but see the protecting hand of God upon His servant Mordecai. What Haman planned to do was no laughing matter, but it is amusing to read chapter six and see God's sense of humour. He turned things around and, through Haman's own pride, had him commissioned by the king to bring honour to the man he intended to kill.

This portion of scripture should allow us to realize the protecting hand of God upon those who serve Him today. It is important to understand that Mordecai was faithful to God and the king he served. He did not deserve what Haman had planned for him, and God protected him. He even gave him a place of greater honour in the king's eyes.

God has promised, "I will never leave thee nor forsake thee" (Hebrews 13:5) and, "In all thy ways acknowledge Him and He shall direct thy paths" (Proverbs 3:6). God is our Protector.

Direction for today: Serve God faithfully, and all things will work together for your good.

Prayer for today: "Thank You, Jesus, that You will never leave me nor forsake me."

March 13: Read Esther 7,8

Key verse: *"Now Esther spoke again to the King, fell down at his feet, and implored him with tears to counteract the evil plot of Haman the Agagite, and the scheme which he had devised against the Jews" (Esther 8:3 NKJV).*

The Jews were still under Haman's decree of death. Unless the order of the king was changed, every Jew would die. Esther sought to save her people by interceding on their behalf. Her intervention saved the Jews, because she went to the only one who could change the situation.

James tells us that "the effective, fervent prayer of a righteous man avails much" (James 5:16). In our most dire circumstances, we can humbly beseech our heavenly Father to change the situation. Nothing is impossible with God. God can heal that sick child, restore that marriage, solve that problem, in response to prayer. Whatever the need, God is able to provide.

Direction for today: Be an intercessor for the needy.

Prayer for today: "Lord, in every circumstance, help me to remember to immediately turn to You."

March 14: Read Esther 9,10

Key verse: *"Therefore the Jews of the villages, that dwelt in the unwalled towns, made the fourteenth day of the month Adar a day of gladness and feasting, and a good day, and of sending portions one to another" (Esther 9:19 KJV).*

It would be difficult to image a more complete reversal of fortunes for the Jews. At one point, they are facing racial extermination, but by royal decree, allowing them to attack the enemies who gather to destroy them, the Jews win a complete victory.

The feast of Purim was instituted as a permanent memorial of the day of triumph. Purim comes from "Pur", a Persian word meaning "lot". Haman had by lot decided this to be the day of the Jews' extermination. God's lot reversed that decision and determined that the day would be one of victory.

Direction for today: Remember that the final decision always rests with God.

Prayer for today: "Thank You, Jesus, that You are always able to bring victory, even in impossible circumstances."

I and II Thessalonians

Paul had been driven from Thessalonica shortly after leading many new converts to the Lord. He sent Timothy back to check on the progress of the church and to encourage the Christians (I Thessalonians 3:2). Timothy returned with a good report of the new work, and brought some questions to Paul from the Thessalonians, especially concerning the return of Christ. The first letter is an answer to those questions, and general encouragement.

The persecutions at Thessalonica continued, as did some of the errors concerning Christ's return, and Paul quickly wrote the second letter to encourage and correct the church again.

March 15: Read I Thessalonians 1-3

Key verse: "For this reason we also constantly thank God that when you received from us the word of God's message, you accepted it not as the word of men, but for what it really is, the word of God, which also performs its works in you who believe" (I Thessalonians 2:13 NAS).

If ever people have needed something in their lives that works, it is now. The world is filled with people desperately seeking for that missing element, that factor that will give them reason for being; for something, or someone, that will "work" for them.

Paul had found both that something, and that someone: the Word of God, and Jesus Christ. Being one of the key religious leaders of his day had not worked for Paul. An excellent education, approval of governmental and religious authorities, power to direct the lives of others — none of these things worked for him.

And then he met Jesus, and made Him the controlling influence in his life. He carried the message of Christ and the scriptures to huge sections of the then-known world, and rejoiced as God's Word began to do its holy work in those to whom he preached, and among whom he ministered.

Direction for today: Let the word of God work mightily in you.

Prayer for today: "May Jesus have as much influence in my life as He did in the life of the apostle Paul."

Memory Verse

"For I know that my Redeemer lives, and He shall stand at last on the earth; and after my skin is destroyed, this I know, that in my flesh I shall see God." Job 19:25,26 NKJV

March 16: Read I Thessalonians 4,5

Key verse: *"Abstain from all appearance of evil" (I Thessalonians 5:22 KJV).*

Here, Paul speaks of the second coming of Jesus Christ, and offers some general guidance concerning appropriate Christian lifestyle.

As we await the return of our Saviour, several things are expected of us. We must warn the unruly, comfort the feeble-minded, support the weak and be patient with all people. These are our responsibilities to others.

Then we must be fair and follow that which is good, rejoicing, praying continually, thanking God for all things. In all things, and at all times, we must be open to the Holy Spirit, open to preaching, and careful to ensure that whatever we do is according to the will of God as revealed in the Bible.

And last, but not least, we are asked to stay away from all appearance of evil. Jesus will help us and empower us to do all of these things. Trust Him to guide your life.

Direction for today: "I can do all things through Christ which strengtheneth me" (Philippians 4:13 KJV).

Prayer for today: "Father, help me to be sensitive to know which things are improper for me as Your child."

March 17: Read II Thessalonians 1-3

Key verse: *"Now may the Lord of peace Himself continually grant you Peace in every circumstance. The Lord be with you all!" (II Thessalonians 3:16 NAS).*

Paul speaks of the turmoil, wickedness and deception that will accompany the coming of the Antichrist. But he says, "The Lord Himself give you peace". This tells us that true peace does not depend on surroundings or circumstances.

Many in the world call for peace, strive for peace, and claim to offer peace. This is a noble concept, but apart from Christ it is doomed to failure, for true peace is never external nor temporal; it is only the product of the Holy Spirit at work in the spirit of a believer. The Lord, and only the Lord, gives us peace, a peace that is so deep and real that it survives any circumstance in which we might find ourselves.

Direction for today: Jesus is the only true source of peace.

Prayer for today: "Father, may I share with someone else the true peace that comes from You."

Why do righteous suffer?

This question has confronted God's people all through history, from the death of Abel (Genesis 4:8) to the sufferings of Paul; from the tribulations facing Christians in our world to the still-to-come times of the martyrs recorded prophetically in the book of Revelation.

More than any other book in the Old Testament, Job answers this question. Job suffered precisely *because* he was a righteous, blameless man, and thus was a target for the attacks of Satan!

Job also suffered because God was allowing him to suffer, that his faith might be proven strong (I Peter 1:6,7), and because God knew that after he suffered a little while, He would raise Job up to a place of eternal glory (I Peter 5:10).

Who was Job? Almost all we know of him is stated in the first verse of the book – he was a righteous man, who worshipped God and lived in the land of Uz. Subsequent verses tell us he was extremely prosperous.

It is certain that Job was a historical character, but it is also obvious that his story has been rendered in poetic form; this book is classed both with the wisdom literature (Proverbs, Ecclesiastes) and with the poetical books (Psalms, Song of Solomon, etc.).

Job lived in early, patriarchal times; perhaps he was a contemporary of Abraham, or lived even earlier. It is probably that he was not a Jew – in fact, if he lived before Abraham, there were no Hebrew people.

We must realize, as we read this book, that although every word is faithfully recorded under God's inspiration, not all of the words are the truth. In other words – the speeches of Job's friends and Job himself are accurately recorded, but often those men were wrong! It is therefore very important to remember the central facts of this book: Job was indeed a righteous man, so pronounced by God (1:8), despite the accusations of his friends. The evils that befell him were *not* visitations from God, despite the accusations of Job, who felt that all things must come directly from God!

The conclusion of the book is a beautiful testimony of faith: Job, still unaware of the enemy, Satan content nonetheless to worship and trust his God. We have much to learn concerning faith from this man Job. We can also (in a negative sense) learn much about counselling and sharing burdens from the mistakes of Job's wife and friends.

March 18: Read Job 1,2

Key verse: "Then the Lord said to Satan, 'Behold, all that he has is in your power, only do not put forth your hand on him'" (Job 1:12 NAS).

These first chapters are absolutely important if we are to understand the remainder of the book of Job. And it is especially important that we realize who is acting here, who it is who brings death and destruction to Job's family, servants and possessions. The enemy of Job, and of life, is Satan.

We must also realize that Job did not acknowledge the existence of Satan. Notice Job 1:21, where he says, "The Lord gave and the Lord has taken away. Blessed be the name of the Lord." Now, we know that this is not true — we have just read that Satan was the "taker-away", not God. Death and destruction are the tools of the enemy of man, Satan.

Job believed that God was responsible for the evil that had befallen him, as did all of his friends. Yet he still remained faithful to God! (Job 1:22).

What a lesson this is to us. We know far more than Job did about the spiritual powers waging war in this world. We know that Satan exists and that he is the accuser, the deceiver, the enemy of God and His people. Yet very often, when a crisis befalls us, we accuse God of being unfair to us. What a contrast: Job honestly thought God was doing these things, yet he remained faithful.

This is a vital lesson to remember in times of crisis. Sin and the devil are still in the world, but the death and resurrection of Jesus are evidence that God has taken the result of those evils upon himself, and triumphed.

Direction for today: In any sorrow, we should not blame God; for He did not cause it but, in Jesus, He has borne it.

Prayer for today: "Thank You, Jesus, for sharing my pain and bearing my sin!"

March 19: Read Job 3,4

Key verse: "If someone ventures a word with you, will you be impatient? But who can keep from speaking?" (Job 4:2 NIV).

Job's friends are a great example of how <u>not</u> to comfort a friend. Although some of the things they say are founded in truth, their general attitude is entirely wrong: they believed that Job was suffering because of his sin. Therefore, they attempted to correct him, instead of comforting him.

It is most important that we remember that it is much more important to comfort and suport a brother or sister in trouble, than it is to try to correct them. God says that it is the work of the Holy Spirit to convict of sin, it is never our job!

Job needed friends who would sit with him, express love and offer compassionate companionship. He did not need lectures or correction, expecially from three men who basically did not know what they were talking about!

When we are with a friend who is hurting, may we be true friends, and not lecturers.

Direction for today: Allow the Holy Spirit to do the work of convicting and changing others.

Prayer for today: "Lord, may I be like Jesus in my compassion and love toward others."

March 20: Read Job 5,6

Key verse: "Behold, happy is the man whom God correcteth; therefore despise not thou the chastenings of the Almighty." (Job 5:17 KJV).

This statement, made by Eliphaz the Temanite to Job, is one that is confirmed by several other references throughout God's Word. Correction and discipline are hallmarks of true love. The writer to the Hebrews states that every child of God must submit to the Lord's discipline if he is to bring forth the fruits of righteousness (Hebrews 12:5-11).

However, the thought that Eliphaz seemed intent on pressing upon Job was that all suffering is the consequence of a person's own sin. This would imply that, seeing that Job was suffering so greatly, he must have committed a grievous sin. This kind of reasoning is not borne out by the teaching of scripture. Jesus is the example of the fact that suffering is not always the result of a person's disobedience or sin. Standing before the Jews, Jesus could say: "Which of you convinceth Me of sin?" (John 8:46). No, Jesus never sinned and yet no one has been called upon to suffer more than He did.

Even in everyday life, we know people that often suffer because of the sins and failures of others or because of circumstances beyond their control. Job did not know why he was called upon to go through such a fiery trial but he still retained his faith in God. It does not seem to require much faith when everything is going well, but when everything looks as if it were falling apart faith is put to the test. Someone has said that, "a Christian is like tea: his real strength only comes out when he gets into hot water."

The Word of God says that if we are corrected for our faults and take it patiently we have nothing to brag about; but when we do what is right and we are called upon to suffer for it and do not retaliate, this is pleasing to God (I Peter 2:19-25). God's plan is to conform us to the likeness of His Son Jesus Christ. Suffering is included in that plan. It is not meant to defeat or destroy us but to strengthen and refine us. Gold becomes valuable after it has been subjected to the melting and refining process. I Peter 1:18 tells us that faith that has passed God's testing will bring praise, honour, and glory when Jesus Christ is revealed.

Direction for today: Faith in Jesus Christ can change our stumbling blocks into stepping stones.

Prayer for today: "Father, discipline me, to restore me, whenever I am out of Your will."

March 21: Read Job 7,8

Key verse: *"What is man that Thou dost magnify him, and that Thou are concerned about him?" (Job 7:17 NAS).*

As we read of the suffering of Job, we are reminded of the suffering and death of our Lord Jesus as He, who was without sin, died for our sins. Jesus changed many things that Job and his friends believed to be true. Job said, "he who goes down to Sheol [hell] does not come up" (Job 7:9). But Jesus did!

Job also asked the question quoted in our key verse. He knew nothing of the infinite grace of God, who was not only "mindful" of us, but who sent His own precious Son to give Himself for us!

Jesus is the answer to the questions asked in Job. Job, although he knew nothing of Jesus, was faithful to God. We, who know about the Saviour, have even more reason to be faithful and thankful.

Direction for today: Praise God for His wonderful plan of salvation.

Prayer for today: "Thank You, Father, that You are more than 'mindful' of me."

March 22: Read Job 9,10

Key verse: *"Behold, He taketh away, who can hinder Him? Who will say unto Him, What doest Thou?" (Job 9:12 KJV).*

Throughout the Bible, there are recorded instances when great men of God went through times of real suffering. Moses, for example, spent forty years in the wilderness. Joseph was thrown into a well by his brothers, sold to Egypt, falsely accused and imprisoned for a number of years. He was forsaken by his brothers, friends and seemingly by God. But "we know that all things work together for good to them that love God, to them who are the called according to His purpose" (Romans 8:28).

We must be aware that the devil is always attacking. Another example can be found in John 9:2-4: "And His disciples asked Him, saying, 'Master, who did sin, this man, or his parents, that he was born blind?' Jesus answered, 'Neither hath this man sinned, nor his parents: but that the works of God should be made manifest in him'."

Job's two friends, Bildad and Zophar, accused him of sin, saying, "Job, you obviously have sinned, or you would not be like this now." The devil will always send someone around to tell you you are suffering because you are living in sin. But, if we have repented of our sin, we know that God has forgiven us and the suffering we are going through is not because of those sins which have been confessed and forsaken. We are told, in I John 1:9, "If we confess our sins, He is faithful and just to forgive us our sins, and to cleanse us from all unrighteousness".

When we get to heaven we will better understand the spiritual struggles we have in this life. Until that time, however, we know that all things work together for good to them that love God. Therefore, when you are hurting, run quickly into the arms of your heavenly Father. He will heal your sorrowing heart, and warm you with the sunshine of His love.

Direction for today: Take heart, "For I reckon that the sufferings of this present time are not worthy to be compared with the glory which shall be revealed in us" (Romans 8:18).

Prayer for today: "Father, if I ever face a 'Job' experience, may I remember the faith of Job and the faithfulness of God."

Memory Verse

"Let everything that has breath praise the Lord. Praise the Lord!" Psalm 250:6 NKJV

March 23: Read Job 11-13

Key verse: "I know that I am righteous" (Job 13:18 TLB).

In the middle of Job's distress, we might expect to see Him looking inward for a reason for his problem. He has already searched his heart and come to this conclusion, "I know that I am righteous". With a clear conscience before the Lord, he was able to tell his accusers that he was guiltless.

Ours is the same God whom Job served. He is able to forgive our sins and allow us to live free of the condemnation that guilt brings. Yes, God is willing to forgive, however, the responsibility is ours to search our hearts and confess those things which need to be forgiven.

A great weapon of the enemy is to accuse us of things which we have done. If they have been forgiven and cleansed from our hearts he has no hold over us. However, if he finds a heart cluttered with sin, Satan lays such a heavy burden of guilt on the believer that he may feel condemnation and defeat.

Because Job was a righteous man, when the trail of his faith came he was not crushed by a burden of guilt.

Direction for today: If your heart is not right before God, change that now, so that the enemy will have no hold over you.

Prayer for today: "Father, by Your Spirit, reveal the truth about my heart and my standing with You."

March 24: Read Job 14, 15

Key Verse: "If a man dies, will he live again?" (Job 14:14a NIV).

Praise the Lord, Yes!

Job was a man of great faith. Although he did not understand all that was happening to him, and often turned to the Lord with questions about his calamaties, his overall trust in God never wavered.

Job did not have the New Testament. He did not know the words of Jesus Christ, promising eternal life to all who believe in Him, or saying that He was going ahead of His followers to prepare a place for them in heaven.

But Job did know that God is a just God. He knew that his faith would be rewarded. He knew that there would be an opportunity to stand before his Lord.

It is constantly amazing to discover the deep and abiding faith of Job, a man who knew only a small part of the truth now revealed to us in Christ. We now know the whole story. We know that Jesus has opened the door to eternal life. We know that He is preparing a place for us, and that He intercedes for us as His own.

Praise the Lord that the truth that Job grasped through faith, is now revealed to us in fulness. Every man, woman and child who dies will certainly live again. And each one who dies in Christ will live forever with Him!

Direction for today: Live your life in the consciousness of eternity.

Prayer for today: "Thank You, Jesus, that You are the Door into eternal life."

March 25: Read Job 16,17

Key verse: *"Even now, behold, my witness is in heaven, and my advocate is on high" (Job 16:19 NAS).*

There is an old proverb, "If you don't have anything good to say, say nothing at all." That would certainly have been good advice for Job's friends. All of their talking was useless to Job - it held no comfort or help for him, and he accused them of being "worthless physicians" (Job 13:4).

Job's friends were sure they understood the problem. They saw that all manner of misfortune had befallen Job, and they were convinced that this must be a judgment from God. This is the growing emphasis of the speeches of the "friends" throughout the remainder of the book of Job.

Job, however, knows differently. He knows that he has been as blameless as was humanly possible (as God had also said, in Job 1:8).

He does not understand why all of these things are happening to him and he continues to believe that God must be responsible: "His anger has torn me and hunted me down, He has gnashed at me with His teeth" (16:9).

Yet, in the midst of the betrayal by his friends and his anguish before God, Job glimpses the true picture. For a brief moment, he sees beyond his apparent circumstances with the eyes of faith: "Behold, my witness is in heaven and my advocate is on high".

We long to say to Job: Now you've got it! Let us tell you Who you just saw. "We have an advocate with the Father, Jesus Christ the righteous" (I John 2:1).

Praise God that, in the midst of turmoil, we know who our Advocate is, and we know that we can turn to God our Father, Jesus our Lord, and the

Holy Spirit our Comforter as three friends far more faithful and wise than those of Job.

Direction for today: When called to comfort a friend, allow the Comforter to minister through you.

Prayer for today: "Father, by Your Spirit, teach me to be a friend."

March 26: Read Job 18,19

Key verse: "For I know that my redeemer liveth" (Job 19:25 KJV).

How beautiful it is that, in the midst of persecution, trials and tribulations, we can know that our Redeemer is alive. What a comfort to know that He is with us at all times and will never forsake us.

This book tells the tragic story of the trials of Job. Determined to rob him from God, Satan did everything he could to Job. But the faith of this persecuted man rested, not on logic, but on the Lord.

"I know that my redeemer liveth"; this was a statement of faith in a time of foulness. This was Job's light in the darkest of darkness. His faith in the Lord brought a confident ray of hope.

What about us today? We have a resurrected Saviour, Jesus Christ, who shed His blood that we might be free from our sins. "I will never leave thee, nor forsake thee", is His promise, as recorded in Hebrews 13:5.

Let us stand on the Word of God today and reach out to Him for our strength. With our hand in that of Christ, we will go forward for Him. As Job was victorious over Satan, so are we through Christ.

Direction for today: Enjoy the blessings of our living God by trusting in Him and expecting results!

Prayer for today: "Praise You, Lord, that my Redeemer lives!"

March 27: Read Job 20,21

Key verse: "Listen carefully to my words; let this be the consolation you give me" (Job 21:2 NIV).

Job's advice, although it may have been tinged with irony toward his wordy friends, is excellent counsel for anyone who is comforting someone in sorrow.

Most people are much better at speaking than they are at listening. We are eager to talk, and many of our conversations are really just dual monologues, as each person impatiently waits for his or her opportunity to speak. We really hear very little that is said to us.

The children of Israel frequently had this problem, and God often had to say, "Hear, Oh Israel!" They weren't listening.

In the Book of Revelation, Jesus says to the churches, "He who has an ear to hear, let him hear", implying that many have closed their ears.

We must learn to listen to God; and if we are to be true friends, we must also learn to listen to people. Only when we really hear, and understand, do we have any right to speak.

Direction for today: Listen to God; listen to people.

Prayer for today: "Lord, give me the patience and the compassion to listen."

March 28: Read Job 22,23

Key verse: *"But He knoweth the way that I take, when He hath tried me, I shall come forth as gold" (Job 23:10 KJV).*

Stripped of all earthly possessions, and bereft of his family, Job is asking, "WHY"? The men who have come to comfort him have sought to wring from him a confession of secret sinning. In spite of his heart-searching, Job still does not have the answers.

God Himself said that Job was a perfect and an upright man, who shunned evil. So the problem was not one of guilt. A ray of spiritual insight seems to shine forth in our key verse. Job recognized that, in all that he was going through, and in spite of his unanswered questions, God was there.

It is not too difficult to express faith in God when things are going well, but when the bottom seems to have dropped out of our world, faith is put to the test.

Watching the prosperity and apparent well-being of self-centred, ungodly men, contributed to Job's unanswered questions. The same can perhaps be said about our own situation as well. Sometimes those who neglect God seem to pass through life with a minimum of problems, while those who love the Lord are subjected to sorrow and trials. But happy is the man whose faith is strengthened by the furnace of affliction.

The book of Job stands as a verification of the faithfulness of a sovereign God. Questions may not always be answered but our God is always there, and faith, when tested, is more precious than fine gold.

Direction for today: Though God may not answer all our questions, He stands by us in the midst of our needs.

Prayer for today: "Father, I confess that Your presence is more important than Your answers."

March 29: Read Job 24-26

Key verse: *"He may let them rest in a feeling of security, but His eyes are on their ways" (Job 24:23 NIV).*

Many skeptics challenge the Christian faith on the basis of apparent injustice in the world. They look around the world and see the same things that Job saw: the wicked often prosper and the righteous are seen to suffer.

Job was able to look beyond the immediate appearances, and see the truth. On the scales of eternity, all things will indeed be just. Those who seem to prosper in their wickedness are in the watchful eye of the Lord, who is the righteous Judge. And those who seem to suffer for their righteousness will spend eternity in blessing and glory, with their Saviour and their Father.

Many Christians believe that they can escape punishment for sins if they keep them secret. But while their pastor or their friends may never know, God does.

Direction for today: Confess any secret sins to God, and repent of them.

Prayer for today: "Father, may I always live in the awareness that Your eyes are upon me."

Memory Verse

"The fear of the Lord is the beginning of knowledge, but fools despise wisdom and instruction." Proverbs 1:7 NKJV

March 30: Read Job 27,28

Key verse: *"My lips shall not speak wickedness, nor my tongue utter deceit" (Job 27:4 KJV).*

Job was determined not to find fault with God, even during severe pain. He was willing to accept hurt and suffering as from God.

James, in his tremendous epistle, sums it up this way: "When all kinds of trials and temptations crowd into your lives, my brothers, don't resent them as intruders, but welcome them as friends! Realize that they come to test your faith and to produce in you the quality of endurance. But let the process go on until that endurance is fully developed, and you will find you have become men of mature character with the right sort of independence. And if, in the process any of you does not know how to meet any particular problem he has only to ask God — who gives generously to all men without making them feel foolish or guilty — and he may be quite sure that the necessary wisdom will be given him. But he must ask in sincere faith, without secret doubts as to whether he really wants God's help or not.

"The man who trusts God, but with inward reservations, is like a wave of the sea, carried forward by the wind one moment and driven back the next. That sort of man cannot hope to receive anything from the Lord, and the life of a man divided loyalty will reveal the instability at every turn" (James 1:2-8 Phillips Modern English).

Job's perseverance through severe testings proved to him that he truly was a righteous man, as God had indicated.

Direction for today: Whatever your circumstances, do not waver. Trust God!

Prayer for today: "Lord, strengthen my faith, even in adversity."

March 31: Read Job 29,30

Key verse: "I cry out to you, O God, but you do not answer; I stand up, but you merely look at me" (Job 30:20 NIV).

Sometimes it seems that not even God cares, for our attempts to get His attention produce no immediate visible results.

Job had lost everything except his life and his wife. And between the complaints of his wife and the pain of his boils, his life was hellish, but his story has a victorious ending.

Within this century, many millions of persons have suffered more than Job: in concentration camps or in warfare they have lost all family, friends and possessions and, finally, life itself. People, seeing this ask, "So, where is your God? Why does He allow this?"

The answer for the mind says, "God gave us free will. We have used that freedom to hurt each other and God allows us to suffer the consequences in this life; but, praise God, there is a heaven hereafter".

Jesus' answer for the heart says, "In this world you will have trouble. But take heart! I have overcome the world" (John 14:33). "I am the resurrection and the life. He who believes in Me will live, even though he dies; and whoever lives and believes in Me will live, even though he dies; and whoever lives and believes in Me will never die" (John 11:25,26). "And surely I will be with you always, to the very end of the age" (Matthew 28:20).

Direction for today: Remember that Jesus has overcome the world!

Prayer for today: "Father, grant me a sense of Your presence in every circumstance of life."

4

The Son Of God

The Son of God lay dead and cold
In a grave.
A huge stone rolled before the door.
But neither death nor hell
Nor all the gnashing hordes
Had power to hold or bind
The Lord of all mankind.
The universe could not contain
The joy of triumph over death,
And as he breathed that first new breath
Of life that lives forevermore,
The stars and planets danced and sang,
The angels laughed, the cosmos rang with praise.
Ancient of days, yet raised anew.
And wonders of wonders,
Life is born through death.
And on that first of all tomorrows,
Joy explodes from greatest sorrow.

– Paul Knowles

April 1: Read Job 31

Key verse: *"Oh, that one would hear me! Behold, my desire is, that the Almighty would answer me" (Job 31:35 KJV).*

The cry of Job's heart in this verse is for an answer from God. He seems to be saying, "I have so many accusing voices, I am not sure where I stand. If God Himself would reveal sin in me I would gladly repent."

The depths of Job's trial seems to continue to deepen. First the losses of family, possessions and prestige, then the unmerciful accusations of his so-called friends. But his deepest test seems to be the silence of God.

Job had said, "Behold I go forward but He is not there; and backward but I cannot perceive Him; on the left hand, where He doth work, but I cannot behold Him; He hideth Himself on the right hand, that I cannot see Him." (Job 23: 8,9 KJV). The great test of Job was not only the silence of God but the seeming lack of any divine intervention or spiritual revelation.

In order to understand this book, it is important that we recognize that Job did receive a great revelation of God just before He restored to him his possessions and position of fellowship.

Direction for today: God has revealed Himself and His will in His Word. Study it enthusiastically!

Prayer for today: "Thank you, Lord, for Your great answer to the problems of mankind: Jesus!"

April 2: Read Job 32,33

Key verse: *"He will pray to God, and He will accept him: that he may see His face with joy, and He may restore His righteousness to man" (Job 33:26 NAS).*

Of the four friends of Job, Elihu is the only one who does not insist that Job's sufferings are the direct result of personal sin. He has a much deeper view of sin and chooses rather to concentrate on the mercy which God extends to those who repent (33:26).

The proper understanding of the problem of suffering seems to be beyond human capabilities. It does not occur to Elihu or any of Job's other friends that the sufferings inflicted upon Job are not necessarily evidence of God's judgment but rather a means of expressing God's confidence in Job.

Christians are not immune to sufferings in the world. Our focus should not, however, be upon why we may be suffering but rather on how we will respond. Peter sums it up best, "Wherein ye greatly rejoice . . . that the trial of your faith, being much more precious than of gold that perisheth, though it may be tried with fire, might be found unto praise and honour and glory at the appearing of Jesus Christ" (I Peter 1:7).

April 3: Read Job 34,35

Key verse: *"If thou be righteous, what givest thou Him? Or what receiveth He of thine hand?" (Job 35:7 KJV).*

Many of the words of Job's so-called friends were unjust. They accused him of things in his life that he considered right before the Lord. However, Elihu picks up some of the accusations Job made against God, points them out ot him and leaves it up to Job to decide whether he is right or wrong.

There is a good lesson for us to learn from this. Rather than accusing others of wrong, would it not be more profitable to point out the need of considering their actions and reactions toward God! Then we can leave it to the Holy Spirit to work in them so that they might decide, in the light of God's Word, what is right or wrong. We only look on outward appearances and sometimes what we see is not what God sees.

The thoughts Elihu gave to Job in 36:7, are some which we should consider also. Job had asked what profit his cleansing from sin would be to God. It seems as if he thought that his surrendering to God was doing God a big favour. Elihu points out that the profit or gain is not to God but to us.

We need to consider this. As much as God wants us, He can do without us, but we cannot do without Him. We daily need the forgiveness, love and strength that He offers us.

Direction for today: Remember, without God, you are nothing!

Prayer for today: "Lord, I confess that I am totally dependent upon You for everything in life."

April 4: Read Job 36,37

Key verse: *"He withdraweth not His eyes from the righteous; but with kings are they on the throne; yea, He doth establish them forever, and they are exalted" (Job 36:7 KJV).*

Elihu's theology seemed excellent, but his judgment of Job was far from correct. Only God knows the hearts of man, and He had said that Job was upright. We would do well to remember the words of Jesus "Judge not, and ye shall not be judged" (Luke 6:37). We can be theologically correct and yet not understand our fellowman.

What a consolation it is to know that God does not withdraw His eyes from the righteous. This is why He is caring for us and it is He who establishes us and exalts us.

The question is asked, "How can I be righteous?" I Corinthians 1:30 says, "But of Him are ye in Christ Jesus, Who of God is made unto us wisdom, and righteousness, and sanctification, and redemption." We stumble over the simplicity, perhaps, but He is our righteousness. When we receive Him we become the sons of God (John 1:12). Receive Him, walk in Him, for He is our righteousness.

Direction for today: Rejoice in the Lord, O ye righteous: for praise is comely for the upright (Psalm 33:1 KJV).

Prayer for today: "Father, help me to be compassionate and sensitive, as well as theologically correct."

April 5: Read Job 38

Key verse: "Where were you when I laid the earth's foundation? Tell me if you understand" (Job 38:4 NIV).

Finding a key verse was for me a difficult task, since I have long felt that the 38th chapter of Job is one of the most magnificent in the entire Bible. The majesty, power and glory of God are so depicted in these verses as to lift the reader from any doubt as to the omnipotence of our God.

Let us read again some verses from this chapter as they appear in the New International Version of our Bible:

"Have you ever given orders to the morning, or shown the dawn its place, that it might take the earth by the edges and shake the wicked out of it?" (verses 12 and 13).

"What is the way to the abode of light? And where does darkness reside?" (verse 19).

"Have you entered the storehouses of the snow, or seen the storehouses of the hail?" (verse 22).

"What is the way to the place where lightning is dispersed, or the place where the east winds are scattered over the earth?" (verse 24).

"Does the rain have a father? Who fathers the drops of dew? From whose womb comes the ice? Who gives birth to the frost from the heavens?" (verse 29).

"Who endowed the heart with wisdom or gave understanding to the mind? Who has the wisdom to count the clouds? Who can tip over the water jars of the heavens when the dust becomes hard and the clods of earth stick together?" (verse 37).

Oh, the greatness of God. Such scripture lifts us out of parochial thinking and into the presence of the Almighty. Praise His matchless Name!!

Direction for today: While we must grow in love and knowledge of the Lord, we must always be careful to avoid taking Him for granted.

Prayer for today: "Lord, I worship You for Your majesty, Your might, Your greatness and Your power."

"Fear God and keep His commandments, for this is the whole duty of man." Ecclesiastes 12:13b NKJV

April 6: Read Job 39

Key verse: "Did you give the horse his strength or clothe his neck with a flowing mane?" (Job 39:19 NIV).

Most of us have sat in schoolrooms and listened to teachers who were convinced that all of creation came into being as a great cosmic accident. One species evolved into another by happenstance. According to many scientists, this chapter expresses some important truths. And in addition to the truths about God's power, there is much here about "the origins of the species".

God claims authorship of these amazing beasts. He says that it is He who has created the mountain goats, the wild donkeys, the wild ox, the ostrich, the horse, the hawk and the eagle.

These are not products of a chance development that assisted in survival; they are the product of the creative intent of a wonderful God, who rejoices in the grace of the eagle and the strength of the horse. Praise Him for His marvellous creation!

Direction for today: When you see things He has made, take time to praise the Maker.

Prayer for today: "Thank you, Lord, for the multitude of wonderful things You have placed in this world."

April 7: Read Job 40

Key verse: "Would you indeed annul My judgment? Would you condemn Me that you may be justified?" (Job 40:8 NKJV).

A favorite question of the unbelieving hearts is: if God is so good and powerful, why does He let innocent children and women die through war, famine or catastrophe? Scripture tells us not to answer after the hearing of the ear nor seeing of the eye but by righteous judgment.

Our answer is found in the key verse. Unbelievers try to make God out to be the culprit. They say that if God is so powerful He could stop this from happening. They say this is what they would do if they were God and since God doesn't do it that way he must be a bad God and one to whom they do not have to answer. That is why God asks Job the question, "Would you indeed annul judgment? Would you condemn Me that you may be justified?"

Man wants to play the role of the hero and let God play the villain. In that way he can say that he doesn't have to answer to a God like that and he will continue in his unbelief.

Direction for today: "Trust in the Lord with all your heart and lean not on your own understanding" (Proverbs 3:5 NKJV).

Prayer for today: "Father, I declare my trust in You, in all circumstances."

April 8: Read Job 41,42

Key verse: "I have declared that which I did not understand, things too wonderful for me, which I did not know" (Job 42:3).

In some ways, the conclusion of the book of Job is not what we would have expected. Throughout the book, we are in the position of a reader of a mystery novel, knowing "who dunnit" while the characters in the book do not: we know that God has not caused all that befell Job, but that Satan is responsible.

Yet, even at the end, God does not reveal that to Job. Instead, talking about the great beasts of His creation, God simply tells him that there are many things far above his understanding.

And Job got the message: our key verse is his confession. In these chapters he rises to a level far beyond mere understanding. Job attains the ultimate of faith: "God, I will trust you even when I do not understand!"

So often we spend time attempting to figure out the reasons for hardship, or for almost any circumstance we face. And sometimes it is true that there are things for us to learn in those circumstances. But perhaps the greatest lesson we can learn is that, whether we understand our situation or not, we can trust God!

Job received something far better than an explanantion — he caught a glimpse of God (42:5), and that was more than enough!

Direction for today: Instead of focusing on the questions, focus on the Answer.

Prayer for today: "Lord, I do not seek to know all things; I only seek to know You."

I and II Timothy

Paul wrote these letters to Timothy, his spiritual son, who was probably pastor of the Church at Ephasus.

In the first of these books Paul gives wise guidance for the church and its officers. He includes warnings against false teachers, instructions for church life and prayer and gives qualifications for those in leadership. Paul then speaks to Timothy about his personal conduct and his relationship to various groups within the church.

Even today, church leaders regard I Timothy as a most useful manual for church planting and building.

II Timothy is a precious book, the last written by Paul as he was imprisoned. In the paragraphs of this letter, we see Paul as he neared the end of his life: weary, but triumphant, sensing that, as the end is near, so is the victory!

April 9: Read I Timothy 1,2

Key verse: "Here is a trustworthy saying that deserves full acceptance: Jesus Christ came into the world to save sinners — of whom I am the worst" (I Timothy 1:15 NIV).

This is a clear, concise statement of the mission of Jesus Christ. Sadly, many people today have missed the point. They see Jesus as a great man, a good teacher, or a wonderful example. And, of course, He was those things as well.

But He did not come first to teach; He was a man, but not only a man. He was a great example, but if He did not also save us, we would be unable to even begin following that example.

Jesus came, first of all, to save sinners. To do that, He had to be not only a man, but also the Creator of man. Only the death of God Himself was big enough to cover the sins of all of the men, women and children who need to be saved!

If Jesus had only come to show us how to live, He would have left us frustrated and doomed, wallowing in our own failure. But He came to rescue us, that we might live.

Paul knew this. and in spite of all that he had accomplished as a great missionary and teacher, He never lost sight of his need for a Saviour. Was Paul really the worst sinner that ever lived? Yes, just as much as each one of us — for each of us has sinned enough to send the Son of God to His death.

Direction for today: Always remember that, without Jesus, you would be trapped in sin, and headed straight for destruction.

Prayer for today: "Praise you, Jesus, that You save sinners like me!"

April 10: Read I Timothy 3,4

Key verse: "Do not neglect the spiritual gift within you . . ." (I Timothy 4:14a NAS).

Paul exhorted Timothy not to neglect the spiritual gift that had been given to him. Should you also be receiving such a challenge?

Too often, those who have received gifts by the Spirit of God fail to use them. Out of fear, shyness, lack fo confidence or lack of faith, we refrain from ministering. But in doing so, we are disobeying God and withholding blessings from other people. We are also missing wonderful opportunities to be ourselves, built up in the faith.

Has the gift God has given you been allowed to wither away or lie dormant? If so, seek the anointing of the Spirit to stir it up and rekindle the coals. Put that gift into use as the Lord grants you opportunity, which He surely will do.

Your spiritual gifts were given to you to glorify the Giver, to bless others, and to build you up.

Direction for today: Do not neglect your spiritual gifts.

Prayer for today: "Father, show me my gifts and give me faith to use them."

April 11: Read I Timothy 5

Key verse: "Do not rebuke an older man harshly, but exhort him as if he were your father" (I Timothy 5:1 NIV).

Timothy was in a difficult position. He was appointed to pastor a church in which he was one of the younger men. Paul specifically instructed him to treat the older men of the church with reverence, affection and respect.

In our day, we live in the midst of what has been called "the youth cult". The media seems to believe that anything worthwhile has to be new, and that the only desirable time of life is youth. Merchandising is directed at the young, or at those who want to appear young.

The Bible stands against this kind of upside-down thinking. It is no accident that leaders of the church are called "elders" — they will usually be older, more mature Christians. The Scriptures instruct younger Christians to realize how much is to be learned from older men and older women.

If there is any place in our world where older people should be given their rightful place, it is within the Christian community.

Direction for today: Express to an older member of your church your appreciation for his or her ministry.

Prayer for today: "Father, thank You for the mature Christian leaders of my fellowship. Bless them in a special way."

April 12: Read I Timothy 6

Key verse: "Fight the good fight of the faith; take hold of the eternal life to which you were called when you made the good confession in the presence of many witnesses" (I Timothy 6:12 RSV).

Paul is reminding Timothy, and us, as we read this, that we are engaged in a fight of faith. There are many, many temptations that attempt to ensnare us. Among these are: self-conceit, a craving for controversy, and the love of money. We should aim instead for: righteousness, godliness, faith, love, steadfastness, gentleness.

When Paul says "I have fought a good fight" (II Timothy 4:7 RSV), he means that he has identified himself with the battle of righteousness and has given himself as a good soldier for Jesus Christ.

The key to taking hold of the eternal life lies in the good confession such as Paul made. That confession is, "Jesus is Lord" (Romans 10:9 RSV) or more specifically, "Jesus is my Lord."

The key to the constant battle is that if we will acknowledge Jesus before man, then He will acknowledge us before His Father in heaven (Matthew 10:32 RSV).

We "fight the good fight" when we tell other people about Jesus and we win the fight as they confess Jesus as Lord and Saviour.

Direction for today: There is power in the name of Jesus to convert people, bring healing and give eternal life. Use His name liberally.

Prayer for today: "Jesus, You are Lord of my whole life!"

Memory Verse

"Also I heard the voice of the Lord, saying: 'Whom shall I send, and who will go for Us? Then I said, 'Here am I! Send me.'" Isaiah 6:8 NKJV

April 13: Read II Timothy 1

Key verse: *"For God has not given us a spirit of fear; but of power, and of love and of sound mind" (II Timothy 1:7 KJV).*

Fear cripples the lives of multitudes of Christians. There are many kinds of fear: fear of failure, of the unknown, of people and of death, to name a few. Fear cripples our Christian witness by demoralizing us (I Samuel 13:5-8), giving us an attitude of defeat (Numbers 13:30-14:2) and silencing our testimonies (John 9:22).

Physically, fear causes us to have overactive adrenal and thyroid glands. Over long periods of time, this leads to malfunctions in our body. Fear plagues us with loss of appetite, sleep and strength. This is not the way God intended believers to live.

The cure for fear is found in two simple Bible truths: God's love and mercy are unending, and He gives authority to every believer. I John 4:18 says that perfect love casts out fear. In addition to God's wonderful love giving us the assurance that we need, we as believers can take authority over fear. We can speak to it and command it to go in the name of Jesus. I had, for many years, been plagued by acrophobia, a fear of height. Even during my walk as a Christian, this fear had increased. Then one day, I realized that I was in bondage to this fear, took my authority as a blood-washed child of God, and was gloriously set free!

Direction for today: Recognize the truth that a Christian need never be dominated by fear, and to be free!

Prayer for today: "Father, set me free from fear to know power, love and a sound mind.

April 14: Read II Timothy 2

Key verse: *"Remember Jesus Christ, risen from the dead, descendant of David, according to my gospel, for which I suffer hardship even to imprisonment as a criminal; but the word of God is not imprisoned" (II Timothy 2:8,9 NAS).*

Paul wrote II Timothy at the end of his life. At a time when many of us are contemplating retirement, extended vacations, and a generally easier life, this great apostle was facing deprivation, prison and death by execution.

Paul's life was not an easy one. From the moment of his dramatic conversion (Acts 9), he turned his back on a secure and prestigious position to adopt that of a persecuted itinerant preacher of a new religion. We know that God miraculously delivered Paul from harm and death time and time again; but we know, as well, that he often suffered sickness, pain, and hardship.

Yet, to the great apostle, these things were never the key issues. He sought to win new Christians, plant new churches and extend the kingdom of God.

Direction for today: The extension of the kingdom of God was the first and only priority for Paul, and should be so for all of God's people.

Prayer for today: "Thank you, Father, that Your word can never be imprisoned, destroyed or stopped!"

April 15: Read II Timothy 3, 4

Key verse: "For I am now ready to be offered. . . ." (II Timothy 4:6 KJV).

The Apostle Paul, in these two chapters, warns us of things to come, reminds us of his sufferings, challenges and then shows how the Lord is his strength and deliverer. What a beautiful testimony of confidence in our living God, especially as Paul reiterates that he is "now ready to be offered".

(1) *He has fought a good fight.* Like a fighter, he has put everything he has into serving Jesus.

(2) *He has finished his course.* The spiritual goals he set for himself have been reached. He has done what he felt Jesus wanted him to do.

(3) *He has kept the faith.* In spite of what Satan tried to do to him, he kept his eyes on Jesus, the author of our faith.

We can learn from this great Apostle that, in spite of opposition, the reality of Christ is manifest in our lives as we serve, obey and trust Him.

Direction for today: "Be thou an example of the believers" (I Timothy 4:12 KJV).

Prayer for today: "Lord, when I reach the end of my life, may I be able to declare that I have fought a good fight, finished my course, and kept the faith."

Psalms

The title of this Old Testament hymn book is from a Greek word, simply meaning "Songs". The Hebrew Bible entitles this collection, "Praises".

These 150 poems must surely reflect every attitude of the human heart, every emotion that human beings ever face. In these psalms we encounter praise to God, awe in the presence of His creation, repentance, confession, despair, sorrow, joy, fear, faith, and peace. And in each and every psalm, God is clearly seen as the source of all good, and the answer to all problems.

These poems reflect a long period of Hebrew history, ranging from the time of Moses to the days after the exile . . . a span of approximately 1,000 years! Many of the psalms were written by David, the poet-king. Others come from Solomon, from Asaph (David's chief musician) or from members of the schools of temple musicians.

The psalms are poetry. English poetry, like that of many other nations, often depends on rhyme as its key feature. This is obviously lost when the poems are translated into another language. But the important element of Hebrew poetry, parallelism, is retained in translation. Thus we can appreciate the poetry even when we read it in English.

Most of the psalms are written in parallel form. That is, an idea is presented, and then repeated another way. In a sense, the poets were rhyming ideas instead of words. Fine examples of parallelism can be found in Psalm 1; verse 1 states one idea three times, in three slightly different forms; verse 2 repeats another idea. Parallelism can take several forms. Sometimes, the same idea is repeated (as in the examples just mentioned); on other occasions, an opposite idea is contrasted with the original statement (see Psalm 1:6).

Be conscious of the creativity in these poems, as you read the psalms. But even more, seek to be open to the outpouring of the Spirit of God, as you lift your heart to the Lord along with these God-loving poets who wrote the greatest praises in the world thousands of years ago.

April 16: Read Psalms 1-3

Key verse: *"For the Lord knoweth the way of the righteous; but the way of the ungodly shall perish" (Psalm 1:6 KJV).*

Throughout these psalms, the writer points to two different ways in which people are going. One is spoken of as the way of the righteous and the other, the way of the ungodly. Those in the way of righteousness are portrayed as seekers of God and truth and justice. Those in the way of the ungodly are shown to be disobedient to God, perpetrators of lies and wicked actions.

The psalmist not only traces the courses of each of these, but also reveals their end. The ungodly fall under the judgment and wrath of God. The righteous come under God's care and protection, even in times of adversity.

Personal faith in God was a very real, practical experience in David's life. His intimate relationship with God is very evident throughout the life of the shepherd boy who became king. His willingness to wait for God's timing, rather than taking things into his own hands, is an expression of this vital trust in the Lord. So also is his intense agony of repentance of the sin which broke his fellowship with his God.

It is not surprising that many people turn to the Psalms for comfort and strength. Here we find struggles and victories, as well as encouragement and warnings which speak to our life situations. The simplicity and practicality of the Psalms are the doorway through which we enter to begin the ascent into the glory and joy also expressed in these wonderful hymns.

Direction for today: Walk always in the way of righteousness.

Prayer for today: "Thank You, Lord, that in every situation, You are there with strength and encouragement."

April 17: Read Psalms 4-6

Key verse: *"I will both lay me down in peace, and sleep: for Thou Lord, only makest me dwell in safety" (Psalm 4:8 KJV).*

"Now I lay me down to sleep, I pray the Lord my soul to keep; If I should die before I wake, I pray the Lord my soul to take." Countless children have prayed that at bedtime, night after night. Perhaps large numbers of them have grown up without knowing that it was David's prayer, too, as he lay down at bedtime.

For David, it was much more than a simple childhood request. His prayer was a statement of his will – I *will* lay my head on my pillow in peace." He knew the Lord was the one who would cause him to sleep safely and in peace.

Far too many of us, far too often, pray for God's safety as we sleep . . . and then toss and turn the night away.

As God's people, we need to pray God's protection and then go one step further and claim for ourselves the words of David – I *will* lay down in peace and sleep *because* God keeps me."

Direction for today: Because of the protection of the Lord, you can live every minute of your life in complete peace and assurance.

Prayer for today: "Thank You, Father, that I can rely on You in every moment of my life."

April 18: Read Psalms 7, 8

Key verse: *"O Lord, our Lord, how majestic is Your name in all the earth" (Psalm 8:1 NIV).*

As a shepherd boy, David had spent most of his early years in the outdoors. He knew the hillsides and streams of Israel well, and wherever he looked, he saw not only the creation, but the Creator.

Mathew Kousal, a Canadian artist who has painted over 13,000 nature paintings and sketches, takes little credit for his artistic productions. Instead, he looks at the natural scenes reflected in his work, smiles, and speaks with awe and affection of "the Creator" who made all things. He understands David's statement that the name of the Lord is declared in majesty in all the earth.

As Christians, we can easily see the hand of God in all of nature. But we should also realize that it is part of our responsibility as Christian stewards to care for this very creation. God gave mankind dominion over the earth, and no one should be more conscious of this than believers.

Let us do all in our power to be sure that the hand of God is plainly seen in the beauties of creation. The enemy would love to destroy that, and obscure the signature of the eternal Artist.

Direction for today: Be a good steward of the environment.

Prayer for today: "O Lord, our Lord, how majestic is Your name in all the earth."

April 19: Read Psalms 9, 10

Key verse: *"The Lord is a refuge for the oppressed, a stronghold in times of trouble" (Psalms 9:9 NIV).*

More than anyone on this earth, the Lord God knows the terrible results of sin. From the time of Adam and Eve on, the sin of humanity has destroyed life and brought terrible hardship all over the world.

Sin will one day be entirely eradicated. God will judge His creations, and everyone who has ever lived, from creation until the end, will be called to account. But God cannot stamp out sin without stamping out the as-yet-unrepented sinners, and His mercy is still extended to all who will seek to be rescued from their sin, through Jesus. Therefore, we will see the results of sin in this world.

But we also have, echoed again and again in the Psalms, the promise that God is our refuge in the trouble and oppression which will occur in our fallen world. No matter what befalls us, we are 'hid in Christ'.

In these two psalms, the theme is repeated. We are told that God will turn back our enemies, especially the eternal enemy, Satan. God will "uphold" us, and will never forsake us. He hears our cries. He is our hope, our helper, our encourager and our defender.

Direction for today: Remember that, whatever the circumstances, God is your refuge.

Prayer for today: "I will praise You, O Lord, with all my heart."

April 20: Read Psalms 11-14

Key verse: *"They have all gone astray, they are all alike corrupt; there is none that does good, no, not one" (Psalm 14:3 NASB).*

I thank God daily for this verse. I thank Him daily for penetrating our very hearts with this truth: "For all have sinned and fall short of the glory of God" (Romans 3:23). "For all of us have become like one who is unclean and all our righteous deeds are like a filthy garment" (Isaiah 64:6). To acknowledge that we are short of God's glory is to acknowledge that we are sinners and in need of a Saviour.

We do have a Saviour, Jesus Christ the Lord.

How do we have our sins wiped away and merit God's love forever? Jesus spoke it very simply, as recorded in Mark's gospel: "The time is fulfilled and the kingdom of God is at hand; repent and believe in the gospel" (Mark 1:15). Paul wrote to the early church in Ephesus: "You have been saved by grace in your faith and not of yourselves, it is the gift of God; not as a result of works that no one should boast" (Ephesians 2:8-9). That gift of God – eternal life – is free to you through repentance. Jesus so loved you that He died for you, cleansing you of your sin in His precious blood. He paid the price of your redemption.

"But as many as received Him, to them He gave the right to become children of God, even to those who believe in His name, who were born not of blood, or of the will of the flesh, nor of the will of man, but of God"

(John 1:12). To be born again simply means that God has called you to repent of your sins, thus avoiding eternal damnation, and invite Jesus to be the Lord of your life. In Revelation 3:20, we read that Jesus says, "Behold, I stand at the door and knock. If anyone hears My voice and opens the door, I will come into him (or her) and will dine with him and he with Me".

Have you committed your life to Jesus? If not, won't you now, without hesitation, say, "Jesus, I am sorry for all my sins. Please forgive me and come and live with me"? Then study His Word and seek fellowship with other Christians.

Direction for today: If we come to God, He *always* receives us!

Prayer for today: "I trust in Your unfailing love; my heart rejoices in Your salvation" (Psalm 13:5 NIV).

April 21: Read Psalms 15-17

Key verse: "I have set the Lord always before me. Because He is at my right hand, I will not be shaken" (Psalm 16:8 NIV).

In many of the larger cities in North America, locksmiths and hardware stores do a booming business in locks for the doors of apartments and houses. Many people have several locks on their doors and windows, as they seek security.

Some have even gone so far as to have guns in their homes – surely a mistaken way to feel secure.

As we well know, none of these things really guarantees security. Our world is spoiled by sin, and the most horrible results of that sin will sometimes invade our lives. But we need not be shaken by whatever comes our way. While in our own strength we have no certain defences, in Christ we are completely secure.

Unfortunately, many of us tend to forget about God until the crisis comes. But this is not the way to genuine security. David said that the Lord was "always" with him. Only when we walk consistently with our Lord will we know true security.

Direction for today: Do not wait for a crisis to call upon the Lord.

Prayer for today: "Keep me safe, O God, for in You I take refuge" (Psalm 16:1 NIV).

April 22: Read Psalm 18

Key verse: "The Lord is my rock, and my fortress, and my deliverer, my God, my rock in whom I take refuge, my shield, and the horn of my salvation, my stronghold" (Psalm 18:2 RSV).

There is probably no one verse that more accurately describes our God and Saviour, Jesus, than this one. Paul describes Jesus as the "visible image of the invisible God" (Colossians 1:15), "for in Him all the fulness of God was pleased to dwell, and through Him to reconcile all things whether on earth or in heaven, making peace by the blood of His cross" (Colossians 1:19, 20).

When we recognize Him as who He is, and call upon His name, we can build our lives upon Jesus and His instructions for our life. Then, no matter what kind of problems, trials or disasters hit us, we can look forward to coming through them. "Every one then who hears these words of Mine and does them will be like a wise man who builds his house upon the rock; and the rain fell, and the floods came, and the winds blew and beat upon that house, but it did not fall because it had been founded on the rock" (Matthew 7:24,25). Build your life upon the rock – Jesus – and you, too, will not fall.

Direction for today: Follow Jesus' advice and enjoy the results.

Prayer for today: "The Lord liveth; and blessed be my rock; and let the God of my salvation be exalted" (Psalm 18:46 KJV).

April 23: Read Psalms 19,20

Key verse: "The heavens declare the glory of God; and the firmament sheweth His handywork" (Psalm 19:1 KJV).

As a man is to be judged by his works, so God can be judged by His. The second verse of this Psalm explains that the heavens and the firmament constantly, day after day and night after night, everywhere in the world, to the total human race, declare the glory and the greatness of God. These have no speech or language, yet they tell of the wonderful works of God.

The constant succession of day and night speaks of a design that was created by God in the beginning: light and darkness, day and night.

As we behold the brightness of the heavens, we may know that God is light. In reading these verses, we must give God the glory for all the comforts and all the benefits we have by the lights of heaven. But we must look above and beyond them to the Son of righteousness. It is God's desire that we, His children, walk in the light and that day after day we should declare to the world His glory.

Direction for today: Like the heavens, let us also declare the glory of God!

Prayer for today: "Let the words of my mouth, and the meditation of my heart, be acceptable in Thy sight, O Lord, my strength, and my redeemer" (Psalm 19:14 KJV).

April 24: Read Psalms 21,22

Key verse: "For the kingdom is the Lord's; and He is the governor among the nations" (Psalm 22:28 KJV).

Psalm 22 is clearly prophetic of the suffering and death of Christ on the cross. The first lines of the psalm were repeated by the Lord as He hung dying, "My God, my God, why hast Thou forsaken Me?" (Psalm 22:1, Matthew 27:46).

There are at least two other places where Jesus' word might be quotations or paraphrases of the words in Psalm 22: "I am thirsty" (John 19:28, which compares to Psalm 22:15), and the final triumphant cry, "It is finished" (John 19:30), which is one possible translation of the last phrase in Psalm 22.

There are many other obvious prophetic references to the crucifixion of our Lord in this psalm: "They pierced my hands and feet" (vs. 16); and "They divide my garments among them, and for my clothing they cast lots" (vs. 18).

Think of it, if Jesus was indeed quoting this psalm to Himself on the cross, He faced His anguish with praise to His Father on His lips, and He knew that He was not forsaken: "When He cried to Him for help, He heard" (vs. 18).

We must imitate the faith and assurance of our Lord, as He suffered for us. Even as He hung in torment, dying a horrible death, He knew that, "The kingdom is the Lord's and He rules over the nations" (vs. 28).

Direction for today: God is in charge!

Prayer for today: "Thank You, Jesus, that You were willing to suffer the agony of the cross for me."

April 25: Read Psalms 23-25

Key verse: "The Lord is my shepherd; I shall not want" (Psalm 21:1 KJV).

There is no greater passage in the history of literature. This marvellous psalm is poetically wonderful, artistically creative, and entirely memorable. But, even better, it is also completely true!

Read this psalm several times today. Read it *aloud* to rejoice in the artistry of David's expression. Read it *slowly* to meditate on the truths in it. Read it *often* to let those truths settle in your spirit.

The Lord is your shepherd. He cares for you in all of the ways a good shepherd cares for his sheep: He gives us peace, supplies our food (physically and spiritually) and guides us in the way in which we should go. No matter what danger threatens, He is our protection.

In fact, His provision is far greater than your need could ever be. Keeping close to this Shepherd will guarantee that our cup will be more than full!

And, praise God, this wonderful provision is not only for the days of our earthly life. We shall also dwell in the house of the Lord, forever!

Direction for today: Stay close to the Shepherd.

Prayer for today: "Thank you, Jesus, that You are with me always, to protect and comfort me."

April 26: Read Psalms 26, 27

Key verse: *"The Lord is my light and my salvation; whom shall I fear? The Lord is the strength of my life; of whom shall I be afraid?" (Psalm 27:1 NAS).*

The Lord is the light of our life. The light of His Holy Spirit illuminates our spirit, His truth gives light to our understanding and His penetrating love gives light to our imperfections and downfalls. It reveals to us our shortcomings and leads us to the foot of the cross to accept His forgiveness and cleansing. Praise His wonderful name!

Scripture says "Greater is He that is within us than he that is within the world." And again the scriptures tell us, "If God be for us who can be against us?" God has surrounded us and placed within us authority and strength by His Holy spirit. We have no need to fear. II Timothy 1:7 reads: "For God hath not given us the spirit of fear; but of power, and of love, and of a sound mind."

No matter what the circumstances, God has made available to us His peace that passes all understanding.

Direction for today: God's peace is always available to you.

Prayer for today: "Teach me Thy way, O Lord, and lead me in a level path" (Psalm 27:11 NAS).

Memory Verse

"Through the Lord's mercies we are not consumed, because His compassions fail not. They are new every morning; great is Your faithfulness." Lamentations 3:22,23 NKJV

April 27: Read Psalms 28-30

Key verse: *"For His anger endureth but a moment; in His favour is life: weeping may endure for a night, but joy cometh in the morning" (Psalm 30:5 KJV).*

It's hard to imagine the despair that gripped the psalmist David when he was running for his life from King Saul. He must have had low moments that we know nothing about and yet, in all, he maintained a childlike faith in God that rebounded in every situation, no matter how desperate it got to be. After a desperate prayer, he would always end with praise and glory to the name of the Lord, together with a statement of his unqualified faith in God's power to deliver.

In these psalms, we can clearly see David's concept of God and his childlike trust in a great, loving Father.

David not only knew the anger of Saul but also the anger of God. He would see that, whereas Saul's anger grew and festered, this was not the way with God. Whereas His anger was only momentary, disappearing as soon as we repent, God's favour was life-giving and life-long.

May each of us come to a place where we realize, deeply within our beings, that God is, and that He is the rewarder of those who diligently seek Him. And let us trust Him as naturally as a child trusts his own father.

Direction for today: Learn to praise God in every circumstance.

Prayer for today: "O Lord, my God, I praise You for who You are".

April 28: Read Psalms 31, 32

Key verse: "Then I acknowledged my sin to You and did not cover up my iniquity, I said, 'I will confess my transgressions to the Lord' – and You forgave the guilt of my sin" (Psalm 32:5 NIV).

It is important that David's pattern of life be known so that it is understood what he is going through here.

David had a relationship with God in which God meant everything to him. Yet, as an imperfect, ordinary man, he failed in that relationship because temporal things at times became more important to him. He didn't just make a little mistake but failed God miserably by sinning against Him.

Does this sound familiar? We must do the same thing that David does in this psalm, for he gives the formula for real happiness.

Sin, David pointed out, was eating away at his life and destroying him. At the same time the hand of the Lord, His spirit of conviction, was upon him. There was only one way he could experience the freedom and happiness God intended for his life. In verse five, he acknowledged his sin and confessed it to God. Then, and only then, could God forgive him and bring real happiness and peace to David's life.

He can, and *will,* do the same for you.

Direction for today: It is foolish to try to hide your sin from God; He already knows all about it!

Prayer for today: "Praise be to the Lord, for He showed His wonderful love to me" (Psalm 31:21).

April 29: Read Psalms 33, 34

Key verse: "I will bless the Lord at all times, His praise shall continually be in my mouth" (Psalm 34:1 NAS).

Praising God is not always easy. It is natural for us to praise Him during the "mountaintop" experiences, when everything is going well. It is when we have to walk through the deep valleys that offering up praises to God truly becomes a sacrifice.

Human nature tends to allow circumstances to control our feelings. Worship, however, is an act of our will. "I *will* bless the Lord at all times." Our circumstances may change, our moods may change, but God never changes. He is always worthy to be praised.

C.M. Ward once said that to accomplish anything for the kingdom of God requires human effort as well as divine inspiration and guidance. "There is no victory without a battle. It takes grit as well as grace to sing praises at midnight." He was, of course, referring to Paul and Silas who, in spite of their desperate plight, offered up praises to God (Acts 16:24, 25).

Praise brings freedom. When we praise God, we are no longer controlled by our emotions, for by praising Him we take our eyes off the circumstances and focus them instead upon God. He wants us to rise above the circumstances and experience the freedom that comes with worship. For Paul and Silas, it meant release from prison bonds. For you and me it can mean release from emotional bonds which may hinder our Christian walk.

Direction for today: God can work through those who praise Him.

Prayer for today: "I bless you, Lord, and praise You for Your wonderful works."

April 30: Read Psalms 35, 36

Key verse: "They shall be abundantly satisfied with the fatness of Thy house; and Thou shall make them drink of the river of Thy pleasures" (Psalms 36:8 KJV).

Serving God brings excitement, abundance and fullness. When we are called by the Lord Jesus Christ, we are not asked to face a dull, unexciting existence but one in which we daily see the hand of the living God.

As a father cares for his child, so does our Heavenly Father care for us. He wants to be able to meet our needs and is more than willing to do so. Whether it is a financial need, healing, or deliverance, God wants to manifest Himself through that need.

All we have to do is ask . . . ask and you shall receive.

If you have a need, why not give it to Jesus today? Give Him the opportunity to meet that need, for the promise is that God will abundantly pour out on you and you shall drink of the river of His pleasures.

Direction for today: Give God an opportunity to meet your needs.

Prayer for today: "Father, as I give my needs to You, I am trusting You to meet them."

5

Stream of Living Water

*There's a stream of living water
That is flowing from the Father.
It brings life in the light
Of the rising of the Son.
There's a promise of the Spirit
And for all of us who hear it,
It brings joy and peace
As He and we are one.*

– Paul Knowles

May 1: Read Psalm 37

Key verse: *"Delight yourself in the Lord and He will give you the desires of your heart" (Psalm 37:4 NIV).*

What does it mean to "delight yourself in the Lord"? One preacher has suggested this acrostic:

D – Daily
E – Everything
L – Laid
I – Into
G – God's
H – Hands
T – Triumphantly

That is the message that comes through again and again in this psalm. We must trust the Lord in all things, actively and consistently relying on Him. He will surely care for us.

And that is the reason for the last word of the acrostic: Triumphantly. We know that trust in the Lord is the true path to victory.

If we believe that these things are true, it is not surprising that we will delight in the Lord, rejoicing in the freedom and peace that are ours as believers.

Direction for today: Delight yourself in the Lord!

Prayer for today: "Lord, I commit my way to You."

May 2: Read Psalms 38, 39

Key verse: *"I said, I will guard my ways, that I may not sin with my tongue; I will guard my mouth as with a muzzle" (Psalm 39:1 NAS).*

David, Solomon, Peter, James and Paul all spoke of the dangers of the tongue. They were well aware of the great harm that can be done by one of the smallest members of our bodies.

We know how we have used our tongues to bless God and to curse men, often at the same time or within a very short period. We know the times we have fallen into gossip, murmuring, backbiting; the times we said things we knew were wrong. It may be that the most widespread disease among human beings is "foot in mouth disease"!

But the situation is not hopeless. Control of the tongue is a matter of control of the Spirit: as the Holy spirit is allowed to reign in our spirits, we will be able to control our tongues. David announced, "I will guard my mouth". He recognized his own responsibility. We, too, need to become "willers", dedicated to obeying God in this matter. We need to determine to keep our tongues from evil and to speak instead that which will bless and build up.

Direction for today: Be slower to speak, and consider in the light of the Spirit what you will say.

Prayer for today: "Lord, I will allow Your Spirit to cause me to control my tongue."

May 3: Read Psalms 40, 41

Key verse: *"Blessed is he who has regard for the weak; the Lord delivers him in times of trouble" (Psalm 41:1 NIV).*

We are called to be like Christ.

This verse deals with a very practical result of that important truth. Just as Jesus focused much of His ministry to the poor, the needy and the weak, so are we as Christians to care for the needy in our world, whether they live next door or halfway around the globe.

Christians do not always live up to this instruction. Too often, our churches are strongholds of the middle class and we are deliberately unaware of the needs that abound around us and in the world.

If Jesus had ignored those in need, we would still be lost in sin and headed for hell! Let us follow the example of our Lord, and reach out, in genuine Christ-like love, to share with and help the weak. When Jesus said that we would do greater things than ever He did, He was not only referring to miracles: He was telling us to continue every aspect of His ministry on this earth.

Direction for today: Show regard for the weak in some practical way.

Prayer for today: "May all who seek You rejoice and be glad in You" (Psalm 40:15).

Memory Verse

"I will give you a new heart and put a new spirit within you; I will take the heart of stone out of your flesh and give you a heart of flesh. I will put My Spirit within you." Ezekiel 36:26,27a NKJV

May 4: Read Psalms 42-44

Key verse: *"Yet the Lord will command lovingkindness in the daytime, and in the night His song shall be with me, and my prayer unto the God of my life" (Psalm 42:8 KJV).*

David, again in trouble, takes time to commune with God. He complains of his circumstances, yet in the midst of this thirsting comes a revelation of the true nature of his Lord. Truly He is a God of loving kindness!

David declares that in the midst of oppression from his enemies he will still have a song in the night and his prayer shall be to God. Job 35:10 tells us it is God our maker who gives songs in the night.

The true heritage of each Christian is not an easy road but peace that passes all understanding *and* misunderstanding (John 14:7). Paul and Silas were true examples of those who had a song in the night. The results were exciting (Acts 16:25).

Many are locked in prisons of their own making, but God has a way out. Are you in bondage today? Won't you surrender your will and trust God to deliver you?

Direction for today: Trust God; He never fails.

Prayer for today: "As the heart panteth after the water brooks, so panteth my soul after Thee, O God" (Psalm 42:1).

May 5: Read Psalms 45-47

Key verse: "O clap your hands, all ye people, shout unto God with the voice of triumph" (Psalms 47:1 KJV).

In Psalm 46: 4-5, the psalmist extolls the greatness of the majesty and grace of God's kingdom and what it means to the people of this earth. He also tells of the confidence that the church can have in the fact that our God is great and a strong refuge of strength; that He is there in trouble when we need Him and is the source of blessing.

God is described as an unending river. The streams make the heart glad of the City of God, because from them flow all of the necessary goodness for the well-being of the people of God. Then, in the first verse of Psalm 47, he says, "O clap your hands, all ye people, shout unto God with the voice of triumph."

The psalmist could contain himself no longer. Some people feel that it is not proper to get emotional about the Lord, but it is very evident in the Bible that those who had a personal revelation of God got emotional. In fact, most people get emotional about something that is important to them.

Yes, there is a place for emotion in one's personal relationship with God. When emotion is outpoured as a spontaneous result of an inward revelation of God it is a healthy part of our Christian experience and we, like the psalmist, can say "Sing praises to God, sing praises, sing praises unto our King, sing praises" (Psalm 47:6). I can almost sense the enthusiasm in his spirit as words come forth from his pen.

Direction for today: Praise the Lord with joy and enthusiasm!

Prayer for today: "Lord, I praise you. You are the King, the Lord Most High. You are greatly exalted."

May 6: Read Psalms 48-50

Key verse: "But God will redeem my soul from the grave; He will surely take me to Himself" (Psalm 49:15 NIV).

This psalm is an amazing example of faith. The Lord chose to reveal Himself to His people long before He showed them anything about heaven or eternal life. C.S. Lewis argues that God chose this approach because He wanted His people to love Him for Himself, not for the things He could do for them.

True love can never be based on promised reward; love must be unselfish.

Yet God's people, as they eagerly sought Him in love, often received glimpses of eternal truths. This psalm is just such an example. The psalmist realizes that "no man can redeem the life of another or give to God a ransom for him – the ransom of a life is costly, no payment is ever enough – that he should live on forever and not see decay."

"Look," says the psalmist, "it is hopeless. Death is inevitable. No one has enough money, or enough righteousness, to buy life in the face of death." But, despite this apparent hopelessness, the writer senses that the Lord can overrule.

The author does not know about Christ. He does not know how God will do it, but he declares, "God will redeem my soul from the grave."

Praise God, he was right! With this writer, who lived about 3,000 years ago, rejoice in the salvation that is ours in Christ. Praise the Lord!

Direction for today: Realize that no one can buy his way out of death; Jesus is the only answer.

Prayer for today: "Thank you, God, that You will redeem my soul from the grave, and take me to Yourself."

May 7: Read Psalms 51-53

Key verse: "Create in me a pure heart, O God, and renew a steadfast spirit within me" (Psalm 51:10 NIV).

In this particular Psalm, David is obviously feeling the weight of his sin. However, he does not allow this weight to destroy him, but brings it to the one who can minister forgiveness and healing. The first half of the Psalm seems to speak of the cleansing that needs to take place. The second half tells of the results of that cleansing.

Too often we want the cleansing, but have no desire to accept the changes it will bring. Cleansing must bring results! David understood this and therefore did not only ask for cleansing but a renewal in his life. He prayed for a steadfast spirit. He was desirous of living a life that constantly revealed his relationship with God so that others could see the result of his faith.

Psalm 51:10 needs to be our daily prayer, for we need not only to be cleansed by God but to live daily for Him.

Direction for today: Dying to self and living for God is a daily process.

Prayer for today: "Create in me a pure heart, O God, and renew a steadfast spirit within me."

May 8: Read Psalms 54-56

Key verse: "In God I will praise His Word, in God I have my trust; I will not fear what flesh can do unto me" (Psalm 56:4 KJV).

Suppose we feel unwell and go to the doctor. Often the first thing he'll ask is, "Let me see your tongue." The condition of the tongue gives the doctor a clue to the condition of the body.

Isn't the same thing true in a spiritual sense? Doesn't the state of our tongues indicate the condition of our souls?

This thought is one main thread running through each of the psalms of our reading today. David, a man "after God's own heart" (Acts 13:22; I Samuel 13:14), is careful to guard and bridle his tongue (James 1:26). He uses this gift of God, the gift of speech, to glorify his God – to tell of His righteousness, power, mercy and truth. He uses his tongue to pray to God, to call upon His Name, to sing His praises, to speak the truth.

Our speech is vitally important.

A Greater than David warns, "Out of the abundance of the heart the mouth speaketh. A good man, out of the good treasure of the heart bringeth forth good things: and an evil man, out of the evil treasure bringeth forth evil things. But I say unto you, that every idle word that men shall speak, they shall give account thereof in the day of judgment. For by thy words thou shalt be justified, and by thy words thou shalt be condemned" (Matthew 12:34-37).

Direction for today: Use your tongue to praise God continually, and you will have no time for anything else.

Prayer for today: "Thank You Father, for Your Word".

May 9: Read Psalms 57-59

Key verse: *"I will praise You, O Lord, among the nations; I will sing of You among the peoples" (Psalm 57:9 NIV).*

David could never have been accused of being shy. He loved God, and made sure that everyone heard about it. When the symbol of God's presence, the ark of the covenant, was returned to Jerusalem, David danced before the procession with such joyful abandon that his wife despised him.

There is no doubt that David meant what he said. He loved God, and he freely and happily acknowledged his Lord before the nations and the peoples. In this, David is a great example to all of us Christians who are afraid to speak our praise to the Lord, even in the safety of a church service.

God has called us to proclaim our faith, unashamed of our Lord and Saviour. David knew that nothing else was more important than his love for God – not the respect of others who might think his actions excessive, nor his own image as a solemn king.

He loved God, and wanted everyone to know it.

Direction for today: Do not be ashamed to proclaim your love and praise for God.

Prayer for today: "I will praise You, O Lord and sing of You among the people."

May 10: Read Psalms 60-63

Key verse: "My soul finds refuge in God alone; my salvation comes from Him" (Psalm 62:1 NIV).

Today, let us think of those two words, "God alone". This verse says something extremely important: the only ultimate answer is in God. Our only refuge, security and peace will be found in Him.

Too many Christians follow the ways of the world, seeking refuge and security in other things. We may worship God, but we attempt to gain security for ourselves through material things. We claw our way up corporate ladders to make more money so that we can be more secure. We hold two jobs to pay for two cars so we will be happier.

Sometimes, we seek refuge in personal relationships. We lean completely on a spouse or a specific friend. But when that person fails – as every person will, sometime or another – our source of security is gone.

There is only one refuge: God. The sooner we realize that, the sooner we will take the first steps toward real personal peace. Too many Christians are ignoring the benefits of their relationship with the Father.

Direction for today: Do not place faith in any false source of security; lean only on the Lord.

Prayer for today: "O God, You are my God, earnestly I seek You; my soul thirsts for You" (Psalm 63:1).

Memory Verse

"Blessed be the name of God forever and ever, for wisdom and might are His." Daniel 2:20 NKJV

May 11: Read Psalms 64-66

Key verse: "Say to God, 'How awesome are Your deeds!'" (Psalm 66:3 NIV).

God's deeds are, without question, worthy of awe. This psalm reviews some of the things the Lord has done; and He continues to do the same wonderful things today!

Verse 3 speaks of victory over enemies. We must certainly praise the Lord for the victory He has won for us over sin, death and hell! In verse 6, the psalmist speaks of the impossible act of turning sea into dry land. Has God done the impossible in your life? Has He healed, or delivered you from apparently impossible circumstance? Praise Him!

Verse 7 tells us that the Lord rules and that we can therefore trust Him to be able to answer. In verse 9, we see that God has saved our lives. The act of saving us, in Jesus, is reason enough in itself to praise Him until He comes.

In verse 12, we are reminded of the abundant life that is ours as children of God. Then, in verse 19, the author offers praise for answered prayer. Do you remember to thank God each time He answers your prayers?

Finally, in verse 20, we read of God's gift of love to us.

Truly, His deeds toward us are "awesome"!

Direction for today: Praise God for His awesome deeds, especially those from your life.

Prayer for today: "Praise be to God, who has not rejected my prayer nor withheld His love from me!"

May 12: Read Psalms 67, 68

Key verse: *"What a glorious Lord! He who daily bears our burdens also gives us our salvation" (Psalm 68:19 Living Bible).*

It is great to know that an almighty, powerful God, who "causes the earth to tremble and the heavens to shake" (Psalms 68:8), reduces this power to an individual level for you and me to appreciate.

God had constantly displayed His power by delivering the Israelites from various dangers and foes. Many times the problems were self-induced. If you and I were the judges, we would say that most often they deserved what they got.

But God does not work that way; He always keeps His promises. His compassion for us reaches far beyond our comprehension, but He does not just bail us out of "tight spots". The same God who promises eternal life will also daily maintain our well-being. He has promised to carry our burdens. What a comfort!

Direction for today: Remember that God always keeps His promises.

Prayer for today: "Thank you, Lord, that You are a father to the fatherless and a defender of widows."

May 13: Read Psalm 69

Key verse: *"I will praise the name of God with a song, and will magnify Him with thanksgiving" (Psalm 69:30 NAS).*

Throughout many of David's psalms, we can discover two streams flowing together. One is the expression of deep inner emotion, arising from experiences which would seem to press in upon him like an overwhelming load. The second is an outpouring of confidence and faith in the God whom he called his Rock, his Fortress.

This deep-seated faith in the sufficiency of God found expression in songs of praise and thanksgiving unto the Lord.

Life for the follower of the Heavenly King is never guaranteed to be exempt from pressure or adversity. In His final message to His disciples, before His death, Jesus made this significant statement: "These things I have spoken unto you, that in Me ye might have peace. In the world ye shall have tribulation; but be of good cheer; I have overcome the world" (John 16:33). Here again, we see the dual streams to which David gives expression in the Psalms. There are the trying experiences of living in a world that is out of tune with God; but there can be an inner peace that is found by being personally in tune with Him.

That is why the same writer, in the same hymn, can write, "Save me, O God, for the waters have threatened my life", and then proceed to our key verse.

Direction for today: Praise God for the peace that supercedes circumstances.

Prayer for today: "Thank You, Lord, that through ever-changing situations, You are always faithful."

May 14: Read Psalms 70, 71

Key verse: "Now also when I am old and greyheaded, O God, forsake me not; until I have shewed Thy strength unto this generation, and Thy power to every one that is to come" (Psalm 71:18 KJV).

David looked upon his old age as simply a continuation of his service to God and his relationship with Him. He specifically asks God for help to continue to be a minister to those that would follow him in a new generation.

His prayers, in Psalms 70 and 71, are typical of many of the prayers of David. There seems a desperation for God to intervene in what seems like a hopeless situation and invariably God did take a hand in David's affairs.

Would to God that none of us Christians, when we reach old age, would lay down our armour and weapons of war, but continue to battle for the Lord in reaching this new generation with the Good News. Who better than an aged person, with many years of experience of walking with the Lord, to relate to the younger generation the faithfulness and unfailing love of God.

May our old age be as fruitful for God as the most energy-filled days of our youth.

Direction for today: Age is irrelevant to God, for anyone of any age can tell of His love and mercy.

Prayer for today: "In Thee, O Lord, do I put my trust" (Psalm 71:1).

May 15: Read Psalm 72

Key verse: "He shall have dominion also from sea to sea, and from the river unto the ends of the earth" (Psalm 72:8 KJV).

Jesus will come back to earth again, some day, to set up His kingdom.

On the day when He returns, tears will be wiped away from the eyes of those who weep. There will be life instead of death, gladness instead of sorrow, and joy will replace crying. "And I heard a great voice out of heaven saying, Behold, the tabernacle of God is with men, and He will dwell with them, and be their God. And God shall wipe away all tears from their eyes; and there shall be no more pain: for the former things are passed away".

Until the time of Christ's return to earth, God set up His kingdom in our hearts when we accept Him as our Lord and Saviour. But we are told, in Ephesians 1:20-23, that God has set Jesus at His own right hand, "far above all principality, and power, and might, and dominion . . . and has put all things under His feet and gave Him to be head over all things in the church, which is His body".

As representative of the Father, Jesus takes up His residence and dominion in us so that every person around us tastes a little bit of what God's kingdom or dominion is like. As God's representative, the suffering one will experience the healing of Jesus Christ through you.

Direction for today: Life your life in the awareness that some day God is going to call history to a halt.

Prayer for today: "Blessed be the Lord God, who only doeth wondrous things."

May 16: Read Psalm 73

Key verse: "Whom have I in heaven but You? And there is none upon earth that I desire besides You" (Psalm 73:25 NKJV).

It's in the refining fires that we come to the place where we realize God must be our first love.

The psalmist saw the prosperity of the wicked and was tempted to let envy take over in his life. Listening to the preacher is good, because it reminds us of what God says. God's word gives us an eternal outlook on life. Heaven is going to be a beautiful place because of who is there – Jesus Christ the Lord!

The hope of the believer cannot be purchased. It is given by our Lord Jesus as we give ourselves totally to Him. Then we can declare, "You will show me the path of life; in Your presence is fullness of joy; at Your right hand are pleasures forevermore" (Psalm 16:11 NKJV).

Direction for today: Put aside anything in your life that comes before God, for that is idolatry.

Prayer for today: "Thank You, Lord that when everything temporal is gone, Your promises continue."

May 17: Read Psalms 74, 75

Key verse: "We are given no miraculous signs; no prophets are left, and none of us knows how long this will be" (Psalm 74:9 NIV).

Would God allow such a thing to come to pass? There certainly have been times in history when He seemed to be strangely quiet. The people of Israel, like Job, went through periods when the voice of the Lord seemed to be stilled, and His hand withdrawn.

Similarly, believers may encounter such times in their own lives. These valleys are difficult to take, especially if they come on the heels of mountaintop times which have included miracles and inspiring words of prophecy.

We do not always know God's purpose for these things. At times, the silence may be caused by our own sin. If this is so, we need to repent in order to sense the Lord again. But this was not the problem with Job, and is not always the cause of our "dry times".

It may be that the Lord is allowing our faith to mature. We need to move beyond having faith because of miracles or other evidence, and come to a place of confidence in God alone, no matter what our circumstances.

Thus it was with Paul, who, although in prison, could sing praise. Thus it was with Jesus, who on the cross commended His Spirit to the Father. Dry times cause plants to put roots down much deeper than they ever would in the rainy season.

Direction for today: In dry times, wait on the Lord, and trust Him, because He is God.

Prayer for today: "Father, give me the patience to wait before You, and to trust You when, like Job, I do not hear Your voice."

Memory Verse

"I will heal their backsliding, I will love them freely, for My anger has turned away from him." Hosea 14:4 NKJV

May 18: Read Psalms 76, 77
Key verse: "Thy way is in the sea, and Thy path in the great waters, and Thy footsteps are not known" (Psalm 77:19 KJV).

God guides His people; sometimes in pleasant paths beside the still waters (Psalm 23:2), sometimes through deep waters (Psalm 77:19). In the midst of difficulties or in moments of uncertainty, God promises to lead us in paths that we have not known (Isaiah 42:16). Sometimes they are like deep waters which cannot be fathomed, or like the ways of a ship at sea which cannot be tracked.

Sometimes, like the children of Israel who were escaping from the pursuing armies of Pharoah, we have only one path to follow: through the sea. At moments like these we must learn to step out in faith, trusting completely in God's resources, remembering that His ways are not always our ways.

When God leads us, He does so with all the tender care of a shepherd (Psalm 77:20). We can walk confidently in the knowledge that, in any circumstances, God's resources are always sufficient.

Direction for today: Wherever God leads, His own sheep follow without question.

Prayer for today: "I will meditate on all Your works and consider all Your mighty deeds" (Psalm 76:12 NIV).

May 19: Read Psalm 78

Key verse: "That they should put their confidence in God, and not forget the works of God, but keep His commandments" (Psalm 78:7 NAS).

There is a vast difference between Christian separation and Christian isolation. As followers of God, we are called to be different from the corrupt world system (II Corinthians 6:17), but we are commanded *not* to be withdrawn or isolated from our fellow human beings (Acts 1:8, Matthew 28:19).

Yet often we find Christians tending to simply withdraw from contact with the world, convinced that all things are going to continue to become worse and worse. Christians at times seem to despair of being a positive influence on unbelievers. We think that each succeeding generation will be worse than the last.

But here, in Psalm 78, we find promises that it need not be so. God spoke to His people and told them that concern for the faith of the children could produce a faithful new generation. In the first verses of this psalm, the Lord tells His people to concern themselves with the children, and to teach them the ways of God. If God's people faithfully reach out to the children, "a stubborn and rebellious generation . . . whose spirit was not faithful to God" (78:8), but will "put their confidence in God . . . and keep His commandments" (78:7).

We need not, we *must* not, give up the young people as lost to the world, the flesh, and the devil. Christians are called to reach out and save young people caught in the descending spiral. In the face of a corrupt world, we must still remember that God is in the business of restoring to Himself lost sheep.

Direction for today: Teach the wonderful truths of God to your children.

Prayer for today: "Lord, please show me how I can reach out, in Your name, to even one child, that he or she might come into the kingdom of God."

May 20: Read Psalms 79, 80

Key verse: "Why should the nations say, 'Where is their God?'" (Psalm 79:10 NIV).

Too often today, the world is looking at a church with no power. Hundreds of Christian fellowships meet weekly, and weakly. There is no sign of the signs that accompanied the people of God in New Testament times. The miracles seem to be gone.

And the unbelievers say, "Where is their God?"

The weakness does not lie with the Lord. He is eager to do the same things through us today that He did through Peter, Paul and indeed Jesus Himself. God has promised this. But He only works through willing channels. Too often, our fear of ridicule or of failure stops the Holy Spirit from working through us.

Jesus promised that signs would accompany the proclamation of the gospel. It is time that Christians began to expect miracles, once again, in every church that preaches the Good News of Jesus. The true works of God are a wonderful answer to unbelievers. In the New Testament, many, many people came to the Lord because of His works. That pattern is to be followed today as well.

Direction for today: Make yourself available to the Holy Spirit.

Prayer for today: "Restore us, O Lord God Almighty" (Psalm 80:19).

May 21: Read Psalms 81-83

Key verse: "I would feed you with the finest of the wheat; and with honey from the rock I would satisfy you" (Psalm 81:16 NAS).

This Psalm begins with great enthusiasm and rejoicing, as Asaph encourages the people to sing and shout and to play their musical instruments in celebration of the goodness of God.

Then we read the words of God, as He reminds His chosen people of all He had done for them, warns them against sin and tells of their waywardness. In verse 13 we read the heart cry of the Father, "Oh, that My people would listen to Me, that Israel would walk in My ways." But this was not the way it was.

Today the Lord says to you and me, "Oh, that you would listen to Me, and walk in My ways." Are we doing that? In our key verse He tells us what He wants to do for us if we would obey Him. He wants to feed us with good things, to provide for us abundantly. He *wants* to bless us . . . only our disobedience stands in His way.

Direction for today: All good things are yours because of God's love. Don't allow disobedience to keep you from that inheritance.

Prayer for today: "My heart and my flesh sing for joy to the living God."

May 22: Read Psalms 84-86

Key verse: "For the Lord God is a sun and shield; the Lord gives grace and glory; no good thing does He withhold from those who walk uprightly" (Psalm 84:11 NAS).

This verse speaks of the greatness of our Lord through Jesus Christ, and how He reaches down to mankind. He is our sun and shield – offering each of us the warmth of His love and security of His protection.

Then He gives us grace – which is defined as unmerited favour. Praise His wonderful name, He not only gives us unmerited favour but also gives us glory!

And the last part of this verse is such a tremendous promise, "No good thing does He withhold from those who walk uprightly." Note that we are not told that we will have *all* things but that we will have *good* things. Our Father knows those things which are good for us. Matthew 7:11, 12 tells us, "If you then, being evil, know how to give good gifts to your children, how much more shall your Father who is in Heaven give what is good to those who ask Him!"

Direction for today: The Lord is our shield; therefore stay near Him, where you are protected.

Prayer for today: "Thank You, Lord, for every good thing!"

May 23: Read Psalms 87, 88

Key verse: "Soon it will be too late! Of what use are your miracles when I am in the grave? How can I praise you then?" (Psalm 88:10 Living Bible).

David pleads with the Lord to extend his life and he promises to praise the Lord for all His miracles.

If you were asked to write your own obituary, what would you include? Would it be all those things you meant to do but never quite got around to? Of course not!

So many historical people have monuments, buildings and parks named after them. Many are inducted into various halls of fame. Doubtless you, too, would be pleased to know you would be remembered in such a way.

But how many people strive to leave a spiritual legacy behind? This should be our ultimate contribution to mankind. Proclaiming the way of salvation and God's life-changing miracles should be our utmost priority.

David knew the importance of praise. He constantly exhorted the people to praise.

Direction for today: Follow David's example, and praise God as long as He gives you breath.

Prayer for today: "Lord, teach me to use every moment for Your glory."

May 24: Read Psalm 89

Key verse: "Blessed is the people that know the joyful sound: they shall walk, O Lord, in the light of Thy countenance" (Psalms 89:15 KJV).

In the preceding verses, the psalmist has been reveling in the might and majesty of the Lord. Then, like a choir director who leads his musicians to a crescendo, he cries out, "Blessed are those who experience the joy of close personal relationship with their God."

The source of overcoming strength and contentment is not human skill or ability, but the all powerful Creator of the Universe. The portions following our key verse have as, their main theme, the reliability of our God. He is pictured as a covenant-making and covenant-keeping king.

David is used as an example of a man who through faith, experienced the faithfulness of the Lord. However, beginning with verse 27 there appears to be a Messianic prophecy. The reference is not to David but the Lord Jesus Christ. He is the One who would keep the covenant with the Father. In return, God would keep His promise to those who would be known as the seed of David, those who would place their faith in God's firstborn, the Lord Jesus Christ. He in turn would keep His promises to them.

This brings us back to our key verse, "Happy are the people whose God is the Lord and who walk in the light of His truth."

Direction for today: Walking close to God is the only way to walk in the light.

Prayer for today: "Blessed be the Lord forever!"

Memory Verse

"And it shall come to pass afterward that I will pour out My Spirit on all flesh; your sons and your daughters shall prophesy, your old men shall dream dreams, your young men shall see visions." Joel 2:28 NKJV

May 25: Read Psalms 90, 91

Key verse: "He that dwelleth in the secret place of the Most High shall abide under the shadow of the Almighty." (Psalm 91:1 KJV).

There is something about a dwelling place that brings security. The place we call home is, for many, a place of security. There the rest of the world can be shut out, warmth can be felt and a sense of belonging is ours. This is because it is our dwelling place, our haven.

For the Christian, the dwelling place that brings security spiritually is in "the secret place of the Most High". It is communion with God that brings peace to our mind and soul. However, it is not just a matter of spasmodic communion. Rather, the communion spoken of here is that which is constant. It is a daily part of life. That is seen in the word "dwelling". The word dwell means "to make one's home; live".

The logical conclusion is that it is the person who lives in the presence of God, or daily abides in the Lord, and who puts confidence and trust in Him, who knows His real protection and love.

Direction for today: Dwell with the Lord; do not merely call on Him in a crisis!

Prayer for today: "Lord, with Your guidance, I will do Your will."

May 26: Read Psalms 92-94

Key verse: "They shall bring forth fruit in old age; they shall be fat and flourishing" (Psalm 92:14 KJV).

It is often said in growing old we become either better or bitter. How unpleasant it is to be in the presence of someone who is continually complaining, expecting others to serve and give them special attention. Thank God, He has something better for His obedient children.

Proverbs 4:18 says, "The path of the just is as a shining light that shineth more and more unto the perfect day." Physicians tell us that a joyful, happy person does not age in body as quickly as the depressed and sad.

Though our bodies are bound to grow old, our spirits can be refreshed as we meditate on the Word. Psalm 1 reminds us that God knows the way of the righteous and we can continue to be fruitful and flourishing. We can think of many examples of this as we recall some saintly Christians whom we have known, or of whom we have read.

Direction for today: Remember that, although your present body may age, your spirit is eternally alive in the Lord.

Prayer for today: "Lord, today I give You thanks, praise Your Name and proclaim Your lovingkindness and faithfulness!"

May 27: Read Psalms 95-97

Key verse: "Forty years long was I grieved with this generation, and said, It is a people that do err in their heart, and they have not known My ways" (Psalm 95:10 KJV).

In the middle of these three psalms of praise, we see demonstrated the grief of our God over His people when they do not hear His voice and because of that, find themselves drawn away, to wander through the wilderness. The heart of our heavenly Father grieves over this. For forty years, this God of all power and majesty grieved over His people because they would not listen to His voice.

God created us in such a way that what we feed our minds affects our feelings. Our feelings push us to take action on the information that our minds have been fed and, because the children of Israel were listening to the heathen and longing after their gods, their hearts pushed them in that direction, towards a life of unbelief. And because of that they were brought suffering.

The struggle that the children of Israel had is ours today. We will either be feeding our minds on truth or with the things of this world. Bombarded by news reports, commentaries and advertising in newspapers and magazines, or on radio or television, your mind is programed and brainwashed. So it is very important what you feed your mind. If you feed truth it will bring life, but if lust and lawlessness it will bring death.

In Jeremiah 10:2 we read, "Thus says the Lord, learn not the way of the heathen, and be not dismayed at the signs of heaven for the heathen are dismayed at them".

Direction for today: Realize that you are capable of grieving God; be sure not to return disobedience for the great love He has shown you.

Prayer for today: "Father, may I always love You, and always hate evil".

May 28: Read Psalms 98-100

Key verse: "O Jehovah our God! You answered them and forgave their sins, yet punished them when they went wrong" (Psalm 99:8 Living Bible).

When a child throws a temper tantrum, do you spank or ignore? When an eight year old knowingly disobeys, should you punish or compromise? When a teenager challenges your authority, should you restrict or negotiate?

We serve a God who strikes a perfect balance between justice and fairness. Our desire as parents should be to teach our children obedience, but we should always administer justice in a fair way.

If we examine this passage, we notice that God took three steps when dealing with His people. First, God answered. Never ignore a problem and expect it to disappear. Try to zero in on the cause of the problem.

99

Often disobedience is only a symptom and a wise answer will bring a happy resolution.

Secondly, God forgave. After you and your child have addressed and resolved the problem, you must forgive. Never bring it up again.

Thirdly, God punished. This is probably the most difficult area, as punishment can take so many forms. Do not think you are doing your child a favour by constantly warning only. Carry out the punishment promised; be consistent and always let the punishment fit the situation.

This is God's pattern. Follow it!

Direction for today: Ask God for wisdom to handle family problems.

Prayer for today: "Praise You, Father, that You made me, and made me Your own."

May 29: Read Psalms 101,102

Key verse: *"I will set before my eyes no vile thing" (Psalm 101:3a NIV).*

How much trouble could be avoided if we would follow the principle stated in this verse!

Christians today are bombarded by all manner of "vile things" — on television, in movies, in music and in books and magazines. It seems that we cannot open our eyes without setting them on moral evil.

Yet, if we think carefully about it, we may begin to realize that we have often invited these vile visions, and that it is we ourselves who have opened the door to them. Christians are appallingly lax in their choice of entertainment. For example, when we watch some television program which we know to be undesirable, we are simply asking for trouble.

Of course, our imaginations are sparked by what we feed our minds, and soon we find ourselves obsessed with the vile instead of the holy.

We must repent of our carelessness, and guard our eyes and our minds. If we avoid all the vile things we can, the Lord will filter out the rest that we find unavoidable!

Direction for today: Be sure everything you see, read and hear is honouring to the Lord.

Prayer for today: "Father give me discernment to know what things I must avoid."

May 30: Read Psalm 103

Key verse: *"Praise the Lord, O my soul; all my inmost being, praise His holy name" (Psalm 103:1 NIV).*

Praise. What does it mean? It means to glorify, worship, extol, or give laud. Simply put, we could say it means to honour God for all He has done and for who He is.

David is suggesting to himself that he needs to put his entire being into worship. He is concerned that he honour God for all the blessings He has given to mankind. Then he begins to list all the blessings of God: forgiveness, healing, love, compassion, redemption, satisfaction of all good desires, renewal, righteousness, justice for the oppressed and the grace of God.

There are times when we need to come to God and do nothing else but praise Him. As you take time to read this psalm today, you will see why. No doubt, as you finish the reading, you will have a desire to praise God. Do so!

Direction for today: Praise the Lord!

Prayer for today: "Praise the Lord, O my soul."

May 31: Read Psalm 104

Key verse: "Let the glory of the Lord endure forever; let the Lord be glad in His works" (Psalm 104:31 NAS).

The main intent of Psalm 104 is to exalt the majesty and providence of God. In other words, to praise God. He is to be praised as a great God of unique and matchless perfection for His glory shall endure to the end of time. His work of grace shall be exalted through eternity in the songs of adoration of the saints as well as of the angels. Man's glory fades away but God's glory is everlasting. Creatures change but with the Creator there is no change: "I am the Lord. I change not" (Malachi 3:6).

Our God is a gracious God. He still rejoices in the works of His hand, the product of His own wisdom and goodness. He saw everything He had made and beheld that it was very good.

We often do things about which we cannot rejoice, or wish we had not done them. However, God always rejoices in His works, because they are all done in wisdom and grace.

Direction for today: Remember that God made human beings, and declared them to be good. He was pleased with His creation, and He is pleased when you live as part of His new creation.

Prayer for today: "Lord, I give You all the glory and honour today."

6

Jesus Only!

All we need is only JESUS!
Saviour! Sanctifier! King!
Blessed Lord! and our Redeemer!
In all hearts sweet joy will bring.

All we need is only JESUS!
Lamp divine! to guide our way. . .
Jesus only is our Saviour!
He will answer as we PRAY!

All we need is only JESUS!
He alone can cleanse all sin!
Peace which passeth understanding
Gives a holiness within.

All we need is only JESUS!
He our Hope! our Power! our Stay!
When we in our hearts accept Him
He'll go with us on Life's Way.

Doris Roberts Moore

"Let justice run down like water, and righteousness like a mighty stream." Amos 5:24 NKJV

June 1: Read Psalm 105

Key verse: *"O give thanks to the Lord, call on His name, make known His deeds among the people!" (Psalm 105:1 RSV).*

We need to step back and remember what the Lord has done for us. It is amazing how short our memories can be. Our lives can be a wreck one minute, then the Lord salvages us and the next minute we are groaning because He doesn't seem to be doing anything.

The whole of Psalm 105 is a diary telling how God has looked after His people in the past. And if He has done this in the past, just think of what He is doing today, if we would only look around and acknowledge it.

Everyone of us should keep a "spiritual diary", not only so we will not forget what the Lord had done but, more than that, so that we can tell others what He has done for us *personally*. That is what a "testimony" is all about: simply telling other people what Jesus had done for you . . . or me.

And, when you do remember to do so, other people will be able to believe in Jesus, find forgiveness and eternal life, all because you have remembered to "make known His deeds among the people."

Direction for today: Praise the Lord for three special things He had done in your life.

Prayer for today: "Lord, I thank You for giving such special blessings."

June 2: Read Psalm 106

Key verse: *"Many times He delivered them, but they were bent on rebellion and they wasted away in their sin" (Psalm 106:43 NIV).*

Too often, this is a verbal roadmap of the life of a Christian. Far too many believers are farther from the Lord today than they were at some time before.

Many can remember a time when God was miraculously and powerfully involved in their lives. Perhaps He delivered them from some terrible problem, or healed them, or restored their marriage or their business.

At the time, they gratefully acknowledged the Lord, and praised Him. But, as the weeks and months went by, they became more and more immersed in secular concerns. When they were reminded of their failing love, they responded in rebellion: "I really don't have all that time to spend on those things any more."

Unfortunately, that is the road to destruction. How many of us would confess we are caught in such a situation, right now?

But the next verse is a great promise: God hears even in our distress, remembers us, and restores us in love. If you have fallen from your first love for God, call on Him; He still hears.

Direction for today: Wherever you are, spiritually, call on the Lord, right now.

Prayer for today: "Save me, O Lord my God, from the traps I have set for myself."

June 3: Read Psalm 107

Key verse: *"Let the redeemed of the Lord say so, whom He has redeemed from trouble" (Psalm 107:2 RSV).*

The psalmist reminds us of a basic courtesy: to say "Thank You" to God when He acts in our behalf.

Psalm 107 is a reminder of the unfaithfulness of God's people in spite of His faithfulness to them, or should I say "us"? The psalmist also reminds us that God had done everything out of His "steadfast love" for us.

God's motivation has always been the same: love. "For God so loved the world that He gave His only Son that whoever believes in Him should not perish but have eternal life" (John 3:16).

This means we can trust Him to save us, heal us and guide us.

No matter how much sin and wrong you have done, remember that, "If we confess our sins, He is faithful and just, and will forgive us our sins, and cleanse us from all unrighteousness" (I John 1:9).

Direction for today: When Jesus has rescued you, healed you or answered prayer, thank Him, and tell someone else about it.

Prayer for today: "Lord, give me opportunities to acknowledge You before others, and I will do so."

June 4: Read Psalms 108,109

Key verse: *"Save us and help us with Your right hand, that those You love may be delivered" (Psalm 108:6 NIV).*

What is your specific need today? How long has that need been a part of your life?

Often we carry problems and troubles with us for weeks, months, or even years. They weigh us down and rob us of joy, yet we do not bring them to the Lord. Perhaps we think this specific need is too small to bother God with. Or, perhaps subconsciously, we think it is too big to be solved.

God is concerned about our needs, large or small. Nothing is too small for the Lord. Remember, He is the God who sees even the tiny sparrow fall. But the enemy would love to have us harbour the small troubles that can clog up our spiritual channels. Satan won't attack with something big like cancer if something small, like a cold, will stop us from serving the Lord. Nothing is too small for God.

And nothing could possibly be too big for the One whose right hand formed this entire world! God longs to deliver you from the things binding your life. Bring them to Him!

Direction for today: Bring your needs to the Father, whether they are big or small!

Prayer for today: "Lord, I bring my needs, troubles and problems to You, right now, and I leave them there!"

June 5: Read Psalms 110-113

Key verse: "Praise the Lord. Praise, O servants of the Lord, praise the name of the Lord" (Psalm 113:1 NAS).

What glorious songs of praise these are! Let us look again at some of the verses we have just read:

Praise ye the Lord. I will praise the Lord with my whole heart (111:1).

His work is honourable and glorious: and His righteousness endures forever . . . the Lord is gracious and full of compassion (111:3,4).

Blessed is the name of the Lord from this time forth for evermore. From the rising of the sun, unto the going down of the same the Lord's name is to be praised. The Lord is high above all nations, and His glory above the heavens (113:2-4).

No matter what your circumstances might be today, God asks that you praise Him. And He inhabits the praises of His people (Psalm 22:3).

Direction for today: "Lift up your heads, because your redemption is drawing near" (Luke 21:28 NAS).

Prayer for today: "Lord, help me to worship You in rightful fear and awe, for this is the beginning of wisdom."

June 6: Read Psalms 114-116

Key verse: "Not to us, O Lord, not to us, but to Thy name give glory because of Thy lovingkindness, because of Thy truth" (Psalm 115:1 NAS).

Those who sang this song were proclaiming a truth which is important to every servant of God. This verse stands as the answer to the greatest sin of man: the sin of pride.

Satan works very hard to trap Christians in this particular sin. It is especially tempting because it can arise from entirely praiseworthy situations.

If the enemy cannot stop us from doing good in the name of the Lord, he will attempt to lure us into taking the credit ourselves. Unfortunately, we are often very easy to lure. That was a problem with those Pharisees who fell into hypocrisy: they were proud of their efforts to serve God, and they began to take glory to themselves.

106

If ever you are tempted to do this remember: pride is the sin of Satan himself. He tried to snatch some of God's glory; this is why he was cast from the heavenly kingdom.

Be sure that all the glory always goes to the Lord. We are incapable of any good thing apart from the Lord, anyway!

Direction for today: Be sure to deflect all glory from yourself to the Glorious One, Jesus our Lord.

Prayer for today: "All glory ad honour and power be unto You, our Lord and Saviour."

June 7: Read Psalms 117, 118

Key verse: "Praise the Lord, all nations; Laud Him, all peoples! For His lovingkindness is great toward us, And the truth of the Lord is everlasting. Praise the Lord!" (Psalm 117 NAS).

This short Hebrew poem is one of the best descriptions of the relationship that God intended to have with mankind.

First, we see the relationship of human beings to the Lord God — we are to praise Him, to speak and to live to bring glory, laud, and honour to the King of the Universe.

Then, we see God's relationship to us — He deals with mankind in great lovingkindness. And we, living in the age that can know Jesus Christ, see this even more clearly than the psalmist did. Jesus is the embodiment of all of the lovingkindness of God toward us; we are to praise and honour Him. And finally, we can be entirely confident that God will never change. All eternal truth is anchored everlastingly in God. It is because God is, that we can be sure of truth. If there were no God, than all that is would be floating meaninglessly in emptiness. But God *is*. And because we can know Him we can be sure of the truth that God loves us, that we can know Him through Jesus, and that He is pleased with our praise.

As the final phrase says, "Praise the Lord". In Hebrew, that is simply, "Hallelujah!"

Direction for today: Praise God that He is God, and He is the source of all lovingkindness and all truth.

Prayer for today: "Lord, You have made this day; I rejoice and am glad in it."

Memory Verse

"On Mount Zion there shall be deliverance, and there shall be holiness." Amos 5:24 NKJV

June 8: Read Psalm 119:1-72

Key verse: "This is my comfort in my affliction, that Thy word revived me" (Psalm 119:50 NAS).

Almost everyone goes through some kind of trouble. The trials will vary from time to time and person to person, but God desires to comfort us, whatever our situation might be. Sometimes relief comes immediately, but sometimes we must endure through a trying situation. Whatever happens, however, He is able to strengthen and keep us, to console and encourage us, and to give us peace.

The psalmist tells of his experience when the scriptures brought life to him in the midst of affliction. God knows what you are going through at this very moment. God uses His word to bring consolation and comfort to those who seek Him. Jesus said, "The words that I have spoken to you are spirit and are life" (John 6:63).

Direction for today: Seek to learn more of the Word of God.

Prayer for today: "Father, help me to hide Your Word in my heart."

June 9: Read Psalm 119:73-128

Key verse: "Your hands made me and formed me; give me understanding to learn Your commands" (Psalm 119:73 NIV).

It is good to remind ourselves of this fundamental truth: God made us. In fact, He is so involved in our individual creation that the psalmists frequently use the image of God forming us with His own hands.

This must affect much about our daily lives and our relationships with other people. Whenever we encounter someone with whom we have a disagreement, it is good to remember that God also made that person. Whenever we are tempted to dislike someone, we need to remember that each person has worth as a creation of God.

And, of course, we need to take a strong Christian stand against abortion, because each abortion is a killing of a person who is created by God. Each aborted baby is also a tiny image-bearer of God.

God made you and He loves you. God made each person on this earth, and He loves each one. God made each unborn baby, and He loves them as well. Let us so live that we demonstrate the love of God.

Direction for today: Express God's love toward one of His creations.

Prayer for today: "Lord, may the evil of abortion be stopped in our land and around the world."

June 10: Read Psalm 119:129-176

Key verse: "I have longed for Thy salvation, O Lord; and Thy law is my delight" (Psalm 119:174 KJV).

Out of the 176 verses of this marvellous psalm, only one (verse 122) does not speak, in some form, of the Word of God. The various word-forms used throughout the other 175 verses are God's law, God's testimonies; His ways, precepts, statutes, commandments, ordinances, or judgments.

"O how I love Thy law! It is my meditation all the day" (verse 97). The writer of this psalm has grasped a mighty truth and mastered a tremendous lesson. He has realized that he is utterly and completely dependent upon the Word of God. This means the end of egotistic self-reliance. It is perhaps the deepest of all truths to learn, the greatest of all lessons.

How so? Because the Word of God must represent God Himself. As A God of truth, One Who cannot lie, He expresses Himself through His Word of Truth. Thus, the more we love the Word of God, honour and obey the Word, the more we love, honour and obey God Himself.

Just as the Bible is the written Word of God (John 10:35), so Jesus Christ is the incarnate ("enfleshed") Word of God (Revelation 19:13). The more we love, honour and obey the written Word of God, the Bible, the more we love, honour and obey the *incarnate* Word of God, the Lord Jesus Christ. "He that hath My commandments, and keepeth them," says Jesus, "he it is that loveth Me" (John 14:21).

Would that we might all experientially learn this great truth uttered in Matthew 4:4 by Jesus Himself, quoting from Deuteronomy 8:3, "Man shall not live by bread alone, but by every word that proceedeth out of the mouth of God."

Direction for today: "This book of the law shall not depart out of thy mouth; but thou shalt meditate therein day and night, that thou mayest observe to do all that is written therein: for then thou shalt make thy way prosperous, and then thou shalt have good success" (Joshua 1:8 KJV).

Prayer for today: "Father, cause me to receive spiritual food from Your word."

June 11: Read Psalms 120-124

Key verse: "My help comes from the Lord" (Psalms 121:2 NAS).

The psalmist recognizes the fact that we are sustained by the power of the living God. Because of His great planning, we are able to enjoy the light of day, cool silence of night, the warmth of the sun, the abundance of things grown in our rich earth. We cannot move or even breathe without touching something God has created for our survival.

How beautiful to know God has done this just for us. And even more beautiful is the fact that Jesus wants to live in and through us that others may be touched. As we submit to His great love, we have the God-given power to encourage someone else.

Today, let us think of someone who needs a lift. Then ask Jesus to help us minister to that person in a way that will give evidence that 'our help cometh from the Lord.'

Direction for today: Allow the Lord to use you to bring help to someone in need of His touch.

Prayer for today: "Be gracious to us, O Lord, be gracious to us" (Psalm 123:3).

June 12: Read Psalms 125-129

Key verse: *"Those who sow in tears will reap with songs of joy" (Psalm 126:5 NIV).*

Commitment to Jesus Christ means commitment to His cross. The lives of great Christians have involved many tears, suffering and hardships.

The gospel is not easily carried to a lost world, for the enemy stands against us to prevent the salvation of people. That battle is hard-fought, and victories come with tears.

The first tears that bring a harvest of joy are those of repentance. Unless we break before the Lord, confessing our sin and seeking His cleansing, we will never be children of God.

The next tears are tears of intercession. As we realize our place in God's family, we will quickly become aware of our friends, family and neighbours who are still apart from Him and therefore on the road to destruction. We must bring them before the Lord and must do our part in presenting the gospel to them.

Too often, we have an insipid Christianity, lacking tears of repentance, of intercession or of joy. We need to make a complete commitment to our Lord, dedicating our efforts, our prayers, *and* our tears to the advancement of the kingdom. Then we will truly reap in joy!

Direction for today: Be sure that you have repented of all sin. Then, spend much time in intercessory prayer for the lost.

Prayer for today: "Lord, give me the tears appropriate to my situation."

June 13: Read Psalms 130-134

Key verse: *"Behold how good and how pleasant it is for brethren to dwell together in unity" (Psalm 133:1 KJV).*

This Psalm may have come into being as King David watched people, from the twelve different tribes, making their way to Jerusalem, for one of the three yearly festivals.

As recorded in II Samuel 2:4, following the death of King Saul and his son Jonathan, the tribe of Judah anointed David as their King. Failing to recognize God's plan, Abner, the general of Saul's army, set up Ishbosheth, another of Saul's sons, as king over the other eleven tribes. II Samuel 3:1 says that, "there was long war between the house of Saul and the house of David." Subsequent events led to all twelve tribes coming under David's leadership.

This song then became their anthem as they would approach the city from the quarters of the land. Their unity of purpose, to worship the Lord who had brought them into the land, evoked a special spiritual fellowship. The psalmist compared this to the anointing which the high priest received when he was set apart to represent the people before the Lord.

This special time of worship finds its counterpart in the New Testament, in the account of the outpouring of the Holy Spirit, as recorded in the second chapter of the book of Acts: they were all of one accord, in one place, and the anointing of the Holy Spirit came upon them.

After the last supper, Jesus prayed for His disciples. In that prayer He said, "Neither pray I for these alone, but for them also which shall believe on Me through their word; That they all may be one; as Thou, Father, art in Me, and I in Thee, that they also may be one in Us: that the world may believe that Thou has sent me" (John 17:20-21).

After centuries of division and misunderstanding in the Christian Church, we are finally seeing a greater spirit of cooperation and fellowship being experienced, as people from various communions begin to pray and worship together.

Direction for today: Christian fellowship is not a matter of uniformity, but of unity.

Prayer for today: "Lord, may Your true believing church be unified in You."

June 14: Read Psalms 135,136

Key verse: "Give thanks to the Lord, for He is good. His love endures forever" (Psalm 136:1 NIV).

All of God's good gifts to us come from His heart of love. God's love is everlasting, and His gifts and promises are eternal. He loves all men and women, and desires to call every person to relationship with Him.

God's miracles are not caused by some divine need to demonstrate His power; His miracles arise from His love. He works wonders as loving gifts to His creations.

His creation is grounded in love. God made the world, the plants and animals and, above all, human beings, because He loves us.

God's deliverance of His people is based in love. He protects and cares for those whom He loves.

God's daily provision for us is not an accident of nature already set in motion. We do not eat because God made wheat or fruit thousands of years ago. We eat today because He loves us today.

Direction for today: "Give thanks to the God of heaven. His love endures forever."

Prayer for today: "Thank You, Father, for everything Your love means to me and has provided for me!"

"I cried out to the Lord because of my affliction, and He answered me. Out of the belly of Sheol I cried, and You heard my voice." Jonah 2:2 NKJV

June 15: Read Psalms 137-139

Key verse: *"Your eyes saw my unformed body. All the days ordained for me were written in Your book before one of them came to be" (Psalm 139:16 NIV).*

God's love goes far beyond parents' love. His plans go far beyond the plans of parents. His plans are eternal. It is His will that every child should live with Him throughout all eternity.

God has a special plan for each child in which everything that makes life worthwhile is experienced. Oh, how precious every little child must be to our Heavenly Father for Him to love and care that much! No wonder Jesus said, "Suffer the little children, and forbid them not, to come unto Me: for of such is the kingdom of heaven" (Matthew 19:14 KJV).

There is a lot of discussion today as to when life really begins. Psalm 139 indicates that God considers that life begins at the time of conception. It is at that time that He begins to keep records in His book. How it must break His heart when He records the date and time a mother puts an end to the life of an unborn child!

Direction for today: If we confess our sins, God will forgive and cleanse us. That is true even of abortion, if there is honest and true repentance.

Prayer for today: "Lord, thank You for wanting to make me. Thank You for wanting me to love You since I was formed."

June 16: Read Psalms 140-142

Key verse: *"Keep me from the snares they have laid for me, from the traps set by evildoers" (Psalm 141:9 NIV).*

Each of these three psalms we are reading today are concerned with the dangers that beset the psalmist. In each psalm, David speaks of snares and traps laid for him. And in each he asks the Lord to deliver him, and to guide him on a straight path.

Someone who is aware of the dangers in the road is actually much safer than someone who is totally oblivious to them.

Perhaps this is why the Bible spends so much time warning us of the dangers that face the believer. We are told much about Satan and his attacks. We are warned of the temptations that will arise from our own flesh, and from the world. We are told that we are involved in spiritual battle. We are cautioned to maintain peace and unity in the church, or

112

stumbling blocks will emerge even there. Whatever the dangers, we will have victory if we face them in the strength of the Lord.

Direction for today: When faced with snares in your path, turn to the One who knows the way.

Prayer for today: "Lord, keep me from the snares and traps that lie in my way."

June 17: Read Psalms 143,144

Key verse: "I remember the days of long ago; I meditate on all Your works and consider what Your hands have done" (Psalm 143:5 NIV).

Psalm 143 expresses trust and confidence in the Lord during a time when David was in need. Even though he was facing struggles, he acknowledged that the strength he needed came from the Lord. Realizing this, he cries to the Lord for mercy. He asks the Lord to teach the way in which he should walk and to deliver him from his enemies.

The reason for David's trust is seen in the key verse, "I remember the days of long ago." Too often, when we are down or discouraged, we forget the goodness of God.

In such times our trust and confidence must come from remembering God's goodness and faithfulness to us at other times. Then we will find the strength to trust Him, realizing that He has always been faithful in the past and so we can trust Him now.

Direction for today: Frequently bring to mind the blessings the Lord has given you in the past.

Prayer for today: "Teach me to do Your will, for You are my God" (Psalm 143:10 NIV).

June 18: Read Psalms 145,146

Key verse: "The Lord is near to all who call on Him, to all who call on Him in truth" (Psalm 145:18 NIV).

Help is just a prayer away. Isn't that a truth worth holding on to? If we maintain a right relationship with God, serving Him in spirit and in truth, then He is always close by and ready to answer.

Of course, we know that God is omnipresent — everywhere at once. That means He is close at hand to the unbeliever and to the rebellious Christian, as well. However, our unbelief or rebellion will block communication with the Father, and He will be unable to answer because of our lack of faith and faithfulness.

But, if through repentance and consistent prayer and worship, we keep the channels open, God will always be there for us.

Remain close to the Lord, in touch and in tune with Him. And at all times, call upon the Lord — He is there to hear and to help.

June 19: Read Psalm 147

Key verse: "He heals the brokenhearted and binds up their wounds" (Psalm 147:3 NIV).

We live in an age of medical marvels. Severed limbs are reattached, or technological arms and legs that work almost as well as the real thing are provided. Hearts are transplanted. Skin is grafted on to burns. Tumours are removed from brains.

The wonders never seem to cease.

But there is one wound that will never be successfully treated by a medical doctor or the staff in the hospital emergency room. No medical insurance covers it, and no operation can cure it. Yet this wound can be more hurtful that any mere physical problem: a broken heart.

Our world is filled with broken-hearted people. Their lives have been ripped apart by divorce; by the loss of a career; by the death of a loved one. They are victims of failed relationships, shattered hopes, lost dreams.

We have something to offer them that they will never find in a medicine cabinet: healing for their broken heart. Let us take Jesus to a brokenhearted world, for He "heals the brokenhearted".

Direction for today: Remember that you know the answer for a broken heart; always be ready to share it.

Prayer for today: "Lord, give me an opportunity to share You with someone who is wounded in spirit."

June 20: Read Psalms 148-150

Key verse: "Let everything that has breath praise the Lord. Praise the Lord!" (Psalm 150:6 NAS).

Today's readings, and the previous four psalms, might be termed a "primer of praise". There is almost no question concerning praise to the Lord that goes unanswered in these seven psalms. For example:

WHOM are we to praise? There is no doubt that we praise the Lord God, and Him alone.

HOW are we to praise? In song (144:9), with musical instruments (144:9, 150:3-5), with thanksgiving (147:7), in holy dancing (149:3), in great joy (149:5).

WHERE are we to praise? Everywhere! (148:1, 150:1).

WHEN are we to praise? The list is practically endless. We are to praise the Lord for His protection and deliverance (144:10, 11); because He is the great God (145:1-3); for His power and awesome acts (145:6);

for His kindness to the lowly (145:14); for provision of food (145:15); because He is absolutely faithful (146:5, 6); for His holy justice and mercy (146:7-9); simply because "it is good to sing praises to our God" (147:1); for His hand bringing rain and good crops, ice and snow (147:8, 16, 17); for all creation (148:1-6).

Perhaps today you could spend a little extra time in your study. On a sheet of paper, write down each of the categories shown in capital letters above, and make a complete list from these seven psalms. It may be that you'll want to add more of your own reasons to praise the Lord. One hint: you won't be able to add anything to "WHOM" — only God deserves our praise — but the potential list under "WHY" is endless!

Direction for today: Praise God, always!

Prayer for today: "Lord, I praise You for every good gift."

Titus

As with the letters to Timothy, this short letter was written by Paul to a young man whom he had trained for ministry and whom was now pastoring a church.

Together with I Timothy, this epistle is regarded as a manual for a healthy spiritual church.

June 21: Read Titus 1-3

Key verse: *"You must charge the senior men to be sober, serious, prudent, healthy in Christian faith and love and fortitude" (Titus 2:1,2 NAS).*

This entire chapter deals with the Christian character in action. The word *sober* is used here literally as a contradistinction to 'given to over indulgence in wine'. The presumption here is that maturity in years enlightens one to what is and what is not true pleasure. And we are told that self-indulgence costs far more than it's worth.

They must be *prudent*. This implies control. The mature have acquired a strengthened, cleansed mind, maintaining instincts and passions in their proper place. Certain recklessness and frivolity are profiles of youth that are pardonable whereas years are to bring wisdom and gravity of life.

And the astute seniors must be healthy in:

Faith - the years teach us not to trust God less but to trust Him more.

Love - sometimes the years tend to take away kindness and sympathy.

Fortitude - years should temper a man like steel, bearing more with quiet tolerance, conquering life's difficulties in God's love.

Direction for today: A mature Christian uses his or her experience to guide and encourage, not to suppress and discourage.

Prayer for today: "Lord, build in me a truly Christ-like character."

Philemon

This, the shortest of Paul's letters, is essentially a Christian love story. It demonstrates the love Paul has for a Christian brother, Philemon of Colosse; the love Paul has for a new convert, won to the Lord himself, the slave Onesimus; and the love of Christ that must grow between the runaway slave Onesimus and his owner and Christian brother, Philemon.

Memory Verse

"He has shown you, O man, what is good; and what does the Lord require of you but to do justly, to love mercy, and to walk humbly with your God?" Micah 6:8 NKJV

June 22: Read Philemon

Key verse: *"Perhaps he was for this reason parted from you for a while, that you should have him back forever, no longer as a slave but more than a slave, a beloved brother" (Philemon 15:16 NAS).*

This small book of Philemon is one of the most personal books in the Bible. The Apostle Paul, who we usually find writing theological epistles to churches, here takes his pen to write a one-to-one letter to his friend Philemon, concerning the runaway slave Onesimus.

What emerges is a touching account of the love Paul bears for each man, and the love that he knows Jesus will bring between them now that they are linked by the Holy Spirit as brothers in the Lord.

It is interesting that Paul says nothing, concerning the evils of slaveholding, but rather than call Philemon to a socially just position, he goes beyond that and tells Philemon that he must love Onesimus as a Christian brother (vs. 16). The love of Jesus is the only means whereby man obtains true freedom from all of the kinds of slavery in which we can be ensnared.

Direction for today: True freedom is available only in Jesus.

Prayer for today: "Father, give me true freedom that I may be free to be Your bondslave."

Proverbs

There is no more practical book in the Bible than this book of Proverbs. It is the ideal "companion volume" to the Psalms; while the psalmists soar to realms of worship and faith in the heavens, the men who wrote the Proverbs are deeply concerned with the practical outworking of that faith in daily living. Much of this book was written by a man whose wisdom was a direct gift from God – Solomon (see Proverbs 1:1, 10:1 and 25:1).

This is not a book to be read quickly. Each chapter may contain dozens of individual proverbial statements, many standing on their own and requiring individual attention. A proverb is basically a short meaningful saying which communicates moral and ethical principles.

This is not to say there is not a theme to the book; the virtue of wisdom can be found throughout. In fact, it would be a good exercise in Bible study to make note of each time "wisdom" appears and what the Proverbs have to say about it.

June 23: Read Proverbs 1

Key verse: *"The fear of the Lord is the beginning of knowledge; but fools despise wisdom and instruction" (Proverbs 1:7 KJV).*

The fifth chapter of James aptly describes the wisdom of the world and the wisdom of God. In worldly wisdom there is strife, envying, confusion and evil works. Wisdom from above is pure, peaceful, loving, gentle, merciful, impartial, full of good works and without hypocrisy.

Nations who have put God out of their thinking have very little value for human life; their word cannot be depended on and their goals are selfish. We need to be so grateful that our nation was founded on the fear of God. This fear is rightly termed respect, or reverence. Let us pray that our leaders will not follow the example of some other countries, but will realize that reverence for God and His laws is just the beginning of knowledge.

The complexity of the human brain and nervous system far surpasses any achievement that technology can reach or conceive. Yet, man, whose very will was given to him by God, in his foolish pride rejects his Creator.

Direction for today: If you need wisdom, ask the Lord to give it to you. It is always His will for us to be wise in His ways.

Prayer for today: "Lord, may I be filled with the Spirit, and thus know Your will."

June 24: Read Proverbs 2,3

Key verse: *"Blessed is the man who finds wisdom, the man who gains understanding" (Proverbs 3:13 NIV).*

Early in the reign of Solomon, God appeared to him in a vision and told him he could have anything he wanted, he just needed to ask. Imagine, he could have asked for wealth, lands, victory over enemies. He could have asked for anything, but Solomon confessed his inability to rule the

people and said, "give Thy servant an understanding heart." What would you have asked for? Would it have been as noble as Solomon's request?

And God did give His wisdom and understanding to Solomon. It may seem a paradox, but it is wise to desire wisdom. Wisdom is given by God directly to our heart or spirit, but mere knowledge appeals to our intellect or soul (Proverbs 2:10).

The Apostle Paul states, in I Corinthians 1:30, "It is because of him that you are in Christ Jesus, who has become for us wisdom from God - that is righteousness, holiness and redemption." Praise God, Jesus has been made unto us wisdom. When we accept Him, we have a direct line to the wisdom of Almighty God to guide us.

Direction for today: No amount of intellectual exercise will make you wise; that is the work of the Holy Spirit in a yielded life.

Prayer for today: "Lord, may I understand more of Your will today."

June 25: Read Proverbs 4,5

Key verse: "Keep thy heart with all diligence; for out of it are the issues of life" (Proverbs 4:23 KJV).

How does one keep one's heart? How do you keep feeling the way that you should feel? How does one control that?

Proverbs 23:7 says, "For as he thinketh in his heart, so is he." Someone has put it this way, "A man is what he thinks about all day long." It is a fact that if you can feed a person's mind certain information a sufficient number of times, that person will begin to feel that it is right. That is what the television and radio commercials are based on: their minds have been over and over again fed positive information on that product so that they are driven to go out and buy it. That method of advertising works so efficiently that billions and billions of dollars are spent each year for commercial advertising on television and radio.

Much of this advertising leads the viewer to dissatisfaction with lifestyle and circumstances. It is said that water dripping on a stone eventually makes an impression. So it is, that we tend to be brainwashed by that which we hear and see over and over again. If we are going to be pleasing to God, therefore, we must feed our minds the right information.

Philippians 4:8 tells us, "Finally brethren, whatsoever things are true, whatsoever things are honest, whatsoever things are just, whatsoever things are pure, whatsoever things are lovely, whatsoever things are of good report, if there be any virture and if there be any praise, think on these things."

God has created your mind to feed on Him. Jesus says, "I am truth, I am the Way." All truth about everything is wrapped up in the very nature of Jesus. You must waken in the morning thinking those things which are right and true, thinking good thoughts about people, good thoughts about life, and open yourself up to moment by moment communication with our Heavenly Father.

Direction for today: Feed your mind only those things that will build you up in the Lord and in His wisdom.

Prayer for today: "Lord, help me to focus my thoughts on You."

June 26: Read Proverbs 6

Key verse: "How long will you lie there, you sluggard? When will you get up from your sleep?" (Proverbs 6:9 NIV).

We live in an age of "something for nothing". Many people are spending a lot of money in efforts to win at lotteries. Others wait for the big break on the stock market. So many dream of the day when they will win big, and be instantly rich.

This spills over into our workday ethic. Many workers today are not interested in doing a good job for their employers. Instead, they do as little as possible for as much money as possible. Such persons are called, in the Proverbs, "sluggards".

Being a sluggard is bad for the character of the person involved. But for a Christian, it is even more serious. We are to be witnesses to the changing power of the gospel to all those around us, including our fellow-workers and our employers. How can we talk of the change Christ has made if we continue to be lazy and slothful?

You cannot be a sluggard and a good witness at the same time!

Direction for today: Work as though the job you are doing is a witness for Christ. It is!

Prayer for today: "Father, may everything I do, including my work, bring glory to You."

June 27: Read Proverbs 7,8

Key verse: "My son, keep my words, and treasure my commandments within you. Keep my commandments and live . . ." (Proverbs 7:1-2 NAS).

The principles of God are everlasting, God called the Israelites to live within those principles by living according to the law. Although we are in the New Testament era and are living in the age of grace, the principles still apply. However, now we obey God from the heart rather than from fear of retribution.

"Keep my commandments and live . . ." By obeying the principles of God's Word, as reflected both in the Old and New Testaments, we have a solid foundation on which to build our lives. The psalmist David said, "Thy Word have I treasured in mine heart that I might not sin against Thee" (Psalm 119:11). This abiding Word in our hearts assures us of life and insures us against the inroads of evil.

And this wisdom was established before the mountains, before the hills were formed, as we read in chapter 7. God established wisdom long before the world; both in creation and in the plan of salvation He used wisdom.

We should wisely apply the principles of God every day to be assured of victorious Christian living. Without the Word, and without the wisdom of God, we are bound to falter and fail.

Direction for today: Acquiring knowledge is never enough; it is only useful when applied with wisdom.

Prayer for today: "Thank you, Father, that Your truths are everlasting."

June 28: Read Proverbs 9,10

Key verse: "Whoever is simple, let him turn in here" (Proverbs 9:4 NAS).

In chapter 9, we have a very perceptive contrast between wisdom and foolishness (verses 1-18). Wisdom is personified as a woman who invites guests into her house. (v. 1-6). Foolishness, similarly personified, does likewise (v. 13-18). There is rivalry between the two as their allurements are set out. Wisdom is a delightful hostess who has prepared a feast. Foolishness is as a lady of the night, lustfully enticing and alluring.

In both of these instances in this teaching, Wisdom and Foolishness assume that the young man being invited is inexperienced in the ways of the world, knowing not the way which leads to life and the way which leads to death.

Wisdom and Foolishness both presume the necessity of choice for the young man. Both invitations are sounding in his ear and in his heart, but it is clear that he cannot have both. He must make a choice. And that is the most urgent and pressing business in life: making a choice.

Wisdom and Foolishness both offer some immediate satisfaction. Wisdom offers a feast (v. 5) while foolishness offers illicit pleasure and indulgence (v. 17). The way of Wisdom leads to a fuller life; the way of Foolishness ends in death.

Two invitations! They are constantly being issued to each generation: the kingdom of God versus the kingdom of evil. How have you chosen?

Direction for today: Every choice presents you with a wise option and a foolish option. The consequences can be eteral!

Prayer for today: "Lord, may I always choose Your way!"

Memory Verse

"The Lord is good, a stronghold in the day of trouble; and He knows those who trust in Him." Nahum 1:7 NKJV

June 29: Read Proverbs 11

Key verse: "The Lord abhors dishonest scales, but accurate weights are His delight" (Proverbs 11:1 NIV).

What mundane things these are. Does God really "delight" in accurate weights? Yes, He does!

Our Christian faith must be reflected in every area of our lives, or it is empty of meaning. It is no good to worship publicly on Sunday, only to cheat our customers or our employer on Monday.

Too many people have accused the chuch of hypocrisy. The error has not been theirs — it has been the people of the church who have been wrong. The accusers have been correct.

Too many Christians have kept the Lord out of their personal financial dealings and their businesses. But the Lord looks at dishonesty, and calls it a sin! He "abhors" dishonest income tax returns, padded expense accounts, extra hours added to a repair bill. These things are not honouring to the Lord.

How can we expect the world to respect, or be attracted to, a church full of cheats? Let us be sure our lives are straight and honest at all times!

Direction for today: Honesty is not ony the best policy, it is the best witness for Christ!

Prayer for today: "Lord, may all of my financial dealings honour You."

June 30: Read Proverbs 12

Key verse: *"A man cannot be established through wickedness, but the righteous cannot be uprooted" (Proverbs 12:3 NIV).*

As we said yesterday, God delights in honesty. Throughout the scriptures, the believer is exhorted to be honest in every area of life. In this chapter, Solomon continues to teach by contrasts. He continues to portray the results of living God's way as opposed to living the way of the world. For example, "The way of a fool seems right to him, but a wise man listens to advice" (12:15). He contrasts truth with deceit; knowledge with folly; diligence with laziness.

Everyone desires to be successful in life. And although each person's definition of success may differ from the other, the scriptural principles given to us to reach our goals are the same: Be teachable! (12:1); Be wise! (12:8); Be industrious! (12:11); Be a listener! (12:15); Be prudent! (12:16).

For the believer, true success is not measured by material possessions. It is, in fact, measured by the testimony of our lives. What we do for God will last. Our success is our treasure laid up in heaven.

Direction for today: Seek success in God's eyes, not in the eyes of te world.

Prayer for today: "Lord. may I always seek to please You."

Rest

There remains now a rest to the people of God,
When life round them boils and matters are hard.
For God has provided the means of the cross,
Deliverance from fear, apprehension and loss.

But through unbelief we miss the Lord's best,
And during the conflict, in Lucifer's test,
When Satan would laugh and our neighbours
would jest,
God has for His own, provided a rest.

The heart's filled with fear and gross unbelief.
This attitude grows, it's the work of the Thief
The end of it all is deep sorrow and grief
But God has provided a rest and relief.

We often are bitter, and sometimes we hate.
Our spirits sink fast, at a terrible rate.
But Jesus has promised, reversing our fate,
With love fills our being, if we on Him wait.

– Cal Bombay

July 1: Read Proverbs 13

Key verse: "A wise son heeds his father's instruction, but a mocker does not listen to rebuke" (Proverbs 13:1 NIV).

This verse can be understood on two levels. The most obvious relates to physical fathers and sons. In our society, it is rare that a child actually listens to and obeys his or her parent. So often, children go their own way, and ignore the instruction of their parents.

This is wrong. It is against the command of the Lord.

If you are a son or daughter still living with your parents, you are commanded to obey them as long as they are not ordering you to disobey God. And if you are a parent with children still under your care, you must seek the Lord's wisdom to teach you to discipline the children to accept your instruction and to obey your directions.

We can also see this verse in the spiritual sense. A wise child of God will accept the instruction of the Lord, through His Word, through His Spirit and through His people. If we fail to do so, we will fall into folly and eventually into destruction.

Direction for today: Children, honour your parents. Parents, be the kind of parent a child can honour.

Prayer for today: "Lord, may our family relationships be according to Your family plan."

July 2: Read Proverbs 14

Key verse: "He who oppresses a poor man insults his Maker, but he who is kind to the needy honours Him" (Proverbs 14:31 NAS).

"Who is my neighbour?" (Luke 10:29) is a question that we need to consider. Whether we like it or not, our own salvation and eternal life may be dependent upon looking after our neighbour — whether he is relatively well off, even wealthy, or especially if he is poor. We are told here that the oppression of the poor is an insult to God and that kindness to the poor is a way of showing honour to God.

This, of course, is what Jesus tells us about the Last Judgment (Matthew 25:31-46). He identifies Himself with the poor. They are His people. When we show kindness to anyone in need, we are showing it to Jesus personally. And if we don't, we can find ourselves on Judgment Day going off into eternal punishment.

"Truly, I say to you, as you did it to one of the least of these My brethren, you did it to Me" (Matthew 25:40). God rewards respect and care of the poor.

"You shall love the Lord your God, with all your heart and with all your soul, and with all your mind. This is the great and first commandment. And the second is like the first. You shall love your neighbour as yourself" (Matthew 22:37-39).

Direction for today: Help given to the poor, needy or sick is help given to Jesus.

Prayer for today: "Father, help me to show Your love to my neighbours around the world."

July 3: Read Proverbs 15

Key verse: "Better a little with the fear of the Lord than great wealth with turmoil" (Proverbs 15:16 NIV).

God's mathematics are different from the mathematics of man, just as His wisdom is entirely different from the wisdom of this world. This verse is a good example of divine mathematics.

The world says: "the more wealth, the better". Anyone who suggested that a poor man is better off than a rich man would be laughed to scorn.

But this verse says exactly the same thing that Jesus' story of the rich man and Lazarus shows in Luke 16:19-31: all the riches in the world cannot add up to eternal life. Lazarus, a poor beggar, died and was taken to heaven; the rich man under whose table he ate was condemned to hell.

Many people in our world spend all of their lives adding up wealth. The material goods, which they thought would bring happiness, result in turmoil and distress. But others, who know true values, spend their lives for the Lord, accumulating little earthly wealth, but laying up great treasure in heaven.

Direction for today: Concentrate your treasure-hunting on eternal rewards.

Prayer for today: "Lord, may I use any wealth and any energy I have for the growth of Your kingdom."

July 4: Read Proverbs 16, 17

Key verse: "A cheerful heart is a good medicine; but a downcast spirit dries up the bones" (Proverbs 17:22 RSV).

In our day, the medical profession is paying a great deal of attention to the significance of the emotional state of people. There is no longer any doubt that emotions can cause illness. Stress is linked to many serious ailments; depression can have physical implications. Unhappiness, in general, is bad for your health. Guilt or bitterness can cause ulcers, heart disease, and all manner of ills.

The Bible, of course, told us this centuries before medical science discovered the same truth! A cheerful heart is truly, in the most physical sense of the word, "good medicine". The peace and joy of the Lord are not merely spiritual suggestions; they are good for our bodily health!

Jesus gives us joy. That joy, according to Nehemiah, is our strength. The surprising thing is joy gives us physical health as well as spiritual power.

Direction for today: Jesus is the healer of all wounds of the spirit.

Prayer for today: "Father, give me Your joy."

July 5: Read Proverbs 18,19

Key verse: *"Many are the plans in a man's heart, but it is the Lord's purpose that prevails" (Proverbs 19:21 NIV).*

In high schools and colleges there are guidance counsellors; in the working world there are career counsellors, vocational advisors, and industrial psychologists. Discuss your future with any one of them and you will probably be invited to share your hopes, desires, ambitions, and wishes, even your daydreams and fantasies. When your feet are back on the ground, you will probably be offered help in working out a practical, step-by-step plan for reaching a certain goal.

But, as Robbie Burns said, "The best-laid plans of mice and men gang aft agley". Life is full of surprises, some pleasant, some painful. There may be a death in the family, or an unexpected birth. There may be an inheritance, or inflation; sickness or a new love.

We have to remember that we are not in control of the universe: the forces of nature are at work and at the same time other free-willed human beings are trying to fulfill their dreams. And, over all, in all and through all, God is at work.

James tells us, "You do not even know what will happen tomorrow . . . you ought to say 'If it is the Lord's will, we will live and do this or that'" (James 4:14f).

Paul tells us, "We know that in all things God works for the good of those who love Him, who have been called according to His purpose" (Romans 8:28 NIV).

Direction for today: Set your own plans aside, and ask the Lord to reveal His plans to you.

Prayer for today: "Father, as I seek Your will, give me opportunities to share You with others."

Memory Verse

"Behold the proud, his soul is not upright in him; but the just shall live by his faith." Habakkuk 2:4 NKJV

July 6: Read Proverbs 20

Key verse: *"Differing weights and differing measures, both of them are abominable to the Lord" (Proverbs 20:10 NAS).*

The Proverbs are a practical guide to living for the followers of God. As we read these wise sayings, penned thousands of years ago, we quickly realize that God is concerned with everything in our lives.

Being a follower of God, involves allowing Him into every single part of our lives. Our key verse today deals with a very practical, earthly matter — fraudulent scales used by merchants to cheat customers. This sort of dishonesty, we are told, is an abomination to the Lord.

"Abomination" is a strong term. There are other things called "abominations" by God — horrible things such as idolatry (Deuteronomy 27:15), sacrifice of children (Deuteronomy 12:31), witchcraft and other occult practices (Deuteronomy 18:9-12), and adultery (Ezekial 22:11). And here, classed with these terrible evils, is the "abomination" of false scales!

As Christians, we stand as living evidence that Jesus Christ is the Way, the Truth, and the Life. Thus, any departure from His way, His standard of truth, His pattern of life, is an "abomination".

Everything we do in life must speak to the truth of Jesus, whether it be concerning huge moral or spiritual issues, or normal, everyday business practice or life at home.

Direction for today: Are there things in your everyday life which are not honouring to the Lord? If so, cast out these abominations.

Prayer for today: "Father, I pray that my life will be completely free of things which dishonour You."

July 7: Read Proverbs 21

Key verse: "Whoso stoppeth his ears at the cry of the poor, he also shall cry himself, but shall not be heard" (Proverbs 21:13 KJV).

In this chapter, many instuctions are given for the proper use of wealth. God does not condemn the possession of riches if they are procured in a legitimate manner and used in a God-honouring way. In fact, in verse 20, the writer states that the wise will have desirable treasure and oil in their home but the foolish man will have squandered it.

In the key verse, one of the proper uses of wealth is presented: to help the poor. If the wealthy do not help the poor when they cry for it, they will themselves cry and not be heard.

This reminds us of our New Testament debt of love, outlined by the Apostle John in I John 3:17, "But whoever has this world's goods, and seed his brother in need, and shuts up his heart from him, how does the love of God abide in him?" (KJV).

We are also reminded of Jesus' parable of the unmerciful servant, in which He said, "Should you not also have had compassion on your fellow servant, just as I had pity on you?" (Matthew 18:33 NKJV). God has been so good to us. In fact, all that we have is a gift from Him and would not be ours had He not given it to us. Likewise, nothing we have can be withheld from Him.

Direction for today: Realize that you have a responsibility to the poor of the world, in the name of Christ.

Prayer for today: "Lord, show me how best to use whatever I have to help the poor."

July 8: Read Proverbs 22

Key verse: *"Rich and poor have this in common: The Lord is the Maker of them all" (Proverbs 22:2 NIV).*

The Lord is the Maker of all people, rich and poor. But while the wealthy and the impoverished have this in common, this is not all they share. Because not only is the Lord their Maker — He is also their Saviour, their Judge, and their Lord.

No matter how much money anyone has, he or she cannot buy salvation. No matter how poor anyone is, he or she cannot be so poor as to merit salvation. Salvation from sin, death and hell only comes through faith in Jesus Christ.

No matter how much money anyone offers to God, they will not be able to buy their way out of judgment. All, rich or poor, who have rejected Jesus Christ, will find themselves judged and condemned to eternal punishment.

No matter how much money anyone has, that person is still coming to a day when he or she must declare Jesus as Lord. That declaration will either be made voluntarily, or angrily: a declaration made before the Righteous Judge.

Our material goods matter not at all; the state of our heart is all that counts!

Direction for today: Do not depend on any material goods; all will come to rot and ruin.

Prayer for today: "Lord, may I be rich in faith!"

July 9: Read Proverbs 23

Key verse: *"Buy the truth, and sell it not; also wisdom, and instruction, and understanding" (Proverbs 23:23 KJV).*

At first glance, the proverbs contained in today's chapter may not seem to have much connection with each other. They may seem to be just a collection of brief pithy sayings, helpful in themselves, no doubt, but yet separate from each other, and each the product of worldly wisdom and human experience.

There is much more to these sayings than that. Concerning Solomon, we are told in the scriptures that Solomon, the author of this proverb, "loved the Lord, walking in the statutes of David his father" (I Kings 3:3). We are told that, at the beginning of his reign, Solomon asked of God, not personal wealth nor fame, but for "an understanding heart to judge Thy people" (I Kings 3:9). This humble request so moved the Lord that He assured Solomon, "I have given thee a wise and an understanding heart; so that there was none like thee before thee, neither after thee shall any arise like unto thee" (I Kings 3:12).

God, in other words, personally rooted and grounded King Solomon in His own divine wisdom. Thus, the proverbial sayings of Solomon, many hundreds of them, may be likened to the living fruit of a tree which God Himself planted by the rivers of wisdom.

This divine rooting and branching of Solomon's wisdom, of course, explains the love which our Lord had for the book of Proverbs. It explains also the fondness for the book entertained by the apostles Peter and Paul, and by the writer to the Hebrews, each of whose inspired letters contain a number of references to the proverbs.

Direction for today: Happy is the person who delights in the law of the Lord.

Prayer for today: "Lord, continue to lead me into truth."

July 10: Read Proverbs 24

Key verse: "Do not envy wicked men, do not desire their company" (Proverbs 24:1 NIV).

Who are your heroes? Who are the heroes of your children? Too often, Christians, especially our teenagers and children, have the wrong people as heroes.

Often Christian teenagers look to music stars with immoral lifestyles, drug problems, and who sing suggestive or plainly evil lyrics. Or they idolize movie stars who have similar problems, and who appear in movies laced with immoral sex, vulgarity and profanity.

Young children often listen to the same music and watch the same perverted music videos. They also have cartoon heroes who are produced by the same kind of minds that churn out the adult-level garbage!

Even adult Christians often choose the wrong kind of heroes: television stars who are on their fifth marriages or involved in homosexual activity; sports stars with lifestyles ordered by greed and immorality.

The Proverbs warns us of the dangers of this kind of thinking. We are not to envy — or idolize — wicked men.

It is time we began to fill our minds, and the minds of our children, with Christian heroes.

Direction for today: Ask yourself: "Do I have the right heroes?"

Prayer for today: "Lord, give me and my family decent, God-fearing "heroes" to look to as examples."

July 11: Read Proverbs 25

Key verse: "If thine enemy be hungry, give him bread to eat; and if he be thirsty, give him water to drink, For thou shalt heap coals of fire upon his head, and the Lord shall reward thee" (Proverbs 25:21,22 NAS).

The most effective response is to do good to one's enemy. In the Sermon on the Mount, Jesus states, "Ye have heard that it hath been said, thou shall love thy neighbour, and hate thine enemy. But I say unto you, love your enemies, bless them that curse you, do good to them that hate you, and pray for them which despitefully use you, and persecute you" (Matthew 5:43-44).

The command to love was present in the Old Testament (Leviticus 19:18) but the context at that verse, as well as our key verse for today, show that it was limited in scope to a fellow-Israelite. However, Jesus removed this limitation and the command to love applies universally.

Direction for today: The Christian is to love all people unconditionally.

Prayer for today: "Lord, may I love others with Your love."

July 12: Read Proverbs 26

Key verse: *"Without wood a fire goes out; without gossip a quarrel dies down" (Proverbs 26:20 NIV).*

The Bible has much to say about gossip. None of it is good! This particular reference suggests that gossip is the fuel that keeps arguments and quarrels going. Without gossip, there would be much less strife.

This chapter also suggests that gossip wounds deep, getting down into the very being of a person (verse 22). This is true of the victim, the person spreading the gossip, and the hearer — all are deeply hurt by this unloving, sinful activity.

The apostle Paul, writing to the Corinthians, stressed that gossip is fatal to the unity of the church (II Corinthians 12:20). worse than that, Paul includes gossips in one of his harshest lists of sinners, in Romans 1:29. He lumps gossip together with murder, deceit, God-hating, ruthlessness and a number of other terrible sins. There is no doubt that the apostle hated gossip, probably because he saw the terrible damage it did to some of his most beloved churches and believers.

Make a conscious effort to purge your lips from gossip. This terrible habit never brings good; it destroys people, churches, and your own reputation.

Direction for today: Do not gossip. If you have done so, confess it as the sin that it is, and if you have deceived anyone, make it right.

Prayer for today: "Father, help me to be free from the sin of gossip."

Memory Verse

The Lord your God in your midst, the Mighty One, will save; He will rejoice over you with gladness, He will quiet you in His love, He will rejoice over you with singing." Zephaniah 3:17 NKJV

July 13: Read Proverbs 27,28

Key verse: "Do not forsake your friend and the friend of your father" (Proverbs 27:10 NIV).

We live in a very mobile age. It is not uncommon for people to move many times in their lifetime, and to live significant parts of their lives thousands of miles from their hometowns.

This has caused a lessening of emphasis on the old-fashioned virture of loyalty. Our relationships are often very transient, because we are always on the move.

But loyal realtionships are very important. They are especially crucial in times of crisis. So often, people in crisis are far from their home and their old friends, and they find they have no one to whom they can turn. We would do well to make the effort to maintain contact with close friends, even if they are many miles away.

This is also important if we are to win old friends to the Lord. Unless we are faithful in our friendships, they will not consistently hear the gospel from us nor see it at work in our lives and our ongoing concern for them.

Let us work to find ways to maintain friendships, even across the miles that separate. And let us be especially conscious of keeping friendships with non-Christians, even though they do not share our faith. For how will they hear without a Christian friend?

Direction for today: Write or call a friend with whom you have not had contact for a while.

Prayer for today: "Lord, give me the privilege of leading an unbelieving friend to faith in You."

July 14: Read Proverbs 29,30

Key verse: "A man who hardens his neck after much reproof will suddenly be broken beyond remedy" (Proverbs 29:1 NAS).

In the tale of two kings (I Samuel 15, 16 and II Samuel 12), we see how Saul and David reacted differently to being confronted with their sin.

Saul, when confronted by Samuel, began to blame his soldiers and to make excuses for his behaviour. On the other hand, when confronted by Nathan, David responded with: "I have sinned against the Lord."

Saul's attitude toward his sin resulted in his loss of the kingship. David's attitude resulted in forgiveness and restoration.

We, too, need to be aware of this when we are confronted by our sin. When we are, is our attitude that of Saul, who made excuses for his behaviour? Or do we, like David, agree with God, confess our sin and stand accountable before Him to suffer whatever consequences?

Direction for today: Keep a gentle spirit, ready to receive correction from the Lord and His people.

Prayer for today: "Father, make me sensitive to my sin so that I might confess it and receive Your cleansing and forgiveness."

July 15: Read Proverbs 31

Key verse: *"Favour is deceitful, and beauty is vain: but a woman that feareth the Lord, she shall be praised" (Proverbs 31:3 KJV).*

This passage describes the attributes of a virtuous woman. Many women reading this would feel they would fall far short. But *remember*: the ability to be this type of woman comes from the Lord. These qualities cannot be achieved by our own human efforts.

The Holy Spirit operating in one's life produces "love, joy, peace, longsuffering, gentleness, goodness, faith, meekness, temperance" (Galatians 5:22). On the other hand, the three previous verses of that chapter describe those things which are not characteristic of the Holy Spirit working in one's life, "Now the works of the flesh are manifest, which are these: adultery, fornication, uncleanness, lasciviousness, idolatry, witchcraft, hatred, variance, emulations, wrath, strife, seditions, heresies, envyings, murders, drunkenness, revellings, and such like".

One of the ways in which a woman can show she is virtuous is by accepting Jesus Christ as Saviour and Lord and asking Him to fill her with His Holy Spirit. In this way, her family will be uniquely blessed, because the Holy Spirit knows the type of woman she needs to be.

By taking the time to talk and fellowship with Jesus, she can open herself up to be filled daily with the Spirit and the fruit of the Spirit will flow from her own life. Then her children and husband will rise up and call her blessed.

Direction for today: God requires that all men and women seek to be virtuous.

Prayer for today: "Lord, in whatever job or vocation I find myself, help me to be honest, virtuous and honourable."

132

Ecclesiastes

Ecclesiastes, often called "The Preacher", is a book that must be considered as a whole. It contains much that on its own is not spiritual truth, but rather is the expression from the empty heart of a man seeking fulfillment from this world. When we understand that the book represents the search of a man for meaning, a search that leads him further and further into despair, we can understand the first eleven chapters of the book – they are indeed a cry for help!

Yet, by the end, we reach what the preacher has discovered is the conclusion of all things: "Fear God, and keep His commandments".

A Christian of our acquaintance read Ecclesiastes in the days before he knew Jesus. In these pages, he saw his own life; he had tried everything to find pleasure and fulfillment, but all was vanity, all was empty. Then he reached this concluding phrase, and realized here was the answer – to love God and to do His will!" "But I can't!" cried our friend. And down deep in his heart something stirred – "One man did . . . He's in the other half of this book in your hand." And our friend turned to the gospels, read about Jesus, believed, and found the answer to the emptiness of Ecclesiastes.

The book states that it was written by "the son of David, king in Jerusalem". While he is not identified by name, this is often assumed to be Solomon, who surely knew the emptiness of vain pursuits of pleasure, and who has also written other Old Testament wisdom literature.

July 16: Read Ecclesiastes 1-3

Key verse: "For God giveth to a man that is good in His sight wisdom, and knowledge, and joy; but to the sinner He giveth travail, to gather and to heap up, that He may give to him that is good before God. This is also a vanity and vexation of spirit" (Ecclesiastes 2:26 KJV).

If anyone could find complete happiness and fulfillment in life, through what can be called secular success, it should have been Solomon. His own accounting of his achievements, as well as the recording of history, is most impressive. He had wealth unsurpassed by any of his contemporaries; fame that had spread internationally, without our modern means of communications; and social acceptance that many would envy.

Yet Solomon's testimony reveals an emptiness and a searching for an object of fulfillment. He set goals, and reached them, only to find that they were like will-o-the-wisps, or bubbles that burst when grasped. The driving urge appears to have been the satisfying of his own personal ego.

In the end, Solomon acknowledged that to fear God and to keep His commandments was the only safe course in life.

The message of the book of Ecclesiastes is as applicable in this twentieth century as when it flowed from Solomon's pen. The false gods of wealth, fame, and prestige still lure weary wanderers with their empty promises, only to leave them broken and deluded.

The conclusion, as recorded in chapter 12:13; "to fear God and keep His commandments: for this is the whole duty of man", is the real answer to personal, national and international ills. Obedience to the commandment to love one another, as He has loved us, will build bridges instead of walls, and bring the blessing of God's favour.

Direction for today: Fear God and keep His commandments.

Prayer for today: "Thank You, Lord, that in Jesus, I can see the true meaning of life."

July 17: Read Ecclesiastes 4-6

Key verse: "Do not be quick with your mouth, do not be hasty in your heart to utter anything before God. God is in heaven and you are on earth, so let your words be few" (Ecclesiastes 5:2 NIV).

It never ceases to amaze me that God's Word is so up to date and speaks to us so clearly today. Many persons make promises to God but do not keep them. The instruction given in these chapters is that any promise we make to God should be carefully thought out.

God's house is certainly a place where we give of ourselves to Him but it is also a place to listen and let Him speak to us. It is a place where we are to do some heart-searching before we commit ourselves to service. In serving God, as in everything else, we need balance.

It is wrong to make no commitment to Him, but on the other hand it is wrong to make a commitment or promise and not keep it.

We are not to make pledges to God hastily in a moment of emotion. Rather, we need to let the Holy Spirit so work in us that as we make a commitment, we will determine with the help of the Holy Spirit, to fulfil it.

Direction for today: Commitment means more than a promise; it means continued action.

Prayer for today: "Lord, help me to speak the truth in love."

July 18: Read Ecclesiastes 7-9

Key verse: "Whatsoever thy hand findeth to do, do it with thy might; for there is no work, nor device, nor knowledge, nor wisdom, in the grave, whither thou goest" (Ecclesiastes 9:10 NAS).

"Only one life, 'twill soon be past; only what's done for Christ will last" (Oswald J. Smith).

Solomon, the writer of Ecclesiastes, had lived long and had been involved in many situations. He had opportunity to observe firsthand the power and the majesty of the God who had given him such great wisdom and authority.

Although Solomon had received all of these blessings, he was not fully committed to the Lord, and indulged in many things which, although they seemed to satisfy the flesh, caused grief to his own spirit and to God.

All through Ecclesiastes, Solomon warns of the dangers of forgetting God and tells of the blessings to those who will obey Him.

Direction for today: Life is too short to do anything but our best for Jesus.

Prayer for today: "Father, help me to serve You with all my might."

July 19: Read Ecclesiastes 10-12

Key verse: "He who watches the wind will not sow and he who looks at the clouds shall not reap" (Ecclesiastes 11:4 NAS).

Common sense is not as common as it should be. Most of us in the human family assess the situation around us, make what we call rational judgments, and then decide on our actions. God has given us the power of observation, an intelligent need to decide the right and wrong, and a determination to reach goals.

Unfortunately, some people spend all their time assessing the circumstances and accomplish nothing. God has not called us simply to observe, but to be involved.

Our key verse is paraphrased in the Living Bible. "If you wait for perfect conditions, you will never get anything done." Obedience to God does not depend on circumstances, but upon His Word. So, let us not wait for perfect conditions but obey Him now and God, who mysteriously, but capably, forms a baby in the mother's womb, will also bring about success through your faithful obedience to Him.

And what is my final conclusion? "Fear God and obey His commandments, for this is the entire duty of man" (Ecclesiastes 12:13).

Direction for today: Service to God is the only thing in life that really counts.

Prayer for today: "Father, help me to serve You with gladness!"

Song of Solomon

Through the history of Biblical interpretation, the Song of Solomon has been read in many different ways. The Jews believed it was an allegory of the love between God and His people, Israel. Christians adapted this to suggest the book showed the love of Christ for His bride, the church.

More recent Christian writing has explored the book for what it was certainly intended to be – a love poem celebrating the love between a man and a woman, identified as Solomon and his Shulamite bride. There is much in the book that can be shared between a husband and wife as they celebrate together the joys of a marriage relationship honoured and blessed by God.

However, it is also true that marriage is a symbol frequently used by God to show, in the Old Testament, His relationship with His people, (especially in Hosea; see also Isaiah 50:1, 62:4, Ezekiel 16:32), and to represent the bond between Christ and His church under the New Testament (Ephesians 5:22-32). Thus, the symbolism can be carried from the passionate love of the man and woman in this poem to the relationship of God to His people.

Memory Verse

" 'Be strong, all you people of the land', says the Lord, 'and work; for I am with you', says the Lord of hosts." Haggai 2:4b NKJV

July 20: Read The Song of Solomon 1-3

Key verse: *"My beloved is mine and I am his, he feedeth among the lilies" (Song of Solomon 2:16 NAS).*

This whole book is considered by most theologians to be an allegory representing Christ's relationship to His bride, the Church.

As God sanctified the union of man and woman, how much more does He sanctify the union of His Son, Jesus, to His bride, whom He has been preparing for centuries.

Far too often, we disregard the intimacy that God wants us to have with Jesus. What depths of understanding and wisdom await us when we begin to learn of God's love and His nature toward us in the person of Jesus Christ. As we grow in understanding of Who He truly is, we will come into the intimacy with Christ that god has planned for us.

In any intimate relationship, there must be cooperation on both sides. If we expect only a mystical sensation through accepting Jesus as Saviour, then we will be greatly disappointed. If, however, we are willing to surrender all of ourselves, then we will come into the inheritance of all for which Jesus surrendered His life.

He died that we might have abundant life now; and then eternal life.

Direction for today: You can know the love of Christ which passes knowledge, and you can be filled with all the fullness of God! (Ephesians 3:19).

Prayer for today: "Lord Jesus, draw me ever nearer to You!"

136

July 21: Read The Song of Solomon 4-6

Key verse: "How delightful is your love, my sister, my bride" (Song of Solomon 4:10 NIV).

There have been many different interpretations of this poem of love. But whether you study it in its natural form, as a love story between Solomon and the lovely Shulamite maiden, or whether you see it as a portrayal of the love between Christ and the Church, you will not find a more beautiful, tender or moving expression of love.

Here we read Solomon's song of love and, while his imagery is not the type we would use today, nevertheless we see that we are God's handiwork. The beauty and truth of God is reflected in His creation.

The marriage relationship must be exclusive in practice and in yearnings of the heart. This is the meaning conveyed by the poetic term used in 4:12, "A garden enclosed . . . is my spouse."

The maiden, having missed her opportunity to welcome her beloved on his unexpected visit, goes out to search for him. Deep within her heart she is certain of his love (6:3).

We can be just as certain of our Saviour's love for us. Though we may fail Him, His love is unfailing and unending.

Direction for today: The love of God for His children cannot even be measured in human terms!

Prayer for today: "Lord, I will show my love for You through my obedience to You."

July 22: Read The Song of Solomon 7-8

Key verse: "I am my beloved's and his desire is toward me" (Song of Solomon 7:10 KJV).

What a wonderful statement to be able to make! We belong to Jesus because He first loved us and continues to love us today. In fact, the Bible tells us that Jesus "is risen again, who is even at the right hand of God, who also maketh intercession for us" (Romans 8:34b).

How beautiful to belong to Him who died and then rose again. How marvellous to know that, in the presence of Almighty God, He makes intercession for us because He loves us. How humbling, yet comforting, to know that it is He who places the desire in our hearts to follow Him and seek righteousness.

When I encountered Jesus Christ, my life was changed. The broken pieces were mended and old desires and temptations were replaced with a hunger and determination to serve Him. As I enjoyed my new freedom and deliverance, I understood, for the first time, that if any person "be in Christ, he is a new creature" (II Corinthians 5:17 KJV).

I owe everything to Jesus Christ, my beloved, for He gave His life for me on the cross of Calvary.

Direction for today: Know that Christ's commitment to you demands a complete, unequivocal commitment to Him.

Prayer for today: "Lord, I commit myself completely to You. I hold back nothing."

Hebrews

The Epistle to the Hebrews is a letter unique in the New Testament. The author of the book is not identified, and scholars have long debated this issue.

Whoever the human author was, we can clearly see the hand of the Holy Spirit in the writing of this marvellous book. Hebrews, which may have been written to Hebrew (Jewish) Christians to keep them true to the salvation by faith in Christ, and not through the law of Moses, is a precise Christology – perhaps the most detailed and accurate outline of the person and continuing work of Christ in the new Testament.

It is also unique in that it has close ties with Old Testament writings, particularly the book of Leviticus.

The intent of the writer is clear in the very first verses: he argues that, while God has spoken in a variety of ways before the time of Christ, His ultimate and complete statement to man is in Jesus and His saving work. The writer proceeds to demonstrate Christ's superiority to angels, prophets, and priests. Christ is shown as the minister of a new, superior covenant.

July 23: Read Hebrews 1,2

Key verse: "God, after He spoke long ago to the fathers in the prophets in many and various ways, in these last days has spoken to us in His Son, whom He appointed heir of all things, through whom also He made the world" (Hebrews 1:1,2 NAS).

The beginning of Hebrews sets the tone for the whole letter. Whereas in the past God spoke through prophets, angels, dreams and visions, in this age He speaks directly through His perfect Son. So we must listen! (See Ephesians 2:1).

But listen to what? To the Word! Jesus is the Living Word, and speaks to us today by His Spirit. The Spirit of God is our promised teacher (John 14:26). The Bible is the written Word of God and, according to Hebrews 4:12, it is this Word which cuts to the very core of our being and brings about a cure. It is the Word which, coupled with obedience, brings about holiness and cleanness of heart (Ephesians 5:26).

This balance of the written and the living Word of God has been instituted by God. The Word Himself is available to help us whenever we have a need.

Direction for today: Everything God ever did in the past has found its fulfillment and conclusion in Jesus Christ.

Prayer for today: "Thank You, Father, that You have spoken to us so clearly in Your Son, Jesus Christ."

July 24: Read Hebrews 3,4

Key verse: ". . . since we have a great high priest who has gone through the heavens, Jesus the Son of God, let us hold firmly to the faith we profess" (Hebrews 4:14 NIV).

The responsibility of the High Priest was to intercede before God on behalf of the people. He offered the required sacrifice for their sins and then entered God's presence to represent them. The people could not offer a sacrifice for their own sin nor enter God's presence on their own. Nor can we, except through Jesus.

Jesus became our High Priest. On Calvary He offered His life as a sacrifice for our sins and forty days later He ascended into God's presence to represent us. I Timothy 2:5 reads, "For there is one God and one mediator between God and man, the man Christ Jesus."

It is because Jesus represents us that we can hold firm to the faith we profess. Because He became man, we can trust Him to understand our needs and sympathize with our problems. We need to daily yield to His will that we may live victoriously through Him.

Direction for today: Trust and surrender go hand in hand.

Prayer for today: "Praise You, Jesus, for being my High Priest and opening the way into heaven for me!"

July 25: Read Hebrews 5,6

Key verse: "So also Christ glorified not Himself to be made an high priest: but He that said unto Him, Thou art My Son, today have I begotten Thee" (Hebrews 5:5 KJV).

The writer of this epistle was building on the fact that the people were thoroughly familiar with the role of the high priest. The position was not one of human choice but of divine appointment.

The duties associated with this office included the offering of specific sacrifices to God. Only the high priest was able to enter into the most holy place, beyond the veil which separated the holy from the most holy.

How we should praise the Lord that our Great High Priest has met all of God's requirements! He has an eternal place in the presence of our Heavenly Father to represent us. The sacrifice which He offered on our behalf was His own life.

The promises of God are reliable because they are grounded in the very bedrock of His divine nature. If it were possible for God to lie He would no longer be God, for truth is an essential quality of His character.

Every evidence that is necessary to confirm the priesthood of the Lord Jesus Christ has been provided: His physical resurrection, the visible ascension from the Mount of Olives, and the coming of the Holy Spirit in fulfillment of His promise.

Direction for today: The Christian faith is anchored to an empty tomb in Israel and an occupied throne in the presence of God.

Prayer for today: "Praise God that Jesus has met every requirement for our justification, sanctification and glorification!"

July 26: Read Hebrews 7,8

Key verse: *"He is able to save forever those who draw near to God through Him, since He always lives to make intercession for them." (Hebrews 7:25 NAS).*

The book of Hebrews has been called the book of better things. The purpose is to show how many of the things which were ordained to be carried out in the Old Testament find their fulfillment in the person and ministry of Jesus Christ.

The priesthood of Aaron, while ordained by God, is revealed as imperfect. One of the proofs of this imperfection is that each of the priests in the Levitical priesthood would die, and have to be replaced by another man. But the priesthood of Jesus Christ is never interrupted because He is alive forevermore (see Revelation 11:18).

Aaron did not choose to become the first High Priest of the Levitical priesthood, but was appointed by God to that office. So also, Jesus Christ received that eternal appointment from His heavenly Father. This was confirmed as He was raised from the dead and taken back into the heaven (Acts 1:9-11).

What a privilege is ours, to know that we have a great High Priest who appears in the very presence of Almighty God for us. The sacrifice He offered on our behalf does not have to be repeated over and over again, as the Levitical priests had to do. His own perfect life given once was sufficient and that cry from the Cross is so wonderful: "It is finished!" (John 19:28-30).

Direction for today: Jesus cannot only empathize with us in our suffering and our needs, for He has gone the way before us, but He can also provide the grace to overcome, for the power is His!

Prayer for today: "Praise You, Jesus, for Your once-for-all sacrifice of Your precious life."

Memory Verse

"Thus says the Lord of hosts: 'Execute true justice, show mercy and compassion everyone to his brother.'" Zechariah 7:9 NKJV

July 27: Read Hebrews 9,10

Key verse: "Not through the blood of goats and calves, but through His own blood, He entered the holy place once and for all, having obtained eternal redemption" (Hebrews 9:12 NAS).

The twenty-second verse of this chapter tells us: "Without the shedding of blood there is no forgiveness." God Himself had ordained that. For this reason, once a year the High Priest took the sacrifice of a spotless lamb into the Holy of Holies. That sacrifice was good for only one year so a similar sacrifice was carried out each year, year after year.

Then the Father sent Jesus, His only begotten Son, to be the once and for all sacrifice for our sins. Never again would there be the need for further sacrifice. Our key verse today says; "He entered the holy place once for all, having obtained eternal redemption." Hebrews 10:12 tells us that, "He, having offered one sacrifice for sins for all time, sat down at the right hand of God." Verse 14 says, "by one offering He has perfected for all time those who are sanctified."

Praise the Lord, there is no need for anyone to go out into a Christless eternity.

Praise the Lord, we don't have to offer any more sacrifices, but only to believe on His name and to accept that He died for our sins.

Praise the Lord . . . Jesus died once; and we are covered, cleansed and made whole by His death on our behalf.

Direction for today: Praise God for the forgiveness that is ours in Christ. Be sure you claim it!

Prayer for today: "Thank you, Jesus, for my eternal redemption."

July 28: Read Hebrews 11

Key verse: "Now faith is the assurance of things hoped for, the conviction of things not seen" (Hebrews 11:1 NAS).

Faith is the focal point of a successful Christian life. Unless the Christian is properly equipped with the "shield of faith", he will not be adequately prepared for spiritual battle. Faith is essential to salvation (John 3:36) and is the key to answered prayer (James 1:6).

Faith is taking God at His word - no questions asked. There are two sides to faith. The first involves our intellect, the second involves our wills. We make an intellectual decision to trust God at His word and to accept Jesus as Saviour. Our wills must then be surrendered to Him as Lord of our lives.

In the face of great adversity, great men and women of faith, like Abraham, Isaac, Jacob, Sarah, Moses and Rahab, determined to believe God and then submitted their hearts and will to *His* will. They worshipped by faith, governed by faith and conquered by faith. They even died in faith!

The final 8 verses of Hebrews 11 form perhaps the most powerful challenge ever written to the believer. Jesus is the *Author* and *Finisher* of our faith. Are you facing an obstacle today? Are you lacking in faith? Stop now and turn to *Jesus*. Through *Him* you can rise above any difficulty or circumstance!

Direction for today: Faith is believing that God tells the truth, and acting on His truth.

Prayer for today: "Lord, I believe You, I trust You, and I will live in the truth of that confession."

July 29: Read Hebrews 12,13

Key verse: "Jesus Christ the same yesterday, and today, and forever" (Hebrews 13:8 KJV).

This is one of my favourite scriptures, for it tells me three things.

First, that Jesus has been, and will be around all the time - from history to eternity. Second, that Jesus, who cared for the lost, the sick and the suffering, is the same one who continues to care for me now. Third, that Jesus hasn't changed. Not only can I trust Him to cleanse me from my sins, but I can come to Him for my healing and deliverance.

How wonderful to be assured that the One who has provided the way to heaven still cradles me in His arms.

Direction for today: Jesus never changes. His love, His faithfulness and His promises are yours today and always.

Prayer for today: "Thank You, Jesus, that I can always trust You."

Isaiah

The book of the prophet Isaiah might well be called "the gospel of the Old Testament". The words and writings of this anointed prophet are filled with references to the coming Messiah, our Lord Jesus Christ. Some specific Messianic sections are unparalleled in Old Testament literature – sections such as Isaiah 7:14; 9:6,7; Isaiah 11:1-10; 53:1-12; and Isaiah 61:1-3, claimed by Jesus in Luke 4:18-19 as the purpose of His ministry.

Isaiah the prophet was probably a nobleman, a resident of Jerusalem in the final days of the northern kingdom of Israel. His ministry, which began with the dramatic call recounted in Isaiah 6, stretched from the death of King Uzziah in 739 B.C. to the reign of evil King Mannasseh, who began his rule in 697 B.C. The time or cause of Isaiah's death is unknown, but tradition suggests that he was martyred by Mannasseh.

The book can be considered in several sections, as the point of view and theme of the prophet shifts. Chapters 1-39 concern themselves more with the times Isaiah and his nation of Judah was living through; chapters 40-55 are a prophetic vision two hundred years ahead, to the time after Judah had been destroyed and exiled by the Babylonians, and were returning to restore their land. The two emphases combine in the final chapters, 56-66. In a miraculous way, Isaiah's vision frequently stretched even farther, to the days of Christ on earth, and even to the final return of Christ and the establishment of His kingdom. Thus, through this divinely inspired prophet, we gain an overview of the working of God with His people from the years around 700 B.C. through the time of Christ to the end of all time and the beginning of eternity.

Some scholars have attempted to prove that Isaiah's clear vision into the time after the exile suggests there are more than one authors involved in writing this book. But the New Testament clearly attributes authorship of the entire work to one man, Isaiah, son of Amoz (see John 12:38, 39). If we recognize the power of God to inspire a prophet by His Spirit, we need not doubt, but instead, must marvel at the work of the Lord through His servant.

July 30: Read Isaiah 1,2

Key verse: "Come now, and let us reason together, says the Lord, though your sins are as scarlet, they shall be as white as snow; though they are red like crimson, they will be like wool" (Isaiah 1:18 NAS).

Isaiah has taken the earlier verses of this chapter to talk about how sinful the nation of Israel really was. The whole head is sick (verse 5), from the sole of the foot even to the head there is nothing sound in it (verse 6), then the culmination in verse 15, "So when you spread out your hands in prayer, I will hide My eyes from you."

But in the midst of this mess, even while Israel was dead in trespasses and sins, God speaks a word of life: "Though your sins are like scarlet, they shall be white as snow."

God is in the business of restoring, nenewing and rebuilding. He wants to do that in our lives as well as He did in Israel's. Restoration and renewal begin with the word of forgiveness, spoken right into the middle of seemingly impossible situations.

That's our God at work for us!

Direction for today: God has invited you to come to commune and share with Him; accept the invitation!

Prayer for today: "Thank You, Father, for Your cleansing and restoration."

July 31: Read Isaiah 3-5

Key verse: *"Let me sing for my beloved a love song concerning his vineyard. My beloved had a vineyard on a very fertile hill" (Isaiah 5:1 RSV).*

As the means to give his prophecy, the prophet uses a parable as if it were a popular love song. He compares Israel to a vineyard which has been planted with great care, but which produces only wild grapes. There is only one thing to do with such ingratitude and disobedience: the owner will destroy it.

The vineyard is the house of Israel on whom the Lord has lavished such care and attention. When He had the right to expect justice there was only bloodshed. When He expected fruit of righteousness He heard only a cry from the oppressed. The warning is clear — the people of God in their vineyard of the Promised Land will be destroyed, as a useless vineyard would be destroyed by the vineyard keeper.

And the same warning holds true for us today.

Jesus shares the parable of the wicked tenants (Matthew 21:33-46) and warns, "Therefore I tell you, the Kingdom of God will be taken away from you and given to a nation producing the fruits of it" (21:43).

When we let Jesus be our Saviour, Lord and God, we become a part of His new vineyard, the Church, and we are responsible to produce healthy fruit. Paul tells us that "the fruit of the Spirit is love, joy, peace, patience, kindness, goodness, faithfulness, gentleness, self-control; against such there is no law" (Galatians 5:22-23).

But the love song still holds true today. The same warning is found in the Revelation of John. "But this I have against you, that you abandoned the love you had at first. Remember then from what you have fallen, repent and do the works you did at first, if not, I will come to you and remove your lampstand from its place, unless you repent" (Revelation 2:4-5).

There is no church in Ephesus today because it did not repent and recover its first love. Let each one of us repent, recover our first love in Jesus Christ, and produce the fruit of the Spirit.

Direction for today: Remain true to your first love, Jesus Christ.

Prayer for today: "Lord, may I never be cool in my love for You; keep me from lukewarm commitment."

8

Transformation

Before
I was like a rose in need of watering;
My petals were so tight their beauty was not seen.
The glorious scent was stifled
by the stench of rotting leaves and petals
that were unable to breathe.
The colour God had so richly mixed
was muddy, dull and uninteresting.
The flower He created to show beauty and splendour
was far from its potential.
I willed myself to die.
Yet God, in all His greatness, had a plan
He was determined to see through.
Eventually, with time, the love and warmth
around me caused me to bloom
as God had always intended.

Now
This once dying rose
is bringing life and joy to others,
for the blossoming is eternal
and the beauty everlasting.

– Nicola Burke

August 1: Read Isaiah 6-8

Key verse: "If you do not stand firm in your faith you will not stand at all" (Isaiah 7:9 NIV).

Here we see the Lord speaking through Isaiah to Ahaz, king of Judah. A large army has been formed, planning to attack and destroy him and his people. With all natural odds stacked against them, these people are obviously shaken with fear.

Then comes the challenge to rely on the Lord and stand firm in their faith.

In hindsight, it is easy to say that this solution was obvious. Why did Ahaz even have to be told? But just stop and be honest with yourself. How many times have you encountered a seemingly impossible situation and had to be reminded of who was really in control?

Whether it is a problem involving marriage, finances or whatever, we must realize God is our source of strength and wisdom. Although we might fail Him many times, He is always faithful and willing to answer our prayers. God has promised to never leave us nor forsake us. Believe that, and trust Him!

Direction for today: Do not allow circumstances to control you; let your faith control the circumstances.

Prayer for today: "Father, as Isaiah saw You, give me a glimpse of the Lord, high and lifted up."

August 2: Read Isaiah 9-10

Key verse: "For to us a child is born, to us a child is given; and the government shall be upon His shoulder, and His name will be called Wonderful Counsellor, Mighty God, Everlasting Father, Prince of Peace" (Isaiah 9:6 RSV).

There is nothing more exciting than a birth announcement. But this is especially true of the birth of the Saviour. There is only one way to describe Him: "His name shall be called Emmanuel, which means God with us" (Isaiah 7:14, Matthew 1:23).

He was to be no less than God in the flesh. Paul describes Him as "the image of the invisible God" (Colossians 1:15). He came to be a ransom for many (Matthew 20:28) in order to pay for our sin on the cross of Calvary.

In order to receive Jesus as Saviour and Lord, all we have to do is "call upon the name of the Lord" (Acts 2:21), which means asking Him to forgive us for any sin we have commited, accepting Him as Saviour and acknowledging Him as Lord. Then He forgives and gives us Eternal Life.

Direction for today: Spend each day filled with gratitude for the great gift of the Son!

Prayer for today: "Thank You, Jesus, for the peace You bring.

August 3: Read Isaiah 11-13

Key verse: *"The Spirit of the Lord will rest on Him – the Spirit of wisdom and of understanding, the Spirit of counsel and of power, the Spirit of knowledge and of the fear of the Lord" (Isaiah 11:2 NIV).*

This same Holy Spirit, who descended upon Jesus in the form of a dove, has descended on every believer since the Day of Pentecost. It is by the Spirit that you are born again; you are then called to be filled with the Spirit.

This verse, written centuries before Pentecost, outlines some of the wonderful ministries of the Holy Spirit – ministries He brought to Christ, and which He also brings to us.

We can rely on the Holy Spirit for wisdom and understanding. By the Spirit we know and understand the will of God for our lives, and we are gifted to minister to brothers and sisters in the Lord, as well as to unbelievers, with supernatural wisdom.

The Holy Spirit is also given to guide us, and to help us in counselling others. And He is the Spirit of power: power to save, power to deliver, power to heal.

The Spirit brings us knowledge of God, of His word, and sometimes specific information we need to minister effectively.

And, perhaps most importantly, He is the Spirit of the fear of the Lord, which is the basis of true worship!

Direction for today: Allow the Holy Spirit to work all these ministries in you!

Prayer for today: "Lord, keep on filling me with the Spirit."

August 4: Read Isaiah 14-16

Key verse: *"The Lord of hosts has planned, and who can frustrate it? And as for His stretched-out hand, who can turn it back?" (Isaiah 14:27 NAS).*

In verse 24 of Chapter 14, the Lord says, "Surely just as I have intended so it has happened, and just as I have planned so it will stand." Our key verse further confirms this. Once God has determined to do something, *IT WILL BE DONE!*

Sometimes we behave as though we serve a weak, powerless God, hampered by the same frailties and limitations that hinder us. But this is not so; our God is the Creator of the Universe, King of kings, Lord of lords, Almighty, Omniscient and Omnipresent. What He says . . . He will do. Against the greatest odds, our God will come through victorious.

Do *you* believe that?

Throughout the New Testament we are told to trust God, to ask in faith . . . not doubting . . . and we shall receive. The promises of God are to those who accept Him as Saviour and *put their trust* in Him. Then will He be our champion, our victorious Lord.

Direction for today: God cannot fail!

Prayer for today: "Praise You, Lord, for Your compassion."

August 5: Read Isaiah 17,19

Key verse: *"In that day shall Israel be the third with Egypt and with Assyria, even a blessing in the midst of the land: Whom the Lord of hosts shall bless, saying, 'Blessed be Egypt My people, and Assyria the work of My hands, and Israel Mine inheritance' " (Isaiah 19:24 KJV).*

What a shocking statement! Isaiah, the prophet of Judah, could have been accused of treachery, perhaps even blasphemy, for such a pronouncement!

The northern kingdom of Israel was destroyed by Assyria during Isaiah's lifetime, and the southern kingdom, Judah, was severely threatened by this powerful empire from the north. Egypt, similarly, had been the symbol of oppression to the Hebrews ever since the time of the Exodus.

Yet here, inspired by the Holy Spirit of God, Isaiah looks beyond the past and future oppressions and invasions by these two great neighbours of Israel, to a day when people from every nation would be called "the people of God."

In this passage, as in many of the verses of this book of Isaiah, the prophet envisions the day to come, the "day of the Lord", when all injustice and oppression will be set right on earth by the coming King and Judge, and when all people who have faith in God will be known as His people, regardless of national origin.

As Isaiah spoke or wrote these oracles concerning Egypt and Assyria, he was gazing far into the future. We must wonder if any of the people of Israel understood this apparent affection toward their enemies. But now we see that God does have His people throughout the world and that more are coming into His kingdom every day.

Direction for today: What are you doing to help to bring all those who do not know of God's love into His kingdom?

Prayer for today: "Lord, may Your gospel be spread abroad to all people."

August 6: Read Isaiah 20-22

Key verse: *". . . He calls to me out of Seir, Watchman, what of the night? Watchman, what of the night?" (Isaiah 21:11 NKJV).*

Watchman is singular. God deals with me as an individual. I am accountable to the Lord for what I have done, not what the other person has or has not done. Each person must answer to God for his own actions, thoughts and words.

Yes, the world I live in is filled with evils and temptations, but God said, "No temptation has overtaken you except such as is common to man; but God is faithful, who will not allow you to be tempted beyond what you are able, but with the temptation will also make the way of escape, that you may be able to bear it" (I Corinthians 10:13 NKJV).

As a faithful servant, I must watch how I conduct my affairs. I want to be ready for His return. I'm anticipating His smile of approval on my life and the work I have done in His name.

Direction for today: Be a faithful watchman for Jesus.

Prayer for today: "Lord, help me to be a faithful watchman, warning the lost of impending destruction."

August 7: Read Isaiah 23-25

Key verse: *"He will swallow up death in victory; and the Lord will wipe away tears from off all faces; and the rebuke of His people shall He take away from off all the earth, for the Lord hath spoken it" (Isaiah 25:8 NAS).*

The story of Tyre, the grand, prosperous and powerful city that found itself laid desolate, reminds us of the vanity and uncertainty of earthly possessions. Tyre's sin was that of pride. God had to remove the source of pride and bring the people to a place of repentance and humility. We must first give ourselves unto the Lord before our talents or possessions can truly become "holiness unto the Lord."

Chapter 25 has been appropriately referred to as "the song of praise by the redeemed." We canot help but see in these verses the prophecy of the grace of salvation offered to us by the sacrifice of our Lord Jesus. Salvation would be offered to *all* people (25:6).The world would be freed from the bondage or veil of sin, by the light of the gospel (25:7). Death would be swallowed up in victory at the cross! (25:8). And then for the believer there will be endless joy, as God shall wipe *every* tear from our eyes! (25:8).

We cannot allow pride to rule in our hearts, for it will only bring us to desolation. We must be humble before our gracious God, looking forward to the time when we shall ever be with Him.

Direction for today: Be glad and rejoice in your salvation.

Prayer for today: "Thank you, Jesus, that death is already swallowed up in victory."

August 8: Read Isaiah 26, 27

Key verse: *"Thou wilt keep him in perfect peace whose mind is stayed on Thee: because he trusteth in Thee" (Isaiah 26:3 KJV).*

In our world, peace seems to be at a premium. No one is able to find peace. Negotiators spend long months at international conferences, only to return no closer to peace than when they started. Scientific discoveries which are supposed to foster peace are turned for use in weapons.

In our cities, people seek the peace of silence, but never escape the din of cars and buses, stereos and televisions.

People flee to the cottage to find peace, only to be assaulted by portable radios and power boats. There is no peace.

Except in Jesus.

If we forget our efforts to find peace in a temporal sense, and set our minds on Jesus, we will know peace: peace with God, peace that is beyond understanding. This is the only peace worth finding; and, once found, it will never be lost if we continue to trust in the Lord.

Direction for today: Seek for peace where it may be found: in the Lord Jesus Christ.

Prayer for today: "Lord, I thank You for peace in my spirit; I pray for peace in our world."

August 9: Read Isaiah 28, 29

Key verse: *"The afflicted also shall increse their gladness in the Lord, and the needy of mankind shall rejoice in the Holy One of Israel" (Isaiah 29:19).*

In our reading today, Isaiah condemns Ephraim and, in particular, its leaders, priests, and prophets, who "are confused by wine, they stagger from strong drink" (Isaiah 28:7). He also tells the rulers of Judah that, because they have tried to protect themselves through earthly alliances rather than faith in God (Isaiah 28:15), the Lord shall judge them with "justice as the measuring line" (Isaiah 28:17).

The prophet goes on to warn Jerusalem of a time of correction and punishment (Isaiah 29:3,4). Isaiah, however, assures the faithful remnant that "the afflicted also shall increase their gladness in the Lord" (Isaiah 29:19).

This assurance, that those who rely on earthly wisdom and who believe their deeds can be hidden from the Lord shall be brought low and that the afflicted and the needy shall be blessed, is beautifully re-affirmed by our Lord Jesus Christ in the sermon on the mount (See Matthew 5).

We must remember that the One we serve is a loving God, but also a just God. Those who look to the world and its rewards will have to answer for their actions; we, however, have an Advocate, God's own Son, who will speak for us (I John 2:1).

Direction for today: All godly suffering will one day turn into great joy!

Prayer for today: "Thank You, Jesus, that You are our Advocate."

"Lay up for yourselves treasures in heaven, where neither moth nor rust destroys and where thieves do not break in and steal. For where your treasure is, there your heart will be also." Matthew 6:20,21 NKJV

August 10: Read Isaiah 30, 31

Key verse: *"Their strength is to sit still" (Isaiah 30:7 KJV).*

It is obvious, from all of Chapter 30, that God will prove Himself powerful on behalf of Israel – as long as they let Him do it. (See verses 15 and 18, as well as 31:1). It is abundantly clear that God will intervene in a dramatic way in the affairs of the restored Israel, and without the cunning plans of man.

This same Israel, which God brought back into existence in 1948 A.D., in spite of their indifferent unbelief (29:12-24, 30:15), will be blessed, restored, strengthened and honoured throughout the world's nations (31:5).

How good, and how right, are the Biblical instructions for us as believers to "pray for the peace of Jerusalem".

Direction for today: "Pray for the peace of Jerusalem."

Prayer for today: "Lord, may Your will come to pass for the nation of Israel."

August 11: Read Isaiah 32, 33

Key verse: *"And a man shall be as an hiding place from the wind, and a covert from the tempest; as rivers of waters in a dry place, as the shadow of a great rock in a weary land" (Isaiah 32:2 KJV).*

The burden of the prophet Isaiah for the kingdom of Judah occurred during the reign of four different kings. The tiny kingdom was under attack from surrounding nations, in danger of being destroyed. In this setting, the key verse takes on added meaning. Early in his ministry Isaiah had been granted a vision of the true king of the universe, and his cardinal desire was to point his people to that King.

In times of distress and adversity, there is a need for an anchoring place for a person's faith.

Isaiah points to a sure anchoring place. He warns against placing confidence in existing political kingdoms and seeks to turn hearts and minds to the Lord. He is likened to a hiding place from wind and tempest and a shade from the burning noonday sun. Not only is He a sheltering place, but He is also the source of life, like a river in a desert.

To place our faith in any other source of help is to invite disaster. Political alliances or sophisticated weaponry are but false security; material possessions are transient, and human relationships can alter or cease to exist. How comforting are these words: "I am the Lord, I change not" (Malachi 3:6) and "Lo, I am with you always, even to the end" (Matthew 28:20).

In spite of all the taunting that might be aimed at those who have put their trust in this King, the Lord Jesus Christ, we can be like Hezekiah. Looking beyond the existing circumstances, he focused his faith on the Eternal God. This faith and confidence in God was not misplaced, for we find that victory was granted.

Our warfare is not against flesh and blood but in the spiritual realm. But this same Lord has the ability to make us more than conquerors. Truly He is the rock that shadows a weary land.

Direction for today: When the enemy would come in like a flood, we have a refuge in the Eternal Rock of Ages.

Prayer for today: "Lord, make me a conqueror, and more than a conqueror in You."

August 12: Read Isaiah 34-36

Key verse: *"And the ransomed of the Lord shall return, and come to Zion with songs and everlasting joy upon their heads: they shall obtain joy and gladness, and sorrow and sighing shall flee away" (Isaiah 35:10 KJV).*

Following this beautiful promise is the terrible threat against Jerusalem by Sennacherib's mighty army. Sennacherib the king of Assyria, had already conquered a number of the walled cities of Judah.

Eight years prior to this, his armies had besieged the city of Samaria for three years before taking it. He had now moved to Lachish, some 35 miles south west of Jerusalem. From here he sent his messengers to discourage and threaten the inhabitants of Jerusalem so that when he arrived it would be an easy victory.

His messengers pointed out that none of the gods of the surrounding cities had saved them, not even the god of the Samaritans.

Sennacherib made two mistakes. His messengers offended God by their over confidence in their own ability to conquer the city in spite of any intervention God might make (II Kings 19:23). He also overlooked a humble, praying king, Hezekiah.

The end of the story reveals the sovereign intervention of our all-powerful God. Sennacherib returned home, leaving his dead army on the fields outside of Jerusalem; there his own sons murdered him as he worshipped in the temple of his god.

God desires to bless and protect His children and to provide for their every need. But often our pride, ambition and lack of surrender cause Him to withhold much that He would like to give to us.

Direction for today: Look for the day of everlasting joy.

Prayer for today: "Thank You, Jesus, that the day is coming when sorrow and sighing will flee away."

August 13: Read Isaiah 37, 38

Key verse: *"I know your sitting down, and your going out and your coming in, and your raging against Me" (Isaiah 37:28 NAS).*

Yes, God knows all about us. He knows what we think; do, or do not do; where we go, and why we go there.

And yes, God knows all about our 'raging against Him'.

What does that mean? God knows each time we question His Word, the Bible; each time we complain about the way in which He made us; each time we grind our teeth because of the circumstances in which we find ourselves. He knows how we handle disappointments; how we feel about those who have done us wrong; how we respond to instruction and correction.

He knows *all* about us. And still He loves us.

Doesn't that amaze you, humble you . . . and bless you? It does me! Every once in a while I'm upset by my response to people, concerned by the irritation which seems to rise so easily within me. I'm disgusted with myself and think: "What does God feel about me *now*?"

And then I realize that, though He must be saddened by my thoughts and behaviour, yet still He loves me, *for I have committed myself to Him.* Because I am His, He loves me with an everlasting love.

Direction for today: God knows your every action, word and thought. Live in that awareness.

Prayer for today: "Thank You, Lord, that although You know me, still You love me!"

August 14: Read Isaiah 39, 40

Key verse: *"They that wait upon the Lord shall renew their strength; they shall mount up with wings as eagles: they shall run and not be weary, and they shall walk and not faint" (Isaiah 40:31 NAS).*

It was most likely during a period of Assyrian pressure, in 701 B.C., that Hezekiah became severely ill. Although Isaiah the prophet warned the king to prepare for death, God intervened. In Isaiah 38:4-6, Hezekiah was promised a fifteen year extension of his life and deliverance of Jerusalem from the Assyrian threat.

In today's reading, we have an account of the acclaim and recognition by surrounding nations of Hezekiah's recovery from illness and his nation's successful recovery from the economic hardships of the Assyrian occupation. The Babylonian embassy was probably duly impressed with the display of wealth in Jerusalem.

But Hezekiah's triumph was tempered by the subsequent warning of Isaiah that succeeding generations would be subjected to Babylonian captivity. Hezekiah, when he received threats from Assyria, went to the temple and prayed for the nation's deliverance. He finished his reign in peace and was buried in honour. With great devotion to the task, he led his people in the greatest spiritual reformation in Judah's history.

Isaiah speaks words of comfort. Isaiah 40:3 foretells the role of John the Baptist and also speaks of the majesty and sovereignty of God, who will come and judge the nations of the earth – a God who not only created the heavens and earth but who shall feed His flock like a shepherd and carry the young lambs in His arm.

Direction for today: Jesus is coming again!

Prayer for today: "Come, Lord Jesus!"

August 15: Read Isaiah 41, 42

Key verse: "Fear not, for I am with you; be not dismayed, for I am your God. I will strengthen you, yes I will help you, I will uphold you with My righteous right hand" (Isaiah 41:10 NKJV).

God told us not to fear. He didn't say there was nothing to fear. If there had been nothing to fear there would have been no need to say, "Fear not". His assurance was that because He is with us we need not fear.

Travelling in Europe, our friends were alarmed that we had not made room reservations in Rome ahead of time. As we travelled, I was reading Hebrews 13:5,6, "Let your conduct be without covetousness, and be content with such things as you have, for He himself has said, 'I will never leave you nor forsake you' " So we may boldly say: "The Lord is my helper; I will not fear. What can man do to me?" Our train arrived late, but we found economical accommodation near to the station. God kept us from harm and danger and once again provided for His own.

In His last discourse with His disciples, Jesus said, "Peace I leave with you, My peace I give to you; not as the world gives do I give to you. Let not your heart be troubled, neither let it be afraid" (John 14:27).

Direction for today: Keep your heart free from covetousness, content and trusting God each step of the way.

Prayer for today: "Lord, by Your Spirit, give me contentment."

August 16: Read Isaiah 43, 44

Key verse: "But now, thus says the Lord, your Creator, O Jacob, and He Who formed you, O Israel, 'Do not fear, for I have redeemed you; I have called you by my name; you are Mine!' " (Isaiah 43:1 NAS).

Later in this chapter God declares, "Before Me there was no God formed, and there will be none after Me." (Isaiah 43:10). Men have tried to create new gods: gods made from wood and stone (see 44:9-20), gods imagined to be on earth, under the earth, and in the skies. But in each case, these gods are gods invented and named by man.

In sharp contrast, the true God, the God of Israel and the Father of our Lord Jesus Christ, is not a *creation* – He is the supreme *Creator*! Man does not imagine Him, nor do we name Him – He names Himself; also He knows each of us by name, individually.

The True God is not an unthinking impersonal deity, but a personal God who seeks a personal relationship with His individual creations. It was the true God who called to a small boy, by name: "The Lord called yet again, 'Samuel' " (I Samuel 3:6). This same Lord called a persecutor of the church by name: "A light from heaven flashed around him; and he fell to the ground and heard a voice saying to him, 'Saul, Saul, why are you persecuting Me?' " (Acts 9:4). And when God chose the leader of His people in the days of the Exodus, He called him by name: "God called to him from the midst of the bush, and said, 'Moses, Moses' " (Exodus 3:4).

And, just as surely, God knows each of us by name. He created us to be the persons we are. And He calls us, by name, to respond to His call. Even more, He tells us that He calls us by *our* name that we might carry *His* holy name: Isaiah wrote that God is gathering "everyone who is called by My name." (43:7).

Direction for today: God has called you by your name, and you are His!

Prayer for today: "Thank You, Lord, that You have claimed me for Your own."

"And He said to them, 'Go into all the world and preach the gospel to every creature. He who believes and is baptized will be saved; but he who does not believe will be condemned.'" Mark 16:15,16 NKJV

August 17: Read Isaiah 45, 46

Key verse: "Turn to Me and be saved, all you ends of the earth; for I am God and there is no other" (Isaiah 45:22 NIV).

Paul, writing to Timothy, says that it is not God's will that any should perish (I Timothy 2:4). It is God's plan for His church that the gospel will be spread throughout the whole world. Sometimes, we have not done such a good job, but praise God, there have always been missionaries willing to risk health, life and their own material possessions to share the news of salvation to all the ends of the earth.

God's message is for everyone, but how will they hear if no one tells them the good news?

Are you willing to carry that message if the Lord calls you to that specific task? Are you helping those already carrying that responsibility, supporting missionaries and ministries in prayer and with funds? That is clearly part of our job as Christians because, if the people of the world are not saved through Jesus, there is no other way!

Direction for today: Play your part in reaching the world for Jesus.

Prayer for today: "Lord, what would You have me to do to help bring those at the ends of the earth to salvation?"

August 18: Read Isaiah 47, 48

Key verse: "If only you had paid attention to My commands . . ." (Isaiah 48:18 NIV).

If only we would have left five minutes earlier, if only I would have paid it, if only, if only, if only. . .

"If only" is probably one of the most widely used phrases of remorse. Through Isaiah, God uses this phrase to give a stern warning to the Israelites who were living idolatrous, wicked lives in Babylon. They had missed out on so much righteousness and peace.

Everything they were involved in had been foretold long before, but they had not heeded the warnings. Now God is going to destroy sinful Babylon, but first give His people a chance to flee.

So many people repeat this same pattern. They constantly reject the call for salvation for fear of missing out on the "good things in life." No matter how much conviction they feel, they will not yield and commit their lives to Christ.

156

The Lord is always willing to take you into the fold but the door of opportunity has closed on many who have procrastinated too long, and are lost in a hopeless eternity.

Have you asked Christ to come into your heart and take full charge of your life? If you have not, why not do it right now?

God knows what is best for you and will direct the way you should go (Isaiah 48:17 NIV).

Direction for today: A Christian has nothing to lose and everything to gain; but an unbeliever has nothing to gain and eternity to lose.

Prayer for today: "Lord, help me always to pay attention to Your commands."

August 19: Read Isaiah 49, 50

Key verse: "See, I have engraved you on the palms of My hands; your walls are ever before Me" (Isaiah 49:16 NIV).

God is so faithful. In spite of the idolatry and sin in the nation of Israel, God did not forget them. Even though He sent them off to slavery with the Babylonians, God did not forget them. He had a plan for His people, a plan that one day, from the lineage of David and the tribe of Judah, would come His Son, the Lord Jesus Christ.

In the key verse we are told that God has, "engraved us on the palms of His hands". No matter what He does, the name of the nation of Israel is before Him. Paul says in Romans, that the Gentile believers are like branches that God has grafted into the tree of God's family. In the same way, our names are before God.

This is a difficult thought for us to understand. The God of this universe, who hung the stars in place and insured that the earth rotates once, not twice, a day, is also so concerned about each of us.

In Psalm 139 David said, "You know when I sit and when I rise; you perceive my thoughts from afar. You discern my going out and my lying down; You are familiar with all my ways." Truly, our God is a great God who not only knows all things but is faithful and just in controlling all things.

Direction for today: You are always in the mind and the heart of God.

Prayer for today: "Praise You, Lord, that I am ever in Your presence."

August 20: Read Isaiah 51, 52

Key verse: "See my servant will act wisely; he will be raised and lifted up and highly exalted" (Isaiah 52:13 NIV).

Isaiah here speaks of the Messiah who was to come and be a servant to mankind. Specifically he speaks of His death, the total surrender that would take Him to the cross and render Him unrecognizable because of the beatings He suffered. What should impress us was His willngness to be a servant, no matter what it cost Him personally. As His followers, are we willing to serve Him the same way?

When Jesus walked upon this earth, the world hated Him. He never went out of His way to cause this; they simply did not accept what He stood for. In John 15:19 He said, ". . . I have chosen you out of the world. That is why the world hates you" (NIV). If someone dislikes us because of our Christian walk, we get discouraged. He said that if we are true servants they will hate us. Should we stop and ask ourselves, how willing are we for this to happen to us because of our love for Christ?

Don't go out looking for others to hate you, but don't crumble if they do so because you serve Him.

Direction for today: Service in Christ means that we must view the world as He did: loving sinners and hating evil.

Prayer for today: "As Christ surrendered in obedience to the Father, help me, Lord, to surrender to You."

August 21: Read Isaiah 53, 54

Key verse: "He is despised and rejected of men; a man of sorrows, and acquainted with grief: and we hid as it were our faces from Him; He was despised, and we esteemed Him not" (Isaiah 53:3 KJV).

Here Isaiah is writing about Israel's Messiah and the fact that He would be rejected. And surely Jesus, Israel's true Messiah, was rejected, despised, wounded, bruised, beaten and finally crucified. Not for His own sins but for ours, and the sins of the whole world.

God is merciful and gracious, always ready to forgive those who come to Him through Jesus Christ, His Holy Son.

As we read these two chapters of Isaiah, we see the nation's rejection of Jesus and then the subsequent pain and sorrow of the Jews. Finally we see that God has not forsaken them but instead fully intends to bring them back into their own land and to bless them in fellowship with Himself.

Direction for today: Consider the sacrifice Jesus made for you.

Prayer for today: "Thank You, Lord Jesus, for bearing my sins, my sicknesses, and my sorrows."

August 22: Read Isaiah 55, 56

Key verse: "Ho, every one that thirsteth, come ye to the waters, and he that hath no money; come ye, buy, and eat; yea, come, buy wine and milk without money and without price . . . Let the wicked forsake his way, and the unrighteous man his thoughts: and let him return unto the Lord, and He will have mercy upon him; and to our God, for He will abundantly pardon" (Isaiah 55:1,7 KJV).

This chapter of Isaiah speaks very clearly of God's unconditional mercy. Mercy is something that is undeserved. It is described, in the Zondervan Bible Dictionary, as, "Forbearance from inflicting punishment upon an adversary or a lawbreaker." That means that your present sin or past sin, no matter what it is, has no bearing on God's forgiveness. He will forgive you if you ask Him to!

In verse one it is quite clear that God makes this offer to everyone, and the offer is free.

However, there is a condition. That is a surrender of self to the Lord; a commitment on our part, of service to Him. "Let the wicked forsake his way, and the unrighteous man his thoughts." When we do this, the Bible promises that God will have compassion on us. He will not bring punishment for the sins we have committed.

So many people live under condemnation of self, even after they have invited Jesus Christ to be their Saviour. They, for some reason, think that God is holding the past against them.

Let us not underestimate the mercy of God. Verse seven states that ". . . He will abundantly pardon." That means God fully pardons. He completely forgives any sin that has been a part of your life. You see, half forgiveness would be no forgiveness at all. God wants us to have freedom in our mind and soul. I John 1:9 says it all: "If we confess our sins, He is faithful and just to forgive us our sins, and to cleanse us from all unrighteousness." The Psalmist said, "As far as the east is from the west, for far hath He removed our transgressions from us" (Psalm 103:121).

Rejoice in the full forgiveness God offers. Learn to forgive yourself when you have turned your sin over to God.

Direction for today: Come to the waters of our Lord.

Prayer for today: "Praise You, Father, for Your provision of spiritual food and drink for all."

August 23: Read Isaiah 57, 58

Key verse: "Is not this the kind of fasting I have chosen: to loose the chains of injustice and untie the cords of the yoke, to set the oppressed free and break every yoke? Is it not to share your food with the hungry and to provide the poor wanderer with shelter – when you see the naked, to clothe him . . ." (Isaiah 58:6,7 NIV).

This is a powerful passage, a declaration by the Lord of things that are very important to Him. We can learn two related lessons from this.

First, God does not want us to come to Him with hypocritical forms of worship. If our lives do not line up, it is not honouring to the Lord to go through empty forms of worship. He does not want fasting without righteousness, any more than He wants sacrifice without obedience or communion without repentance.

Second, God expects His people to relate in very practical ways to the needs of the world. Christians tend to spiritualize many things, but this passage is clear in its intent: we are to stand against injustice, feed the poor and clothe the needy. The commandment could not be more plain.

Direction for today: Oppose injustice in the name of the Lord.

Prayer for today: "Lord give me an opportunity today to obey the lesson of Isaiah 58."

Memory Verse

"Then He said to them all, 'If anyone desires to come after Me, let him deny Himself, and take up his cross daily, and follow Me.'" Luke 9:23 NKTV

August 24: Read Isaiah 59, 60

Key verse: "Behold, the Lord's hand is not so short that it cannot save; Neither is His ear so dull that it cannot hear" (Isaiah 59:1 NAS).

Sin separates us from God. It is the greatest obstacle which we must overcome. It blinds the unsaved to the truth of the Gospel and can hinder the believer from being victorious in his or her Christian walk.

But, no matter how great the sin, God's grace is greater still! We are never too far away for Him to reach us, neither are we too far away for Him to hear our cry. While our sin may hide God's face from us (59:2), our face is never hidden from God! He is ever reaching out in love.

The loving grace of God is beyond mere human understanding. "For behold the darkness shall cover the earth and gross darkness the people: but the Lord shall arise upon thee, and His glory shall be seen upon thee" (60:2).

No matter how spiritually and morally darkened our world may be, the light and the glory of the Lord will be seen in us if we will but stand for Christ and serve Him with all our heart.

Turn to Him today. Renew your commitment to live for Jesus. Forget the past. Press on!

Direction for today: Claim God's promises as you encounter them in scripture.

Prayer for today: "Lord, give me one promise that I can claim from You today."

August 25: Read Isaiah 61, 62

Key verse: "For as the earth bringeth forth her bud, and as the garden causeth the things that are sown in it to spring forth; so the Lord God will cause righteousness and praise to spring forth before all nations" (Isaiah 61:11 KJV).

If you are a gardener, this portion of scripture will mean a lot to you. In the spring we face the soil which has been battered by the elements through the winter. There is work to be done to prepare the soil and then we commit good seed to it. Carefully we keep it weeded, as new plants spring forth. In what could have been a multitude of terrible weeds, we see beautiful flowers, fruit and vegetables that develop before our eyes.

It is always a miracle how God can take a tiny seed and have it grown into a beautiful pumpkin, cucumber or tomato plant. An even greater miracle is when God plants His seeds in the lives of men and women that righteousness and praise will spring forth unto all nations.

Direction for today: Be sure your heart is good soil for the Gardener to work in.

Prayer for today: "Lord, soften my heart."

August 26: Read Isaiah 63-64

Key verse: "For since the beginning of the world men have not heard, nor perceived by the ear, neither hath the eye seen, O God, beside Thee, what He hath prepared for him that waiteth for Him" (Isaiah 64:4 KJV).

The blessings of God are right beyond our human understanding. Isaiah, in his prayer, tells us that since the beginning of time men have not been able to perceive fully the blessings of the Lord that are available to those that believe (Isaiah 64:4).

The apostle Paul, however, tells us in I Corinthians 2:10, that God has revealed His blessings to us and how He continues to do so.

Paul says that when we look through the eyes of the spirit of man, we can only see the things of this world and its desires; we are blind to the things of God (I Corinthians 2:11 and 14).

The day of Pentecost changed all of this, as the Lord poured out His Holy Spirit on **all** believers. The result is that we can, through God's Spirit in us, "know the things freely given to us by God" (I Corinthians 2:12). We are no longer spiritually blinded.

Direction for today: A Christian operates by enlightened faith, never by blind faith.

Prayer for today: "Thank You, Lord, for Your revelation of truth to me."

August 27: Read Isaiah 65, 66

Key verse: "Before they call I will answer; and while they are yet speaking I will hear" (Isaiah 65:24 KJV).

Today's reading contains beautiful poetic language describing the Kingdom of heaven which King Jesus established when He came to be our Good Shepherd, Saviour and King.

Paul quotes from these verses, confirming the taking of the Gospel to the Gentiles also. The language used in expressing the great difference in this new kingdom (Isaiah 65: 17-25), describes the standard of right-eousness that comes by faith through grace as opposed to trying to keep the law.

Isaiah 66:7 says that Zion is in labour. She gives birth to a Son. A nation is born in a day. Pentecost is the Church's birthday and empowering day. Since then, God has used supernatural, godly means of supply for His people in His Kingdom. Isaiah saw it from his vantage point and could not understand. The people of Jesus' day listened to Him and did not understand, but we know we are in the victorious kingdom. We are doing His work until the King returns! Hallelujah!

Direction for today: Before you even call, God's answer is on the way.

Prayer for today: "Thank You, Father, that You hear and answer!"

James

This short letter, written by James, brother of Christ and leader of the Jerusalem church (see Acts 12:17, Acts 15:13-21, Matthew 13:55), has caused many problems for Christian scholars, who did not understand the complete thrust of the writing. James places heavy stress on works in the life of the Christian, and this raises questions concerning Paul's argument that we are only saved by faith and not by works (Ephesians 2:8).

However, James is clearly not speaking of the way to salvation, but rather about the normal Christian life: a life lived through faith, which, if it is real, will produce works worthy of the name of Christ.

We do not read this book to discover how to be saved; but it is invaluable as instruction concerning how to live once we are saved. And we all benefit from his basic question: if our lives show no works arising from faith, do we really have saving faith at all?

August 28: Read James 1,2

Key verse: *"But be ye doers of the word, and not hearers only, deceiving your own selves" (James 1:22 KJV).*

The Book of James is filled with very practical applications of divine principles. The first principle we see here is that of faith. James points out very clearly that faith and doubt are incompatible. Just as light and darkness cannot remain in the same place, neither can faith and doubt.

The application of this truth is certainly relevant in our relationship to our God. Hebrews 11:6, tells us that "without faith it is impossible to please Him: for he that cometh to God must believe that HE IS, and that He is a rewarder of those who diligently seek Him."

This faith is also very practical in our associations with other people. It is the touchstone which keeps us from being deceived by just what we see and hear. The presence of this faith will demonstrate itself in our actions as well as our reactions to the circumstances in which we find ourselves.

While good works are not the basis of faith or of acceptance with God, they are certainly compatible with faith and are an essential demonstration of that faith. James certainly has much to say about everyday living.

Direction for today: There are many spiritual benefits from facing persecutions.

Prayer for today: "Lord, I bring my brothers and sisters who are in persecution to You. Work Your will in their situation."

August 29: Read James 3-5

Key verse: "Confess your faults one to another, and pray one for another, that ye may be healed. The effectual fervent prayer of a righteous man availeth much" (James 5:16 KJV).

The epistle of James is a very practical one. It deals with everyday problems and tells how to correct them.

Our key verse is in the context of a common experience: sickness. James looks at sickness from a viewpoint often overlooked. Medical science deals with illness from a physical aspect but James perceives that the emotional and spiritual realms can be involved as well.

Human relationships can play a key role in a person's overall well-being. Repentance to God and a proper relationship with other people can bring about a healing that medication cannot. The spiritual area is both vertical, toward God, and horizontal, toward our fellow men.

Direction for today: Pray for one another, that you may be healed.

Prayer for today: "Father, I bring a member of the family of faith to You, one who needs Your healing touch."

Jeremiah

Jeremiah lived and ministered to the kingdom of Judah 70 years after the time of Isaiah. Isaiah had lived in the political instability of the kingdom of Judah, and had watched the northern kingdom of Israel fall and be carried into exile. Jeremiah had an even harder task – he was anointed prophet by God to live and preach in the kingdom of Judah even as that very nation was attacked, defeated and carried into exile by the Babylonians.

His was a demanding and depressing role: he spoke for the Lord to people who did not want to hear the word of the Lord. He gave advice which, if followed, would have saved the kingdom . . . but even as he prophesied, he knew the leaders of Judah and the remaining people of God would not listen.

He was imprisoned and tortured for his stand for the Lord, and was finally carried into Egypt by the very people he had warned not to turn to Egypt for help. Yet he continued to stand and call God's people back to the Lord – a call which was ignored by his hearers, but which the Lord God can use even today to restore His people to Himself.

The Israelites did not listen; but as we read Jeremiah together, let us determine in our hearts to hear the word of the Lord through His prophet.

August 30: Read Jeremiah 1, 2

Key verse: *"I will pronounce My judgments on My people, because of their wickedness in forsaking Me, in burning incense to other gods and in worshipping what their hands have made" (Jeremiah 1:16 NIV).*

When many of us think about breaking the Ten Commandments, we think immediately about stealing, adultery and murder, and we have a tendency to pat ourselves on the back if our consciences are clear on these matters. However, let's remember that there are sins against God as well as sins against our fellow-men; and many of us who have kept the last five commandments have disobeyed one or more of the first five.

Jeremiah saw that Israel's troubles stemmed from transgression of the first three commandments, which warned against idolatry. Like other prophets, he called it spiritual adultery, because the worship of false gods involved unfaithfulness to the Lord.

Few today are in danger of bowing down before idols of wood or stone; but there are many who look to science or government or economic reform or to some other human endeavour for solutions to problems, whether on the world level or the personal level. Sometimes we rely on another human being, sometimes on our own intelligence. May God deliver us from all these idolatries and move us to look to Him only for help.

Direction for today: If there are any idols of any kind in your life, destroy them.

Prayer for today: "Father, reveal to me any sin of idolatry in my life. I will immediately repent and turn from such sin."

Memory Verse

"I in them, and You in Me; that they may be made perfect in one, and that the world may know that You have sent Me, and have loved them as You have loved Me." John 17:23 NKJV

August 31: Read Jeremiah 3, 4

Key verse: *"Return, O backsliding children,' says the Lord, 'for I am married to you' " (Jeremiah 3:14a NKJV).*

This verse reminds us of the wonderful intimacy of our relationship with God through Jesus Christ. We who are Christians are referred to as children of God, and as His bride.

As children, we are dependent upon God our Father. He is our supplier of all needs. Jesus promised that if we seek the kingdom of God above all else, everything we need will be supplied to us. Our Father is our protector, our teacher, our leader.

As the bride of Christ, we are in a close love relationship with Jesus our Saviour. Over and over again, throughout scripture, believers are referred to as the bride of God. There is no more loving, close, intimate relationship than that between a loving husband and a loving wife. They share every aspect of life together; so, too, are we to share our lives with Jesus.

But Jeremiah speaks forth a warning: the bride's love has grown cold; the children are backslidden. But because of God's mercy, the word is not that they are cut off, but that they are to "return".

Have you ever loved Jesus more than you do today? Have you ever been more dependent on God than you are right now? If so, you have slid back, away from your closest love. To you, too, God says, "Return".

Direction for today: Repentance must be wholehearted.

Prayer for today: "Lord, may my love for You, as child and bride, grow ever stronger."

9

Jesus

To my Saviour, Lord and King,
Let all creation praises bring.
Cornerstone and great High Priest
Loves all, from greatest to the least.

Living Word and Bread of Life
Came to settle all our strife.
The Door, the Life, the Truth, the Way
Will guide us in our walk each day.

The Good Shepherd who loves His sheep
Us safely in His arms will keep.
The Broken Bread, the Cup of Wine
So we can at His table dine.

Living Water, Bread from Heaven
To us Himself has freely given.
Son of God, born Son of Man,
Came to earth to fulfil God's plan.

By His stripes we can be healed
He with His death our freedom sealed,
Jesus of Nazareth, King of the Jews.
Will you Him now as **your** *Saviour choose?*

– Karin Bouma

September 1: Read Jeremiah 5, 6

Key verse: "To whom can I speak and give warning? Who will listen to me? Their ears are closed so they cannot hear. The word of the Lord is offensive to them; they find no pleasure in it" (Jeremiah 6:10 NIV).

Very few people hear what God has to say to them. And the communication breakdown is never at God's end of the line!

This is certainly true of unbelievers who live in North America – many of them have indeed heard the word of the Lord many times, and have closed their ears to it. But that doesn't mean that believers have a right to stop telling them the word of the Lord, because it may be that they will repent of their hardness, turn to the Lord and be saved.

But, shockingly, there are also Christians who are hardened to the voice of God. It may be that the Lord has spoken to them for years about a particular sin, and they have refused to obey. Eventually, they don't hear God at all. Or it may be that the Lord has spoken to them about a ministry or a gift which He has for them, and they refuse to receive it. Again, their ears have become stopped up.

A child can get into terrible trouble by refusing to listen to a parent. So, too, a child of God is headed for catastrophe if he or she no longer hears the Lord.

If you have rejected a message from the Lord sometime in the past, repent, receive the word of God, obey it, and re-open those channels of communication with Him.

Direction for today: Listen to the Lord; if you have blocked up the channel for communication, repent and restore communion.

Prayer for today: "Father, I long to hear from You. If I have sinned to prevent that from happening, I repent, and ask You to forgive me.

September 2: Read Jeremiah 7, 8

Key verse: "Obey My voice, and I will be your God and you will be My people; and you will walk in all the way which I command you, that it may be well with you" (Jeremiah 7:23 NAS).

Chapter seven begins what is known as Jeremiah's "Temple Sermon".

God told His prophet to deliver this message at the gate of the temple of the throng of entering "worshippers". Although the Israelites were outwardly devout, as frequenters of the house of God, yet Jeremiah was charged to tell them that their hearts were in rebellion against the Lord and His Word.

Mere external religious practices, such as temple attendance, would never satisfy God. Nor would these protect the people from His judgment against secret sin. What God sought was, not the outward (hypocritical) observances of an inward rebel, but the pure inner heart of the man whose spirit was committed to God's honour and glory. Such a person's outward life would naturally correspond to this inner spring of motivation.

Oh, for such a heart towards God! How David sought this, with bitter tears, after his terrible lapse with Bath-sheba. "Cast me not away from Thy presence," he cried. "Take not Thy Holy Spirit from me. Create in me a clean heart, O God. . ." (Psalm 51:11, 12).

Which of us has not had to pray, with David, such a prayer? We'd be wise to pray it daily.For that's the prayer that God delights to answer by 'sending forth the Spirit of His Son into our hearts, crying, "Abba, Father" (Galatians 4:6).Bless His Holy Name!

Direction for today: Be sure your worship comes from the heart.

Prayer for today: "Father, give me a clean heart to worship You."

September 3: Read Jeremiah 9, 10

Key verse: "Oh that My head were waters, and My eyes a fountain of tears that I might weep day and night for the slain of the daughter of my people!" (Jeremiah 9:1 NKJV).

Our Lord weeps over the rejection and unbelief of His own people: "O Jerusalem, Jerusalem, the one who kills the prophets and stones those who are sent to her! How often I wanted to gather your children together, as a hen gathers her brood under her wings, but you were not willing!" (Luke 13:34 NKJV). Jesus was deeply saddened by the rejection He suffered at the hands of His own people in Israel. But where He might have lashed out in anger, He wept instead.

Jeremiah, "the weeping prophet", knew something of the same sorrow, as the Holy Spirit implanted the sorrow of God in his heart. The prophet sensed at least a measure of the compassion of God, and the sorrow our Lord feels when people turn away from Him.

God is just; He will punish sin, and He will not tolerate iniquity. But His mercy is as great as His justice, and He has already carried our punishment as He died on the cross. There, justice and mercy meet.

Yet many still turn from the Lord. His sorrow continues, His compassion is still as strong, and His mercy is yet available. If you have caused our Lord to weep over your sin and rejection, turn to Him today. If you are right with God, through Jesus, ask Him to give you a heart of compassion, that you may intercede for those who still rebel.

Direction for today: Remember: your Father weeps over your sin and rebellion.

Prayer for today: "Lord, give me a contrite heart that will respond to Your still, small voice."

September 4: Read Jeremiah 11-13

Key verse: "But if they will not obey, I will utterly pluck up and destroy that nation, saith the Lord." (Jeremiah 12:17 KJV).

How often do we read very similar statements made by God, through His chosen messengers, to His chosen people? God's laws were written, and disobeyed. God made covenants with man, and man was the felon. Now, in this day of grace, He has written His law in our hearts, and still the flesh, in its weakness, breaks God's laws.

Jeremiah cried out his heart for Israel to listen, and to obey – but their hardened hearts chose their own way – a way of destruction.

Jesus repeated the same principle to His disciples when He said, "If you love Me, you'll keep My commandments."

There is simply no cure for the disobedience of man. Even the apostle Paul found himself doing in the flesh what he would prefer, by his spiritual perceptions, not to do.

Thus it appears that the only answer for disobedience is "forgiveness", by God's grace!

Direction for today: God's grace not only forgives, but enables us to obey from the heart.

Prayer for today: "Lord, I am willing to obey You in all things."

September 5: Read Jeremiah 14, 15

Key verse: *"The Lord said, Verily it shall be well with thine remnant . . ." (Jeremiah 15:11 KJV).*

What a comforting word to receive from the Lord, especially in such a time of trouble. Jeremiah had been faithful before the Lord and was now deeply concerned. A famine encompassed the nation, drying the earth and bringing destruction (see chapter 14:1-7).

When all around us it seems like our world is caving in, though we are doing our best to serve the Lord, what do we do? Jeremiah sought and listened to God. Although the false prophets were prophesying lies that itching ears wanted to hear, the true prophet came humbly before God.

God heard Jeremiah and knew his works and his heart. "It shall be well with thine remnant," He promised. "I will deliver thee out of the hand of the wicked, and I will redeem thee out of the hand of the terrible" (Jeremiah 15:21 KJV).

Because of Jesus Christ, we can look forward, despite troubled times, to a great promise of God ". . . Blessed be the God and Father of our Lord Jesus Christ, which according to His abundant mercy hath begotten us again unto a lively hope, by the resurrection of Jesus Christ from the dead" (I Peter 1:3 KJV).

Direction for today: "My God shall supply all your needs according to His riches in glory by Christ Jesus" (Philippians 4:19 KJV).

Prayer for today: "Father, I pray for my family. Bring them all safely into Your heavenly kingdom."

September 6: Read Jeremiah 16, 17

Key verse: *"The heart is deceitful above all things, and desperately wicked; who can know it?" (Jeremiah 17:9 KJV).*

This is an extremely well-known verse. It contains a very important truth: the fact that we cannot trust our own hearts to lead us into righteousness, for sin has invaded the very core of our being, and we are sinners!

But as this verse stands alone, it contains no hope. The heart is deceitful, wicked, and no one understands it. We cannot trust ourselves, we cannot trust our friends and neighbours, and we can only be sure of falling into evil.

We need to continue reading. The next verse gives us the answer: "I, the Lord, search the heart." As always, when the answer is not in us, we find it in the Lord. He, and He alone, knows our heart. That is why He can call us to repentance, and why only He can cleanse our hearts.

Direction for today: While you cannot trust your own inner motivations, you can trust God to know you, inside and out.

Prayer for today: "Thank You, Father, that You know my heart.Show me areas where I need to repent, and I will do so."

Memory Verse

"Believe on the Lord Jesus Christ, and you will be saved, you and your household." Acts 16:31 NKJV

September 7: Read Jeremiah 18, 19

Key verse: *"Return now every one from his evil way, and make your ways and your doings good" (Jeremiah 18:11b NKJV).*

Too many Christians have a faith that makes absolutely no difference in their lives. Like the people of Jeremiah's day, they confess faith in God, but continue in evil practices and wicked lives.

The word of Jeremiah is a word for the church today. Turn from evil, and do good. The message of James, I John, and many other books of the New Testament is: a faith that is talked about but not lived out is useless, empty and ultimately fatal.

No one can "do good" on his or her own. Our hearts, according to this same prophet, are deceitful and desperately wicked. But when the Holy Spirit comes to reside in our lives, He transforms us into new creations, people who are indeed capable of doing good, as God works through us. We have no excuse for following evil.

Direction for today: Turn from evil, to good!

Prayer for today: "Father, Your will be done."

September 8: Read Jeremiah 20, 21

Key verse: *"Then I said, I will not make mention of Him, nor speak any more of His name. But His word was in mine heart as a burning fire shut up in my bones, and I was weary with forbearing, and I could not stay" (Jeremiah 20:9 KJV).*

The house of Israel had become very prosperous, a blessing of God, which was given to them by God because God loves to bless His people. In the middle of their prosperity however, they turned their hearts away from God toward idoltary, the worst types of sin and the oppression of the poor. They were, in fact, filled with greed; God, therefore, had to judge them because God hates sin.

Before God sends judgment, He sends a prophet to warn people of their need for repentance and His need to judge them. Because God does not *want* to punish people, He would rather that they repent and turn from their sins.

When Jeremiah brought the message of judgment to the people of Israel, they had become so accustomed to rejecting messages from God that they rejected Jeremiah also. They in fact threw him into prison. Discouraged and feeling "what is the use?," he decided not to say any more. God allowed Jeremiah to feel the things that He feels and to see the things that He was seeing.

As he watched the sin and heard the things the people were saying, the message from God burned within Jeremiah's bones until he could no longer keep it within him and he had to speak it out again. God wanted to warn the people through him and give them a chance to repent. This cost Jeremiah a great deal of hardship and suffering but God suffered with him. God's suffering however, was far greater, as His heart was broken because of His concern for His people.

When we speak God's message to the people around us, some may receive it but some may react with anger. Yet the message must be presented. I believe it was because of Jeremiah's persistent message of God's judgment that Daniel, Shadrach, Meshach and Abednego repented. It was worth Jeremiah's persistence to see these four men used by God in later years.

Direction for today: When God speaks to us about our sins and His judgment, it is good for us to listen even though we may not want to hear it.

Prayer for today: "Lord, by Your Spirit, cause Your word to burn in me, too, that I may eagerly share it with unbelievers."

September 9: Read Jeremiah 22

Key verse: *"I spake unto thee in thy prosperity; but thou saidst, I will not hear" (Jeremiah 22:21a KJV).*

The northern ten tribes of Israel had been taken into captivity a number of years before the events of this chapter. God, in His mercy, sent the prophet Jeremiah to warn Jehoiakim, King of Judah, of impending defeat and captivity at the hand of Nebuchadnezzar, King of Babylon, unless the lifestyle of his people changed quickly and dramatically.

The history of Israel during the previous several hundred years indicated that their relationship to God resembled a roller coaster. Sometimes they were obedient and worshipped Jehovah, but often they worshipped other gods. Under the leadership of Josiah, God was honoured. However, when his son Jehoiakim ascended the throne, he led the people into selfishness, and idolatry. The poor, widows and orphans were oppressed. It was to this king that God sent Jeremiah to deliver the stern warning, "Reform or be taken into captivity from which you will never return" (verses 10, 27).

Is God warning the nations of North America today? Truly, He has prospered us. But have we honoured and worshipped Him? It seems that so many ways we have strayed so far from the principles upon which our great nations were established.

We praise God for the modern outpouring of His Spirit and the thousands who have in recent years come into His kingdom. Let us continue to pray for revival and reformation across North America such as swept England under Whitfield and Wesley.

Direction for today: Do not let prosperity get in the way of your relationship with God.

Prayer for today: "Lord, if there are any material things ahead of You in my life, show me, and I will get rid of them."

September 10: Read Jeremiah 23

Key verse: "They keep saying to those who despise Me, 'The Lord has said, "You will have peace" '; and as for everyone who walks in the stubbornness of his own heart, they say 'Calamity will not come upon you' " (Jeremiah 23:17 NAS).

After having promised to send the Messiah, God Himself goes on to denounce false prophets. Our key verse is part of this denouncing, which starts in verse 9 and continues for 32 verses to the end of chapter. He makes us know how displeased He is by those who speak easy things rather than truth. In verse 16, He cautions, "Do not listen to the words of the prophets. They are leading you into futility".

There are many false prophets around today. They are not only found in the cults but even in some Christian churches. They preach that God is a loving God, therefore He would never let anyone go to hell; that if people are charitable and help the poor . . . theirs is the kingdom of heaven. They offer false hope rather than preaching the truth of God's Word. In verse 21, God says, "I did not send these prophets, but they ran. I did not speak to them, but they prophesied".

It is very clear that God is angered by false prophets. Let us be sure to check out the scriptures to ensure that all that we are told is according to His Word.

Direction for today: Be aware that there is much false teaching in the world today.

Prayer for today: "Father, help me to know Your truth and to discern error."

September 11: Read Jeremiah 24, 25

Key verse: " 'You have not listened to Me', declares the Lord, 'in order that you might provoke Me to anger with the work of your hands to your own harm' " (Jeremiah 25:7 NAS).

The prophet Jeremiah makes good use of images to convey his messages – note his use of good and bad figs in Chapter 24. The good figs, *very* good (24:3), stand for the exiles; the evil, *very* evil, too bad to be eaten, symbolize Jerusalem. The exiles are to be restored (24:4-7); the homefolk to be destroyed (8-10). The exiles are to be wholly reborn of heart and are to become God's people.

Jeremiah rightly understood that God used the Babylonians to bring judgment against Judah and the nations. Not only is judgment to come through Babylon, but judgment will come also upon Babylon. The wine cup (25:15-22) is the symbol of God's inescapable wrath to be poured over Judah and other nations.

Note that the fury of the Lord *begins* with Jerusalem and extends to other nations which also deserve correction.

Direction for today: We face many choices; choosing wrongly can become habitual. The only safe way is always to seek the Lord's help in choosing correctly.

Prayer for today: "Father, have mercy on our land, and spare it that our people may yet turn to You."

September 12: Read Jeremiah 26-28

Key verse: "Now it came to pass when Jeremiah had made an end of speaking all that the Lord had commanded him to speak unto all the people, that the priests and the prophets and all the people took him saying, thou shalt surely die" (Jeremiah 26:8 KJV).

Jeremiah was well aware of the price he might have to pay in speaking what God commanded him to speak. But still his love for God was greater than his desire to be accepted.

In today's society, the influence of commercials has told us that we must conform to the world's ideals. But God tells us that when we become His children we are no longer the world's (John 17:17, Romans 12:2).

When we say we have given our hearts to Jesus, then we must realize that Jesus will want to change our hearts, and give our lives new directions. There may be times when He will want to use us in areas that are unpleasant. Those are the times that He sees how committed we truly are.

God is looking for a people who will speak His words, whether they be encouraging or chastising. He is looking for those who will show their love by being obedient, no matter what the cost.

Direction for today: Do I show the Lord my love by being obedient to His commands in my life?

Prayer for today: "Help me, Lord, to obey You, whatever the personal cost."

September 13: Read Jeremiah 29, 30

Key verse: "And ye shall seek Me, and find Me, when ye shall search for Me with all your heart" (Jeremiah 29:13 KJV).

The Lord is speaking to the Israelites who are presently in Babylonian captivity. He has just promised them freedom to return to their own land. Immediately He points out to them the fact that when they call on Him in prayer, He will listen to them. Then He qualifies this statement by pointing out the need of placing themselves totally at His disposal in order to receive the full benefits of their relationship with Him.

The same is so true today with our relationship to God, in Jesus Christ. God has promised us freedom from sin. That is a promise to everyone who will invite Jesus Christ into his life. Not only does He promise freedom from sin, He promises that when we come to Him and give ourselves totally to Him as Saviour and Lord, when we seek Him with our whole hearts, we will find Him. In other words, He will reveal Himself to us, and we will know His direction and leading without a shadow of doubt.

It is important that we learn to daily surrender totally to Him, and seek Him with all our heart. God desires people who want Him first in their lives, over everything and everyone else. That can only happen when we seek Him, search out His ways and daily dedicate our lives to Him.

Direction for today: It is not enough to only begin to serve God; there must be a daily surrender to Him.

Prayer for today: "Help me to search for You with all my heart."

Memory Verse

"For the wages of sin is death, but the gift of God is eternal life in Christ Jesus our Lord." Romans 6:23 NKJV

September 14: Read Jeremiah 31

*Key verse: "For everyone shall die for his own sins . . ."
(Jeremiah 31:30 NIV).*

This message from the Lord is a warning of what lies ahead for His people. Up until this time the Israelites had been like dependent children, needing constant care. They wanted to follow the way of the Lord but relied heavily on the opinions of others to guide them.

But soon it would be different. Each person would be accountable only to God. They would have the opportunity of knowing Him personally and He would forgive and forget their sins.

It is basically the same as changing from a carefree child to a responsible adult. Although children should be encouraged to make decisions, the parents are ultimately responsible for their actions. When little Johnny breaks Mrs. Watson's window, Dad and Mom have to take care of the replacement cost. But, when Johnny is old enough to drive a car he must pay his own tickets and assume full responsibility for mistakes.

Many adults would still like someone to make all their decisions as well as accept responsibilities. But God says there is a day of reckoning, when all will be responsible for their own lives.

Man's natural inclination is to do wrong (Jeremiah 17:1). However, God has allowed us to change this by inviting Jesus, His Son, to come into our lives. Then He will forgive and forget our sins and give us the desire to "honour Him" (Jeremiah 31:33).

Direction for today: You are responsible for every sin that is not confessed and covered by the blood of Jesus.

Prayer for today: "Lord, reveal to me any sins that may be hidden in my past, that I may confess them, repent, and be completely clean."

September 15: Read Jeremiah 32

Key verse: "Behold, I am the Lord, the God of all flesh; is anything too hard for Me?" (Jeremiah 32:27 RSV).

From a human point of view, this is an incredible question to try to answer.

First of all, Jerusalem had come under judgment because of the people's idolatry (32: 22-29) and disregard of God's law (verse 33). They would be taken in to captivity. Those of us who disregard God's law and gospel will also expose ourselves to His judgment.

Secondly, there was a promise of restoration. True to His name, God would gather His people back from their captivity and bring them again to their homeland (32:37-38). But, more than that, He would give them a heart to fear Him (32:39) and make an "everlasting covenant" with them to do them good (32:40-41). And, of course, because Jesus came and established that "everlasting covenant", we can have the promise of Eternal Life when we turn to Him. "If we confess our sins, He is faithful and just, and will forgive our sins and cleanse us from all unrighteousness" (1 John 1:9 RSV).

Try it and see that nothing is too hard for our God . . . not even the restoration of our lives.

Direction for today: Nothing is too hard for the Lord!

Prayer for today: "Praise, You, Lord, that You are the God of the impossible!"

September 16: Read Jeremiah 33, 34

Key verse: *"Behold the days are coming, says the Lord, when I will fulfill the promises I made to the house of Israel and the house of Judah" (Jeremiah 33:14 RSV).*

And we can receive the promise of peace and joy for our day too, for this is the living Word of God. We groan in our time under the heavy burden of inflation and economic uncertainty, breeding insecurity in our future as a people of God. "Iniquity, like the wind, carries us away." (Isaiah 64:6). Famine, earthquake and threats of war surround us. But our hope remains in the joy of the Lord, forever. This is His promise.

As we remain steadfast in a disposition of contriteness and repentance for our failure and wanton sinfulness ". . . there shall be heard again the voice of mirth . . . and of gladness, . . . of the bridegroom . . . and of the bride, the voices of those who sing" (Jeremiah 33:11).

God promises that the branch of righteousness will grow up into David, assuring us that he ". . . shall never want for a man to sit upon the throne of Israel" (Jeremiah 33:17). And, from the branch of righteousness in the line of David, we have One who forever sits upon the throne of Israel: Jesus, Lord of Lords and King of Kings; Jesus, the Alpha and the Omega; Jesus, the Eternal High Priest!

One major trumpet sounding through the airwaves, bouncing to the satellites, bearing the Good News to the captives, to the afflicted and to the uninformed, is the daily sixty minutes of prayer, testimony and praise through television at 100 Huntley Street.

The rallying call has sounded. Let us all increase our support for His ministry which He has raised up in our time. Prayerfully, of course, but financially as well.

Direction for today: God always keeps His promises.

Prayer for today: "Father, pour out Your Spirit on me!"

September 17: Read Jeremiah 35, 36

Key verse: *"This is what the Lord Almighty, the God of Israel, says: 'Go and tell the men of Judah and the people of Jerusalem, "Will you not learn a lesson and obey My words?" ' declares the Lord" (Jeremiah 35:13 NIV).*

God, in His love and mercy, has given us His Word so that we can avoid the pitfalls and many disasters of life. He even tells us that if we will obey His Word we will live forever.

God shows us, in our reading today, an amazing thing. Some people are willing to obey and order their lives by the words and commandments given by men. Whereas these, if kept, will help them in life, such people often completely disregard the requirements of God.

God has given us His Word to guide us, not only through this life but to Eternal Life as well.

God says in His Word that, "He so loved this world that He gave His only begotten Son, that whoever believes in Him should not perish but have everlasting life" (John 3:16). Even in these chapters of Jeremiah, we see that God was reluctant to bring judgment. For this reason, He sent His Word to give them an opportunity to repent and receive life and blessings from Him.

Direction for today: Since God knows our tomorrows, let us trust Him and His word, today.

Prayer for today: "Lord, I am willing to learn from You."

September 18: Read Jeremiah 37, 38

Key verse: "Neither he nor his attendants nor the people of the land paid any attention to the words the Lord had spoken through Jeremiah the prophet" (Jeremiah 37:2 NIV).

Jeremiah was able to read the "signs of the times". He could see that the two super-powers of his generation, Egypt and Babylon, were on a collision course; that Judah was in the middle and that, even from a human point of view, war and destruction were highly likely.

But Jeremiah also knew the history of his people and the ways of God. He could see that the coming troubles were brought about through Jewish idolatry, greed and violence, and that God would use Babylon to chastise Judah, just as he had used Assyria to chastise Israel.

For many years Jeremiah had tried to help his people see the situation as he saw it: from God's point of view. But no one listened; no one repented. What God said to Ezekiel came true for Jeremiah also: ". . . they hear your words but do not put them into practice" (Ezekiel 33:32).

Direction for today: We cannot call the Lord, "Lord", and ignore His directions to us.

Prayer for today: "Father, when people reject You, may I not be angry or scornful, but sorrowful unto intercession and prayer."

September 19: Read Jeremiah 39, 41

Key verse: "'For I will surely deliver you, and you shall not fall by the sword; but your life shall be as a prize for you, because you have put your trust in Me,' says the Lord" (Jeremiah 39:18 NKJV).

When we read this verse with the eternal perspective granted to us by the Holy Spirit, it will help us to re-orient our priorities. Here, God promises deliverance for His people, and He tells them that their lives will be spared.

In this passage, the Lord does not go beyond that promise. He seems to feel that a promise of deliverance and life, is enough.

In our day, too many Christians try to add to that by seeking after many material possessions, prestige or a place of importance. But the Lord knows that those temporal things are of no importance at all.

God's promise to every believer is that He will deliver us from the bondage of sin, the bonds of death and the hold of hell. He promises us life, life beyond anything we know on earth – eternal life in heaven, lived in the presence of the Father, the Son and the Holy Spirit!

Think about this, and then ask yourself: "What more could anyone possibly want?"

Direction for today: God has promised deliverance, and life!

Prayer for today: "Father, thank You for Your wonderful gifts of deliverance and eternal life. Thank You that I will spend eternity with You!"

September 20: Read Jeremiah 42-44

Key verse: "So Johanan the son of Kareah and all the commanders of the forces, and all the people, did not obey the voice of the Lord, so as to stay in the land of Judah" (Jeremiah 43:4 NAS).

We read of the terrible folly of the people of Israel, and we are appalled that God's people could so deliberately and so foolishly ignore the direct command of the Lord. God, speaking through Jeremiah, had promised the people that if they would trust Him and remain in the land of Israel despite the apparent military threats, He 'would build them up and not tear them down, plant them and not uproot them' (Jeremiah 42:10). But God had also warned the people that if they put their trust in the military might of Egypt instead of in Him, they were doomed to defeat and destruction (41:16).

Yet the people ignored the word of the Lord, turned their backs on His promises and fled to Egypt, forcing even the faithful Jeremiah to accompany them. And destruction came upon them, even as God had promised.

We are suprised that the people of God could be so deliberately disobedient when they had been warned of the dreadful consequences. Yet if we reflect on our own lives, we may see the same pattern. God has shown us His will (see for example, I Thessalonians 5:15-22; Ephesians 5:17-21). We know His will; we know that He demands our obedient love. Yet often we turn and go our own way.

Direction for today: To obey is better than sacrifice.

Prayer for today: "Lord, today I will go *Your* way."

Memory Verse

"Or do you not know that your body is the temple of the Holy Spirit who is in you, whom you have from God, and you are not your own? For you were bought at a price; therefore glorify God in your body and in your spirit, which are God's." I Corinthians 6:19,20 NKJV

September 21: Read Jeremiah 45-47

Key verse: *"But fear not thou, O my servant Jacob, and be not dismayed, O Israel: for, behold, I will save thee from afar off, and thy seed from the land of their captivity . . ." (Jeremiah 46:27 KJV).*

As we read of the conquest of Egypt and the destruction of the Philistines, the love of God stands out in His promise to those who serve Him. His servant Jacob was no exception and was recipient of great comfort. God promised to "save him from afar off" and gave the assurance that his whole family would be brought out from their land of captivity.

This is also what God promises us today. When He sent us Jesus Christ, the promise was Eternal Life to all who believe. But not only that, we are also assured that there is salvation and deliverance for the whole family.

As I write, I sense the Lord wants to give a special hope for loved ones who are captive to certain of Satan's traps. Believe now in Christ's delivering power. Expect Him to touch your family members!

Direction for today: "Believe on the Lord Jesus Christ, and thou shalt be saved, and thy house" (Acts 16:31 KJV).

Prayer for today: "Lord, save and protect my family."

September 22: Read Jeremiah 48

Key verse: "The fall of Moab is at hand; her calamity will come quickly" (Jeremiah 48:16 NIV).

This chapter, like others in Jeremiah, is horrible to read. It contains such graphic descriptions of suffering, of destruction, of the outcome of rebellion and disobedience against God.

But perhaps we should read such descriptions frequently. For this is only a temporal judgment; the horrors of hell far surpass these earthly sufferings which would befall this nation who stood as enemy to God and God's people.

Read the passage again, this time realizing that people who choose hell over heaven will face far worse than this. Allow the Holy Spirit to use it to bring a holy and fearful compassion to your heart, so that you will eagerly share the gospel with the lost, saving them from a fate that is truly worse than death.

Direction for today: Think about the reality of hell.

Prayer for today: "Lord, may I always remember that those who do not know Jesus are headed for an eternity of suffering."

September 23: Read Jeremiah 49

Key verse: "Behold, He shall come up and fly like the eagle, and spread His wings over Bozrah; the heart of the mighty men of Edom in that day shall be like the heart of a woman in birth pangs" (Jeremiah 49:22 NKJV).

To a young bird, a shadow cast by wings can mean two completely different things. One shadow, which those babies know well, means that mother or father is returning to the nest, bringing food and providing protection. But another shadow – which might look exactly the same to an untrained human eye – signals danger, the attack of a predator, and the chicks cower in fear.

Throughout the Bible, the image of "the wings of God" frequently appears. Here too, people react in two very different ways. For the Lord comes as Protector and Provider to those who are His; but He comes as Judge to those who reject Him.

In today's reading, the Lord's judgment is pronounced on several nations. Our key verse portrays the fear in the hearts of unbelievers as the shadow of His wings approaches.

The believer never need fear, in this way. Our fear of God is reverence, and awe, but never terror. Instead, we can seek the refuge, safety and joy that we find under the wings of our Lord (Psalms 17:8, 57:1, 63:7). We can depend on Jesus to carry us from danger, as He did the Israelites from Egypt: "I bore you on eagles' wings and brought you to Myself" (Exodus 19:4 NKJV). We can even come to Him for the healing that is in His wings (Malachi 4:2).

Direction for today: God comes in judgment upon those who reject Him, but in love to those who bear His name.

Prayer for today: "Thank You, Father, for the refuge in Your wings."

September 24: Read Jeremiah 50

Key verse: "Behold I am against thee, O thou most proud, saith the Lord God of hosts: for thy day is come, the time that I will visit thee" (Jeremiah 50:31 KJV).

These are some of the most awesome words that could be spoken. To have the Lord God as an adversary is to be doomed to eternal loss. This message was to the exalted Babylonian empire, but it is just as applicable to an individual today.

Proverbs 16:18 says, "pride goeth before destruction and an haughty spirit before a fall." God's Word has many other things to say about the sin of pride. It traces this malady to its original source: Lucifer, the archangel who lifted himself up against God.

To follow in the path of pride is to be found in the wrong camp. The way that meets with God's approval is very beautifully outlined in the words of Philippians 2:5-11. Jesus Christ is not only the Saviour but also the divine pattern for a life approved by a holy God.

Pride was a cancer that brought God's judgment upon the Babylonian empire. Do not let it destroy your life. Let Jesus Christ become your refuge and security.

Direction for today: Give pride no place in your heart.

Prayer for today: "Lord, I boast only in Jesus."

September 25: Read Jeremiah 51

Key verse: "My people, go ye out of the midst of her and deliver ye every man his soul from the fierce anger of the Lord" (Jeremiah 51:45 KJV).

The Lord has used godless Babylon to bring judgment upon His people Israel. Babylon had conquered and taken into captivity many of the people of the ten northern tribes. However, in this chapter we see that God, through His prophet Jeremiah, pronounces judgment upon Babylon. Two reasons are given; her refusal to be reformed (verse 9) and her extraordinary cruelty towards Israel (verses 34, 35).

While God used Babylon to punish Israel, He commanded the exiles to be a witness to the Babylonians (Jeremiah 10:11). However, when the Babylonians refused to listen and turn from their idols, the judgment of God was pronounced upon them. This would also provide release for the Israelite captives.

So we see that God used this wicked nation to punish His own people and at the same time give the Babylonians an opportunity to repent. Only when they would not was His judgment pronounced. How merciful our God is!

We live in a world that is being given yet another chance to repent. As Christians, we are to proclaim the message of the one true God and the foolishness of worshipping any other. Those who listen and repent will be saved; those who insist on rejecting the true God and worshipping their idols of wealth, popularity, pleasure, etc., will receive the judgment of God as surely as the Babylonians did.

Direction for today: We are called to be witnesses to our nation.

Prayer for today: "Lord, open the eyes of millions in our world, that they may see the glorious gospel of Jesus Christ, repent and be adopted into Your family."

September 26: Read Jeremiah 52

Key verse: *"So Jehoiachin changed his prison clothes, and had his meals in the king's presence regularly all the days of his life" (Jeremiah 52:33 NAS).*

In II Kings 24:6-15 we read of Jehoiachin coming to the throne at the age of 18 and being captured and taken away to Babylon by Nebuchadnezzar eight years later. Now, after thirty-seven years of exile, Jehoiachin, king of Judah, was released from captivity.

Can you imagine how he must have felt? For thirty-seven of his sixty-two years he had been a disgraced exile. Now the new king of Babylon, Evil-merodach (he doesn't sound very evil, does he?) shows him mercy and kindness; raises him up to a position of honour and takes care of him for the rest of his life.

And this is what Jesus does for us. He brings us out of captivity, breaking asunder the chains of sin that bound us, and seats us in heavenly places with Himself. Oh, praise His wonderful name!

Direction for today: We are no longer slaves but free, through the shed blood of Jesus Christ.

Prayer for today: "Lord, I am Your willing servant. Please use me".

I and II Peter

I Peter is a "well-balanced epistle"; the apostle writes to Christians who are facing severe persecution, and outlines the sources of their needed strength: God the Father, God the Son, and God the Holy Spirit (1:2).

II Peter contains sharp warnings about the danger to the church brought by false prophets, and promises concerning the coming of the Lord.

September 27: I Peter 1, 2

Key verse: *"Like newborn babes, long for the pure milk of the Word, that by it you may grow in respect to salvation" (I Peter 2:2 NAS).*

The thrust of today's message is growth through the Word.

And we are instructed to "Be diligent . . . approved to God as a workman who does not need to be ashamed handling accurately the Word of truth (I Timothy 2:15). How vital it is for us not only to feed daily on the pure milk of the Word, but also to receive sound doctrine, not desiring to "have our ears tickled" in accordance to our own desires.

Coupled with sound teaching and solid direction, we are urged to receive the Word simply and honestly as "the seed in the good ground: these are the ones who have heard the Word in an honest and good heart and hold it fast, and bear fruit with perseverance" (Luke 8:15).

We are persuaded to be alert and aware of the Power of the Word within us for, "Greater is He who is within you than he who is in the world" (I John 4:4). These are difficult days in which we live, and they could be frightening days. But we who are in Christ should have no fear, for we live and experience the righteousness and victory of Calvary.

Direction for today: A successful Christian life can only be lived by consistently feeding on the manna of the word.

Prayer for today: "Lord, give me an increasing love for Your word."

Memory Verse

"So let each one give as he purposes in his heart, not grudgingly or of necessity; for God loves a cheerful giver." 2 Corinthians 9:7 NKJV

September 28: Read I Peter 3-5

Key verse: *"Casting all your care upon Him for He careth for you" (I Peter 5:7 KJV).*

Our reading today instructs us in human relationships at home as well as with others. It is said the true test of one's Christian character is revealed in the home. We are to be at one, loving and humble. And, if suffering comes, let it be undeserved; let it be for doing good and not evil.

We may feel this is a high standard, but Jesus Himself set the example and will enable us by the Holy Spirit to follow in His footsteps.

Christian character, a meek and quiet spirit, is, in God's sight, of great price. We are reminded that prayer is hindered when the husband is overbearing and does not treat his wife with gentleness. Pastors are to feed the flock, willingly, not just for salary, not lording it over them, but being an example to them. All human relationships must be controlled by that divine love imparted to us by the Holy Spirit.

With this pattern of living, we can cast all our care (the things we cannot handle or control) upon God, because He cares for us. We can be confident that the devil can only roar at us. He cannot harm us. "Submit yourself to God, resist the devil, and he will flee from you" (James 4:7).

Direction for today: Do not waste precious time trying to solve problems you should simply give to Jesus!

Prayer for today: "Lord, help me to truly cast my cares on You, and leave them there!"

Lamentations

This book contains five poetically crafted elegies, or songs of mourning, which were probably written by the prophet Jeremiah (compare II Chronicles 35:35). The poems were written following the destruction of Jerusalem, which included the complete devastation of the magnificent temple constructed by Solomon, and the exile of the people by the conquering Babylonians.

The first four chapters are each acrostic poems, in which each section begins with a succeeding letter of the Hebrew alphabet. This is a distinctive feature of much Hebrew poetry.

Each poem therefore has twenty-two stanzas (there being twenty-two letters in the Hebrew alphabet). The final poem, chapter five, is not alphabetical, but nonetheless contains the same number of stanzas.

This book has been described as "the death wail of Jerusalem", yet in the midst of destruction God's spokesman still finds reason to hope in the Lord: "The Lord's loving kindnesses indeed never cease, for His compassions never fail" (Lamentations 3:22).

September 29: Lamentations 1, 2

Key verse: *"My eyes fail because of tears,*
My spirit is greatly troubled;
My heart is poured out on the earth,

> *Because of the destruction of the daughter of my
> people,*
> *When little ones and infants faint*
> *In the streets of the city" (Lamentations 2:11 NAS).*

Not many of God's prophets lived to see the prophecies fulfilled in their own lifetime, as Jeremiah did. He prophesied that judgment was coming, God was going to bring the Babylonian army against Jerusalem and the destruction would be terrible. This message was very unpopular among the people and resulted in much persecution for Jeremiah.

The book of Lamentations displays, however, that Jeremiah was, in every sense of the word, a prophet who understood the heart of God. "Say unto them, As I live, saith the Lord God, I have no pleasure in the death of the wicked; but that the wicked turn from his way and live" (Ezekiel 33:11 KJV).

Jeremiah could have said, "It serves them right", but instead, in both chapters 1 and 2, he says that tears will not stop flowing from his eyes because of the suffering of the people of God. Although those who would be suffering were those who had at one time laughed at him, Jeremiah did not laugh at them, but besought God to lift the judgment, stop the suffering and show them mercy.

Can you hear the weeping in the voice of Jesus, as you read these words? "O Jerusalem, Jerusalem, thou that killest the prophets, and stonest them which are sent unto thee, how often would I have gathered thy children together, even as a hen gathereth her chickens under her wings, and ye would not!" (Matthew 23:27).

This was the same attitude which Jesus had towards his persecutors.

Direction for today: When warning people about coming judgment, do so with love and compassion.

Prayer for today: "Lord, give me genuine sorrow over the lost."

September 30: Read Lamentations 3-5

Key verse: "The Lord's lovingkindnesses indeed never cease,
For His compassions never fail.
They are new every morning;
Great is Thy faithfulness (Lamentations 3:22,23 NAS).

We are surprised to find this familiar praise in the desperate context of the sad book of Lamentations, "Great is Thy faithfulness".

Would it be more likely that the people of Israel, including the author of these poems, would turn against God, or accuse Him of injustice and a lack of compassion? They experienced sufferings at the hand of God unlike any the nation had faced before. Jeremiah himself, because of his loyalty to the Lord, had faced persecution at the hands of his own people, the very leaders who not long before sought advice from him.

But the lamenter does not shake a fist in the face of God. Instead, he realizes that in good or ill, in triumph or defeat, there is but one thing that does not change, but one rock in which to find refuge – the unchanging compassion and faithfulness of God.

This is our answer: no matter what our circumstances, the ultimate solution for our lives is found in dependence on the Lord. Any other refuge will fail.

It is because we know that God is the Lord, our faithful and just God, that we can trust Him.

Direction for today: God's faithfulness is truly great!

Prayer for today: "Lord, may I awake tomorrow morning praising You for your lovingkindness and faithfulness."

Expectations

How grateful we all can be that God does not have great expectations of us. . .

Expectations
> *of oneself usually turn out to be*

Limitations
> *that inevitably curb our*

Effectiveness,
> *leading most of us to*

Frustration,
> *a state that gives way to*

Discontent
> *with life, in general, and with oneself.*

Unbelief
> *is then able to creep in,*

Confidence
> *can fall to an all-time low,*

Insecurity
> *becomes commonplace and*

Defeat
> *has overcome again.*

That is why God simply loves us — for what and who we are . . . no strings attached. If only we could comprehend the overwhelming depth, completeness and cleansing power of His love, how far we could go. Truly the sky is the limit when there are. . .

No expectations,
> *giving us*

No limitations
> *on what we can do or be;*

Effectiveness
> *is at its height,*

Happiness
> *and*

Contentment
> *are ours,*

Confidence, security and belief return.

Victory
> *has become reality!*

– Nicola Burke

Ezekiel is perhaps the premier visionary prophet of the Old Testament. The book begins with the dramatic words: "While I was by the river Chebar among the exiles, the heavens were opened and I saw visions of God". That is a strong statement of call and of inspiration, and the book of Ezekiel lives up to these claims of prophetic vision.

Ezekiel ministered in the early years of the Babylonian exile: the days after the southern kingdom of Judah had been carried off by her Babylonian captors. At the same time, Jeremiah was ministering his sorrowful message as a few of the Hebrew leaders forcibly abducted him to Egypt.

Ezekiel was taken in the opposite direction, exiled to Babylon. He keenly felt his absence from Jerusalem, for he was of a priestly family and now could no longer carry on his life's work, as he lived far removed from the holy city whose temple lay in ruins.

Yet physical distance is no barrier for God; Ezekiel, although living in Babylon, was given divine visions of Jerusalem, and much of his prophecy concerns those visions.

The writings of Ezekiel are yet another example of the two-fold ministry of the prophet. Most of the opening chapters of the book are prophecies of doom: God's people will suffer because of their sin (chapters 1-24), as will foreign nations who oppose the Lord (25-32). Yet Ezekiel looks beyond the present despair to the new age of the Lord, when apparently dry bones will spring up to a new Spirit-filled life. The latter sections of Ezekiel's prophecy primarily deal with the age when God Himself will be the Good Shepherd of His sheep, and the nation will be restored as a faithful people of God.

Ezekiel and the book of Daniel are the two books of the Old Testament often linked with the Revelation of John as the keys to end times prophecy. Clearly, Ezekiel's visions span the entire vista of history, as he contrasts the Jerusalem of his day, lying in ruins, with the New Jerusalem, ruled by God Himself.

October 1: Read Ezekiel 1-3

Key verse: "Son of man, I have made you a watchman for the house of Israel; therefore hear a word from My mouth, and give them warning from Me" (Ezekiel 3:17 NKJV).

The watchman reported the news. If no enemies loomed on the horizon, he declared that all was well. But, if an enemy appeared, the watchman immediately sounded the warning, so that the defences of the city could be set in order.

God called His prophets to be watchmen. Over and over again, men like Ezekiel, Jeremiah, Elijah and Amos sounded the warning to the people. God said that if the people refused to listen, the responsibility for their downfall was their own; but if the prophet failed to sound the warning, every lost life was on his account!

God has called Christians to be watchmen. We know there is an enemy lurking near and so we must sound the alarm. We must warn people that Satan is luring people to their deaths, that their eternal lives are threatened. And we are to announce the good news of escape in Jesus Christ!

Watchman, are you asleep at your post?

Direction for today: You are called to be a watchman!

Prayer for today: "Lord, may I be faithful to Your calling."

October 2: Read Ezekiel 4-6

Key verse: "And they that escape of you shall remember Me among the nations, whether they shall be carried captives because I am broken with their whorish heart, which hath departed from Me, and with their eyes which go a whoring after their idols: and they shall loathe themselves for the evils which they have committed in all their abominations" (Ezekiel 6:9 KJV).

In the chapters read today, the justice of God is revealed. Because Israel had turned her back on God and allowed idolatry to become her way of worship, God would stand it no longer. His justice had to be poured out in judgment. The mountains of Israel, which had been holy mountains, were now turned into places of idol worship. I Corinthians 3:17 says, "If any man defile the temple of God, him shall God destroy".

Through Moses, God had in the past spoken to Israel. In Exodus 20:3,4, we read that God had given them His principles of worship, "Thou shalt have no other gods before Me. Thou shalt not make unto thee any graven image . . . for I the Lord Thy God am a jealous God".

The justice of God will bring judgment against unrighteousness and sin. However, He is also a God of mercy. In some way, God was going to allow a remnant to escape the judgment. There were those who would not be slain but would be scattered among other nations.

Is it not true that God sometimes allows pressures in our lives to make us aware of our sin and need of repentance? This is what was prophesied for this remnant: in the midst of other nations, they would remember God. Through God's grace their hearts would be touched, their attitudes changed and they would repent.

How would it be known that they had actually repented? Verse nine states, "They shall loathe themselves for the evils which they have committed". True repentance brings about change through sorrow for sin. True repentance is an "about face", a complete turning from sin to righteousness.

God at times uses harsh means to awaken us to our spiritual needs. But He does this in order that we might listen to His Holy Spirit and come to true repentance.

Direction for today: God's love and mercy never discounts His justice.

Prayer for today: "Praise You, Lord, for Your justice and righteousness".

October 3: Read Ezekiel 7-9

Key verse: "I have done as You commanded" (Ezekiel 9:11 NIV).

As Paul realized that his life was almost over, he was able to write: "I have fought the good fight, I have finished the race, I have kept the faith" (II Timothy 4:7 NKJV). He might have said it in the words of our key verse: "I have done as You commanded."

How many believers are going to be able to stand before God and speak those words, knowing that the Lord knows our every thought and action? But, although we sometimes fail, we must never abandon the goal of obedience to Jesus.

The Lord said that we show our love for Him if we keep His commandments. Christian love is always active love; this is why Paul can tell us that, although salvation comes only through the grace of God, we must still work out our salvation. Another way of saying that might be, let your salvation work in you, producing obedience to Jesus.

Even if you have sinned in disobedience, you can be forgiven. And you can begin to obey the Lord, by the power of His Spirit, and live your life so that you can say to God, "I have done as You commanded".

Direction for today: Obey the Lord!

Prayer for today: "Lord, enable me, by the power of Your Holy Spirit, to obey You".

October 4: Read Ezekiel 10-12

Key verse: "And the glory of the Lord went up from the midst of the city, and stood upon the mountain which is on the east side of the city" (Ezekiel 11:23 NAS).

Ezekiel saw, in many prophetic visions, the judgment of God about to be outpoured upon the city of Jerusalem. The idolatry and disobedience of the nation had led the people far from their God.

God's presence had been with them in the Shekinah glory which was present over the Ark of the Covenant. As long as the nation obeyed the principles that were embodied in the Law (engraved on the two stone tablets resting in the Ark), God's presence was with them.

Because of their rebellion and disobedience, as had been revealed to Ezekiel, the nation was being rejected by the Lord. His presence, enshrined in the Shekinah glory, was being removed from the city of Jerusalem and the people would be left to face their enemies alone.

God cannot allow His presence to abide in the midst of sin and disobedience. The cry from His heart is, "Return unto Me and I will return unto you!"

192

Direction for today: God dwells in our praises; He is near to us through our obedience.

Prayer for today: "Father, Your kingdom come!"

"But the fruit of the Spirit is love, joy, peace, longsuffering, kindness, goodness, faithfulness, gentleness, self-control. Against such there is no law." Galatians 5:22,23 NKJV

October 5: Read Ezekiel 13-15

Key verse: "Son of man, prophesy against the prophets of Israel, prophesy and say to those who prophesy out of their own minds: Hear the Word of the Lord" (Ezekiel 13:2 RSV).

This contrast between genuine and spurious prophecy is one which we should all take very seriously.

Praise God that we are living in a time when He . . . "pours forth of My Spirit upon all mankind" (Acts 2:17). Praise God, His gifts of the Holy Spirit are being manifest and much prophesy is evident. However, we are cautioned by God's Word, "Do not believe every spirit, but test the spirits to see whether they are from God; because many false prophets have gone out into the world. By this you know the Spirit of God; every spirit that confesses that Jesus Christ has come in the flesh is from God" (I John 4:1,2).

How is the line of demarcation to be drawn between truth and falsehood in this sphere, according to Ezekiel? His answer, frankly, is simple but not all that satisfactory. The false prophet, he declares; "follows his own spirit and has seen nothing" (Ezekiel 13:3). If he has seen a vision it is not one that God has provided; it is a projection of his own mind. The false prophet is like a jackal or coyote among the ruins and debris, seeking a snug burrow among the rubble, or pouncing on a corpse. The jackal is unmoved by catastrophe; he is seeking only his own advantage.

The true prophet, on the other hand, bridges the gap, and builds a hedge for God's people, even in battle. May we all take to heart the Berean lesson! Paul and Silas preached to the people of Berea in the synagogue of the Jews and ". . . they received the word with great eagerness *examining the Scriptures daily,* to see whether these things were true" (Acts 17:11). All prophetic utterances without exception which contradict the scriptures are false and not truly from God.

Direction for today: God will never tell you something privately that contradicts Scripture.

Prayer for today: "Lord, may I always recognize Your voice, and never be led astray by deceit."

October 6: Read Ezekiel 16, 17

Key verse: "The word of the Lord came to me: Son of man, confront Jerusalem with her detestable practices. . . ." (Ezekiel 16:27 NAS).

One of the greatest acts of love is to confront in a spirit of meekness, those who are doing wrong. Many times, God brings to our attention those things that are hurtful to our well-being. God knows that sin is destructive to individuals, families and nations. Solomon tells us, "Open rebuke is better than secret love" (Proverbs 27:5).

God confronted the Israelite elders with the idoltary in their hearts, hoping they would repent. He reasoned with Jerusalem and reminded them of His goodness. He expounds on the wickedness of their waywardness. "Come now, and let us reason together, saith the Lord, though your sins be as scarlet, they shall be as white as snow; though they be red like crimson, they shall be as wool" (Isaiah 1:18 KJV).

As Christians, we might boast in our born-again experience, but we are cautioned, "Little children, keep yourselves from idols" (I John 5:21 KJV).

Direction for today: "Do not be afraid to confront sin in your community.

Prayer for today: "Lord, may my life, first of all, be clean of detestable practices."

October 7: Read Ezekiel 18, 19

Key verse: "Get a new heart and a new spirit. Why will you die, O house of Israel?" (Ezekiel 18:31b NIV).

People are born with congenital heart disease; every person born since the sin of Adam and Eve has had a dying heart.

This verse does not refer to our physical heart, of course, it speaks of the centre of our being, the heart of our life. And that central part of each person is dead from birth.

God offers to do open heart surgery. It is the will of the Lord to give each of us a new heart, a new spirit, a new centre to our life. That centre is Jesus Christ. He will come into our hearts, and bring life. He will cleanse our spirits, and rescue us from death.

Perhaps Jesus is now at the centre of your life. If so, take a moment and thank Him specifically for bringing you wonderful deliverance from death.

But if you still suffer from a dead heart, take the advice of Ezekiel the prophet: go to God, and get from Him a new heart and a new spirit.

Direction for today: And rejoice in these great gifts from God.

Prayer for today: "Lord, thank You for Your gift of life, and for the new life that Jesus has brought to my heart."

October 8: Read Ezekiel 20

Key verse: "And you shall know that I am the Lord, when I deal with you for My name's sake, not according to your evil ways, nor according to your corrupt doings, O house of Israel, says the Lord God" (Ezekiel 20:44 RSV).

There was no doubt about the "evil ways" of Israel, nor about their "corrupt doings". In chapter 20, the Lord rehearses the history of their rebellions: in Egypt; in the wilderness; and in Canaan. Yet, despite all His people's disobedience, the Lord restrained the full measure of His wrath against them.

Four times in chapter 20 (verses 9, 14, 22, 44), God says He withholds His hand of judgment on Israel, "for the sake of My name, that it should not be profaned in the sight of the nations among whom they dwelt . . . in whose sight I had brought them out." Matthew Henry says, "When nothing in us will furnish Him with a reason for His favours, He furnishes Himself with one."

Praise Him for His mercy and His love!

Direction for today: God's blessings to us imply nothing about our own worthiness!

Prayer for today: "Thank You, Father, that You give me so many good gifts, even though I deserve none of them."

October 9: Read Ezekiel 21, 22

Key verse: "The sojourner suffers extortion in your midst; the fatherless and the widow are wronged in you . . . the people of the land have practiced extortion and committed robbery; they have oppressed the poor and needy, and have extorted from the sojourner without redress" (Ezekiel 22:7,29 RSV).

What did the nation of Israel do wrong? According to these chapters in Ezekiel, practically everything! Their entire lifestyle was an abomination to the Lord; their religious practices, social habits, economic system, and family relationships were all in sharp contrast to the laws of God. Those who bore the name of "God's people" were in reality far, far away from living as the people of God.

It is important to realize that not all sin of Israel was what we might see as "spiritual" transgression against God. Over and over again, God expresses His anger and judgment for their acts against their fellow men, both Israelites and Gentiles. God is full of wrath because of the economic injustice practiced by His people for they have oppressed the poor and gained wealth dishonestly.

This is a valuable lesson for us, in our world of vast differences between the rich and the poor.

It is crucial that we realize that we in North America are among the rich minority, and that we have God-ordained responsibility to the poor of the world. If we fail to minister meaningfully, in the name of the Lord, to the multitude of the poor, we too fall under His condemnation.

Direction for today: Does everything I have belong to Christ?

Prayer for today: "Lord, I yield all my material possessions to You."

October 10: Read Ezekiel 23

Key verse: "For thus saith the Lord God; I will bring up a company upon them, and will give them to be removed and spoiled" (Ezekiel 23:46 KJV).

Using the example of two women who become adulteresses, Ezekiel portrays the spiritual condition of the divided kingdoms of Israel and Judah. Reference is made to both of them beginning their wayward devices while they were still in Egypt.

The picture of the lover who becomes their destroyer is very graphic. Viewing their present positions as bondsmen in a strange land added credence to Ezekiel's message.

Unfortunately, the application of this parable is not exclusive to a bygone generation; the same sad condition exists in our own society. Many a person who has a spiritual heritage has committed spiritual adultery. Leaving sound Biblical principles, many have adopted a humanistic philosophy; turning their backs on Jesus Christ, they have given themselves to unbridled passions and pursuits only to find these leaving them empty and frustrated.

God's purpose in allowing Israel to go into bondage was not to destroy but to restore. His desire for the redemption of wandering and broken lives is still the same today.

Direction for today: Recognize God's purposes in everything He allows you to go through.

Prayer for today: "Lord, fill with Yourself all the empty spaces in me."

October 11: Read Ezekiel 24, 25

Key verse: "I the Lord have spoken. The time has come for Me to act. I will not hold back; I will not have pity, nor will I relent. You will be judged according to your conduct and your actions, declares the Sovereign Lord" (Ezekiel 24:14 NIV).

There are three connected themes in chapter 24: The parable of the rusty cooking pot (verses 1-14); the sign of the death of Ezekiel's wife (15-24); the end of the prophet's dumbness (23-27).

The knowledge of the siege of Jerusalem (verse 2) again illustrates Ezekiel's supernatural gift, and would constitute a public confirmation of his prophetic office. The city of Jerusalem is like a cooking pot whose 'rust' (verse 6) cannot be removed. The only thing that can be done is to set the pot upside down on the fire (verse 11). However, its heavy deposit has not been removed, not even by fire. Similarly, Jerusalem must be destroyed in order to be cleansed.

Ezekiel was to hide his grief and show no mourning (verse 17) following his wife's death. This caused his fellow exiles to ask him the meaning of his conduct. It is explained in verses 20-24. Jerusalem and its sanctuary are as dear to them as a wife to a husband; when they hear of its destruction and the loss of their relatives, they, too, must bow in silence before God, for it is God's judgment.

Direction for today: God gives us these harsh warnings, through the Old Testament prophets, to keep us close to Himself.

Prayer for today: "Lord, I pray that anything in me which is not honouring to You would be put to death."

Memory Verse

"And do not be drunk with wine, in which is dissipation; but be filled with the Spirit." Ephesians 5:18 NKJV

October 12: Read Ezekiel 26,27

Key verse: "'I will make you a bare rock; you will be a place for the spreading of nets. You will be built no more, for I the Lord have spoken,' declares the Lord God" (Ezekiel 26:14).

What a judgment on proud Tyre! Throughout these two chapters we read of what God will do to this prosperous trading port. In our key verse, God pronounces, "you will be built no more". Even today, the ruins stand as stark testimony to the reality of the judgment of God.

I am reminded of the contrasts given in the book of Proverbs, where we see the rewards of the just compared with the punishment of the unjust. Today, we might be questioning God as to why the ungodly seem to enjoy such prosperity while we, perhaps, are having difficulties and heartaches. But God will not be mocked; He will repay man according to his righteousness or his wickedness.

Direction for today: Anyone who stands against God, will fall.

Prayer for today: "Lord may I always stand with You, never against You."

October 13: Read Ezekiel 28, 29

Key verse: "Thou wast perfect in thy ways from the day that thou wast created, till iniquity was found in thee" (Ezekiel 28:15 KJV).

The description of the king of Tyre given in the 28th chapter is very revealing. The basic attitude of this powerful, influential king is traced to its original source. The expression of pride and the lust for power, was at the root of Satan's rebellion against God. Isaiah 14:12-15 gives a further description of this fallen angel who was called Lucifer, son of the morning and the anointed cherub (Ezekiel 28:14). In our key verse, we read that in his creation this high order of angelic being was perfect until iniquity was found in him. The desire to usurp the position of God led to him being expelled from God's presence. Ephesians 6:11-12 tells us that our warfare in now against the wiles of the devil.

To the person who refuses to submit to the authority of God there comes the subtle temptation of the arch deceiver. This would appear to have been the tragedy of the kingdom of Tyre.

Where there is no evidence of a genuine repentance toward God, there still hangs over an individual, or a nation, the warning of coming judgment. When warnings are repeatedly ignored, there finally comes the outpouring of that judgment. The island fortress of Tyre, including its coastal territorial possessions, was completely destroyed. So it will be for the unrepentant sinner.

This is not God's will, for He is not willing that any should perish. In fact God has done everything possible, and necessary, to keep man from destroying himself. In Jesus Christ, He has provided the way out, and into that place of acceptance and fellowship with Himself.

Direction for today: We do not always need to learn from our own experiences; the Bible has been given to us to save us that kind of pain!

Prayer for today: "Lord, help me to accept your principles and apply them in my life."

October 14: Read Ezekiel 30,31

Key verse: *"Thus will I execute judgements in Egypt: and they shall know that I am the Lord" (Ezekiel 30:19 KJV).*

"For the time will come when they will not endure sound doctrine; but after their own lusts shall they heap to themselves teachers, having itching ears; And they shall turn away their ears from the truth, and shall be turned unto fables" (II Timothy 4:3,4). There is only one God, and His love has been manifested to us in His Son, Jesus Christ. The Godhead was completed with the Holy Spirit.

The Bible says, "For whosoever shall call upon the name of the Lord shall be saved" (Romans 10:13). Jesus said, "I am the way, the truth, and the life: no man cometh unto the Father, but by Me" (John 14:6).

When people have "itching ears", their lusts produce fables and they take unto themselves other gods, even gods made of their own hands. When this occurs, terrible destruction is imminent, as it was for Egypt and the other nations against which Ezekiel prophesied.

Let us search our hearts and keep ourselves always open to the true God, that our experience might be that of blessing, not judgment.

Direction for today: May I have ears only for the truth of God.

Prayer for today: "Lord, may Your truth always be in my ears, my heart and my spirit."

October 15: Read Ezekiel 32, 33

Key verse: ". . . as I live, says the Lord God, I have no pleasure in the death of the wicked, but that the wicked turn from his way and live" (Ezekiel 33:11 RSV).

Some people seem to think that God is out to get them. They see God, not as a loving Father, but as some kind of cosmic ogre who has set out to destroy them completely, and torture them as He does so.

They have believed a lie. God is indeed the Father of all who will be His children. The Lord tells us, in our key verse, that He has no pleasure in the death of the wicked. God does not want anyone to die! He cares so much that He, in the person of Jesus Christ, took the deaths of the whole world — including your death! — upon Himself.

Jesus said that He did not come to condemn the world, but to save it. Paul told Timothy that God wants everyone to come to repentance.

God is not in the condemnation business; He is in the restoration business! He takes pleasure in our repentance, when we turn from our path of wickedness and death and receive His gift of life and peace.

Direction for today: Be careful to avoid any vengeful spirit that would rejoice in the end of life of someone who has been your enemy.

Prayer for today: "Lord, may I see all people through Your eyes only; heal me of any vengeful spirit that rejoices in the suffering of others."

October 16: Read Ezekiel 34,35

Key verse: "I will seek My lost ones, those who strayed away, and bring them safely home again" (Ezekiel 34:15-16 NIV).

The Lord has allowed Israel to fall into the hands of enemies who tortured the people and desecrated the land.

In this portion, God, through Ezekiel, rebukes the leaders of His people. He had expected them, as shepherds, to lovingly guide and rebuild the nation in a responsible fashion. But, rather than showing care and compassion, they are greedy, neglectful scoundrels, treating the people with cruelty.

This angers the Lord, and He passes judgment on the leaders. He Himself assumes the role of shepherd and promises to heal the people and make their land peaceful and prosperous once again.

God promises He would not only provide nourishment and security, but spiritual provision as well. This was a beautiful promise of hope for a needy people.

Direction for today: Be very diligent to care for any God has placed under your leadership.

Prayer for today: "Lord, I bring to You all those for whom I am responsible."

October 17: Read Ezekiel 36, 37

Key verse: "A new heart will I give you, and a new spirit will I put within you: and I will take away the stony heart out of your flesh, and I will give you an heart of flesh. And I will put My spirit within you" (Ezekiel 36:26,27b).

Just as the Lord promised Israel that He would cleanse them for the sake of His holy name, so He tells us today.

Perhaps as you read this you have not been living the type of life you know the Lord requires of you. Like Israel, you have become involved in worldly things, have entered into friendships or deeper relationships which are not honouring to His name. Read again Chapter 36: 20-28. Let these verses speak to your heart.

God is gracious and merciful. He desires your love and fellowship but He also requires your faithfulness and obedience.

Today, take unto yourself afresh those last words of verse 28: "ye shall be My people, and I will be your God".

Direction for today: Claim those words of relationship for yourself: "You shall be my God, and I will be Your person."

Prayer for today: "Father, You are my God; and I am your servant."

October 18: Read Ezekiel 38-40

Key verse: "'And I will not hide My face from them any longer, for I shall have poured out My Spirit on the house of Israel,' declares the Lord God" (Ezekiel 39:29 NAS).

Chapters 38 and 39 are unique in Old Testament prophecy, for they desicribe the assault of foreign powers against the chosen people of God after the commencement of the Messianic kingdom. In chapter 38, verses 8-14, Ezekiel shows the nation of Israel as being resettled in their land and transformed into a prosperous community.

The opening of both chapers is very similar. Both emphasize the miraculous nature of Israel's deliverance. Both Israel and the other nations will, in this way, learn of the power of God. Over and over again this is repeated (38:16,23; 39:6,13,21-23,25-29).

Throughout the centuries, God's chosen people have rejected the Messiah. But the time is coming when that shall change. Praise the Lord!

Direction for today: Allow the Lord to fill you with His Holy Spirit.

Prayer for today: "Praise You, Lord, for the gift of Your Holy Spirit."

Memory Verse

"For to me, to live is Christ, and to die is gain." Philippians 1:21 NKJV

October 19: Read Ezekiel 41, 43

Key verse: "Son of man, describe the temple to the people of Israel, that they may be ashamed of their sins . . ." (Ezekiel 43:10 NKJV).

Sin is something of which we sould all be ashamed. The purpose of describing the Temple to these people was to change their ways. In thinking of the Temple as a place of holiness and a place in which God was present, these people would be ashamed of their sin. But being ashamed was not enough. A change had to take place whereby this shame caused them to follow the regulations of the Temple.

The scripture reveals that our bodies are the temple of the Holy Spirit (I Corinthians 6:19). We need to allow Jesus Christ to totally control our lives, so that the direction He has set down in His Word will bring about necessary changes.

Direction for today: Consider your sins only long enough to be thoroughly ashamed of them.

Prayer for today: "Lord, help me to see sin through Your eyes."

October 20: Read Ezekiel 44,45

Key Verse: "And the Lord said to me, 'Son of man, mark well, see with your eyes and hear with your ears, all that I say to you concerning all the ordinances of the house of the Lord and all its laws. Mark well who may enter the house and all who go out from the sanctuary" (Ezekiel 44:5 NKJV).

God wants us to pay attention to what He expects of us. He wants us to use the members of our body to glorify Him.

Paul says, "I beseech you therefore, brethren, by the mercies of God, that you present your bodies a living sacrifice, holy, acceptable to God, which is your reasonable service. And do not be conformed to this world, but be transformed by the renewing of your mind, that you may prove what is that good and acceptable and perfect will of God" (Romans 12:1,2 NKJV).

Direction for today: Be a good steward of all aspects of your life, living each moment for the Lord.

Prayer for today: "Lord, may my body be a holy temple for the Holy Spirit."

October 21: Read Ezekiel 46, 48

Key Verse: *"You are to allot it as an inheritance for yourselves and for the aliens who have settled among you and who have children" (Ezekiel 47:22 NIV).*

Instruction is given here for the division of the land which Israel now occupied. It is interesting to note that any stranger who had settled among them and had children was to be equally considered in the division of the land. Obviously, these strangers had accepted Israel's way of life and were living under God's rule. God had promised Israel this land but He also includes those who had accepted their way.

This should speak to us about the gospel. Matthew Henry states, ". . . all the subjects of Christ's kingdom have obtained like precious faith." It doesn't matter whether we are male or female, Jew or Gentile, in Christ our inheritance is the same. Romans 10:12 reads "For there is no difference between Jew and Greek — the same Lord is Lord of all and richly blesses all who call on Him."

The inheritance in Christ is the same for all who will trust Him as Saviour and Lord. He came to the Jew first but opened the same door to all.

Direction for today: God's kingdom always has room for more.

Prayer for today: "Thank You, Lord, that You have received strangers — like me!"

October 22: Read II Peter 1-3

Key Verse: *"The Lord knows how to deliver the godly out of temptations and to reserve the unjust under punishment for the day of judgment" (II Peter 2:9 NKJV).*

God has not promised to deliver us *from* temptations, but *out of* them. We will never be completely free from temptations, until we are past the possibility of sinning, in heaven. The Bible tells us that even Jesus was faced with temptations, yet He did not sin.

That tells us that it is no sin to be tempted. The devil would like to convince you that temptation is the same as sin: that once an idea has come to you, you are guilty. This is simply not true.

The question is, what do we do when we are confronted by temptation? We have only three choices:

1) We can dwell on that temptation, and thus fall into the sin that is presented to us.

2) We can try to fight the temptation in our own strength. This will usually lead straight into the sin, as well.

Or, 3) we can accept God's gift of deliverance from temptation. James says, "Submit yourselves therefore to God. Resist the devil, and he will flee from you" (James 4:7).

Only through reliance on the Lord can we come through every temptation in victory!

Direction for today: Take the advice of Peter and James: resist the devil by drawing close to God.

Prayer for today: "Lord, lead me out of temptation, and deliver me from evil."

Daniel

God is in charge! That is the key message of this book, and the theme that ties together its two diverse sections.

The book is named for its author and main character, Daniel, the Israelite exile who lived in Babylon from about 606 B.C., the time of the first deportation of Jews from Judah, until about 540 B.C. Jesus Himself attested to Daniel's authorship of this book (Matthew 24:15).

The first section demonstrates God's control, as the Lord miraculously intervenes in the affairs of Daniel and his three Hebrew friends. Here we have the accounts of the fiery furnace, and of Daniel in the lion's den. In the first section of the book, Daniel is frequently given the interpretation of dreams. In the latter chapters (7-12), he himself receives visions. These important visions and dreams are Old Testament keys to the final days of history. They are a prophetic roadmap to the empires of the world, and they all point to the final destruction of earthly political systems, as the Lord Himself comes to rule the world.

Many of the prophetic symbols and images of Daniel are repeated in the New Testament book, the Revelation of John. We can learn much about the years to come by careful interpretation of Daniel and the other prophetic books, but we must be careful to realize that only God knows all concerning the end of history as we know it.

October 23: Read Daniel 1,2

Key verse: "But Daniel purposed in his heart that he would not defile himself with the portion of the King's meat, nor with the wine which he drank: therefore he requested of the prince of the eunuchs that he might not defile himself" (Daniel 1:8 KJV).

The name Daniel means, "God is my judge". It was a name well suited to this man of God. Herein lay Daniel's key to a successful walk with God. His example of determination strikes at the heart of every believer.

In the opening chapters of the book, Daniel's commitment is put to the test. The commandment to eat from the king's table placed Daniel and his three friends in an awkward position. To eat and drink of this food would violate their consciences. In the midst of their captors they were loyal to God. Nebuchadnezzar could change their names but he could never change their nature. And so Daniel boldly challenged the chief steward to a ten day test; whereupon he and his three friends proved to be ten times better "in all matters of wisdom and understanding".

We are commanded to come out of the world, be separate and purify ourselves from all that may contaminate the body and the spirit (II Corinthians 6:17, 7:1).Daniel's stand, and ultimate victory, shatters the argument of any believer who would blame defeat on worldly surroundings. Here we see that, if we are willing to take a stand for God, we will see victory.

Direction for today: Compromise in spiritual matters means making a deal with the devil!

Prayer for today: "Help me, Lord, to purpose in my heart not to compromise."

October 24: Read Daniel 3,4

Key verse: "If we are thrown into the blazing furnace, the God we serve is able to save us from it, and He will rescue us from your hand, O King. But even if He does not, we want you to know, O King, that we will not serve your gods or worship the image of god you have set up" (Daniel 3:17-18 NIV).

Over and over again we hear, or say, "Why doesn't God do something?" Often, underneath this question is the unspoken assumption that God must make life comfortable for us, that He exists to provide for and protect us. We tend to forget that there is a war on — the war between good and evil, betwen the true God and false gods — and in a war there are casualties on both sides.

Shadrach, Meshech and Abednego had seen the ruin that came upon Jerusalem after the Jews had fallen into astrology and other forms of idol worship. They were determined to be loyal to the Lord. They knew with Isaiah that His ways are not our ways (Isaiah 55:9). They knew with Moses that God is sovereign and He will have mercy on whom He will have mercy (Exodus 33:14) and so they were able to say with Job, "Though He slay me, yet will I hope in Him" (Job 13:15).

Jesus, too, suffered, though He had committed no sin. When He died and was buried, it looked as though evil had won. But on Easter He rose again; and, if we die with Him, we shall also live with Him (Romans 6:8).

Direction for today: "If you suffer for doing good and you endure it, that is commendable before God" (I Peter 2:20 NIV).

Prayer for today: "Father, I trust you in life and in death."

October 25: Read Daniel 5,6

Key verse: "Now when Daniel knew that the writing was signed, he went into his house; and his windows being open in his chamber toward Jerusalem, he kneeled upon his knees three times a day, and prayed and gave thanks before his God as he did aforetime" (Daniel 6:10 KJV).

Daniel was a good and faithful servant of King Darius. The scriptures even say his accusers tried to find fault with him but, "forasmuch as he was faithful, neither was there any error or fault found in him" (Daniel 6:4 NAS). Daniel was also faithful to God. He knew that, under the decree from King Darius, he risked his life each time he prayed and sought God.

How privileged we are to live in a country where we are not persecuted for our beliefs.

Daniel was not only faithful to God but knew God would be faithful to him. He had confidence that no matter what the outcome, God was in control. Paul said it so well, "to live is Christ and to die is gain" (Philippians 1:21). God's faithfulness to us is far beyond our own understanding.

Direction for today: Give thanks that you live free from persecution, but be prepared to face it if it comes.

Prayer for today: "Lord, may my faith be strong enough to stand in persecution; and strong enough to go forward *without* persecution!"

Memory Verse

"As you have therefore received Christ Jesus the Lord, so walk in Him, rooted and built up in Him and established in the faith, as you have been taught, abounding in it with thanksgiving." Colossians 2:6,7 NKJV

October 26: Read Daniel 7,8

Key verse: "And to Him was given dominion, glory and a kingdom, that all the peoples, nations, and men of every language might serve Him. His dominion is an everlasting dominion which will not pass away; and His kingdom is one which will not be destroyed" (Daniel 7:14).

This is a picture which is a far cry from the political and social systems of our world of today. Here, in Daniel's vision, we see a world united under one Ruler, a King who will reign forever in a kingdom which will not fall.

When we compare this eternal rulership of Jesus Christ to the kings, presidents and prime ministers of our present world, the most glorious empires of history pale into insignificance. Only under the dinvine reign of our Lord Jesus Christ will the vision of benevolent rule, properly used power, and unity of all peoples, be realized.

Under King Jesus, all subjects will live in joy and harmony. There will be no more military superpowers, no Third World countries, no poverty and starvation. In His eternal kingdom, we will truly live as His creations were intended to live.

Direction for today: The peace that the whole world will know when Jesus rules the world can be ours, right now, if we allow Jesus to rule our lives.

Prayer for today: "Praise You, Lord, that Your kingdom is everlasting."

October 27: Read Daniel 9,10

Key verse: *"So I gave my attention to the Lord God to seek Him by prayer and supplications, with fasting, sackcloth and ashes" (Daniel 9:3).*

Daniel was a man of prayer. He knew the importance of regular communication with his heavenly Father, and his humility and dedication caused the people to hold him in respect. Little wonder then, that God chose him to receive the visions of which we read in Chapters 7 and 8. Then, in Chapter 9, verses 21-27, Gabriel is sent to 'give him insight and understanding'.

If we hear from God, we too must be prepared to faithfully spend time in earnest prayer, to confess our sins and humble ourselves before Him. Daniel confessed not only his own sin but the sins of the nation.

Today, God needs His people to stand up and be counted; to intercede on behalf of our nations and to call people unto repentance. He calls us to look beyond our immediate spheres of family and friends, beyond our church fellowships, of prime importance though they may be, and to pray for our government leaders and other elected officials, those in our legal systems, the police, schoolteachers and all others in authority.

Direction for today: Prayer and fasting should play a significant role in your spiritual life.

Prayer for today: "Father, teach me to pray."

October 28: Read Daniel 11,12

Key verse: *"And they that be wise shall shine as the brightness of the firmament; and they that turn many to righteousness as the stars forever and ever" (Daniel 12:3 KJV).*

This is a fitting conclusion for the book of Daniel. In the opening chapters we see Daniel and his friends making important decisions in their lives. Choosing to place God first exposes them to real tests of their faith, but it also opens the way for the Lord to prove Himself to be their sufficiency.

Burdened by the opposition his people are experiencing in Jerusalem, Daniel becomes an intercessor. In answer to his fervent prayers, God grants Daniel a glimpse into the future. He reveals national struggles, and their impact upon the people for whom Daniel was praying. There would be powers that would rise and fall but, through it all, God's hand would be over Daniel's people. What a long-range weapon is the power of prayer!

The fact that Israel has not lost its national identity is verification of Daniel's vision. In spite of all attempts to obliterate the seed of Abraham, they will survive. This is not because of their worthiness, but is evidence of the faithfulness of God. To point men to the living Lord is the essence of wisdom. Coming to know Him produces righteousness.

In a day of fluctuating values, the message of Daniel is still crystal clear. When the God of the universe is given His rightful place in human lives, He will confirm His reliability. Social, political, and economic structures may change, but the God of Daniel remains the same. When national, or international, scenes are gloomy and depressing, the *uplook* is still as bright as the promises of God.

Daniel had learned the secret, early in life, of rising above circumstances. The testing of this faith had produced a man of sterling qualities. This daily communion with his heavenly King equipped him to stand before earthly kings. It is not so surprising that some of the secrets of the future, were given to him in those times alone with God.

Direction for today: The people of God will always survive.

Prayer for today: "Lord, may my faith in You shine to the world."

I, II and III John

These letters, written by the apostle John (who also penned the gospel of John, and the Revelation), are a concise, precise guide to the Christian live. Their content is firmly anchored on one theme: love. This is the love Christians receive from the Father through Jesus, and the love that we then must share with one another, if we are truly Christian.

October 29: Read I John 1-3

Key verse: "Little children, let us not love in word or in speech but in deed and in truth" (I John 3:18 RSV).

It is a perennial temptation to all of us to substitute talk about love for deeds of love. In an even more subtle form, we are often tempted (in pride or in ostentation) to 'love' in deed but not in truth, having only the appearance of loving. "If I speak with the tongues of men and of angels . . . If I give all my possessions to feed the poor . . . but have not love, it profits me nothing" (I Corinthians 13:1-3).

Christian giving, or good deeds, differs in two ways from worldly giving. Firstly, the presumption is that the material things which God created are good in themselves. Secondly, for the Christian, giving or loving in deed and in truth presumes that the motivating impetus begins in God's love.

Private property is understood by the Christian to be God-given and that over which the Christian has been given stewardship. It is through giving that God builds fellowship and community and, indeed, unites His Body, the church. Shakespeare understood this: "They do not love, that do not show their love." (Two Gentlemen of Verona, Act 1, Scene 11). Deeds done that are in truth are genuinely Christian deeds. "When therefore you give alms, do not sound a trumpet before you, as the hypocrites do" (Matthew 6:12).

Good deeds or giving and sharing, without love and truth as their foundation, flounder on self interest or pride. To do good deeds in truth presumes God's love in your heart.

To spread the Good News of the invitation to the repentant heart to recieve this love is the ministry of 100 Huntley Street. And this ministry is totally dependent on this love and overflowing in your prayer and financial support.

Direction for today: Practice love in action.

Prayer for today: "Lord, give me opportunities and means to demonstrate my love for You and others."

October 30: Read I John 4,5

Key verse: *"Hereby know ye the Spirit of God: every spirit that confesseth that Jesus Christ is come in the flesh is of God" (I John 4:2 KJV).*

There are many false doctrines today. A sure way to discern those that are true, is to listen to what they say about Jesus. False doctrines will always make Him less than God by referring to Him as a god or an angel. The Bible, however, calls Him - God.

I John 5:7 indicates that God the Father and God the Son are completely inseparable. When we pray to God the Father, we are also praying to God the Son and God the Holy Spirit. They all hear our prayer and respond cooperatively.

Nature is filled with many examples of creation existing in a trichotomy (that is, a division into three parts). The planet earth consists of land, water and air. One cannot exist without the other. Our bodies are made of flesh, bone and blood. Each part relies on the other for existence. We are also made up of body, soul and spirit.

Jesus is God, He is the Son of God. Remember that He came in the flesh in order to save you and me: in order that we might spend eternity with Him.

Direction for today: Allow the love of Christ to flow over you.

Prayer for today: "Thank You, Lord, for sending Jesus."

Hosea

Hosea is the first of 12 books, the final writings of the Old Testament, that are often grouped together as "The Minor Prophets". They bear this title only because of their length, not because of their significance: some of the most powerful prophetic proclamation is found in these relatively short books.

The 12 books appear in apparently random order, although it is possible to identify the date and historical setting for most of them.

Hosea was a prophet who lived in the northern kingdom of Israel at the same time that Isaiah was ministering in Judah to the south. He was the only "writing prophet" in the north who addressed his own people. The northern kingdom was even more wicked than the south, and fell to oppressors sent by the Lord as judgment a century and a half before Judah suffered that fate.

Hosea's ministry occurred in the years just before this attack on the north by Assyria. He prophesied from about 750 to 725 B.C.; the Assyrians destroyed northern Israel in 722 B.C.

Hosea enacted a graphic example of the unfaithful nation of Israel; the book tells us that he took a wife who was a prostitute, and who was subsequently unfaithful to him. This was a picture of the relationship between God, as husband, and His unfaithful wife, the children of Israel. Scholars disagree as to whether Hosea actually married a prostitute, or whether this is an allegorical image. Either way, the book is a powerful picture of waywardness by the people of God, contrasted with God's faithful love for His own.

October 31: Read Hosea 1-4

Key verse: *"I will have compassion on her who had not obtained compassion, and I will say to those who were not My people, 'You are My people!' and they will say 'Thou are my God!'" (Hosea 2:23 NAS).*

The lesson of Hosea is found in the names of his children. The name of the third child, Loammi, meaning "Not my people", is the result of God's people rejecting God.

The terms of God's covenant were, "I will be your God, and you shall be My people" (Jeremiah 7:23). By their sinful acts of spiritual adultery, of chasing after other gods like an adulterous woman, and their sins, immorality and unwillingness to follow God's commandments, Israel rejected God.

By calling Israel, "Not My people", God dissolved His covenant with them, but He also promised to make them His people again (3:23). He achieved that through Jesus Christ. Paul points this out clearly when he talks about those saved under the New Covenant, "even us whom He has called, not from the Jews only, but also from the Gentiles" (Romans 9:24-26).

When we believe in Jesus Christ as Saviour and Lord, we are transferred from being "not His people" to being "His people", from the Kingdom of darkness to the Kingdom of light (Colossians 1:13).

Direction for today: You are a product of the compassion of our loving God!

Prayer for today: "Praise, You, Father, that You have made me Your child."

11

The Anointed

The void was deep
        When you called my name

In the silence I wept –
        Then slowly came
                To your throne
                        And hid my face.

Your voice rang out
        Stand! –
                I anoint Thee Son!

He wrapped me in His grace
        And I slept
                Safe
                        In my Father's embrace.

– Bonnie Knowles

November 1: Read Hosea 5,6

Key verse: *"Come, let us return to the Lord" (Hosea 6:1 NIV).*

In today's reading, we see the utter depravity of man and the continuing love and mercy of God.

The Israelites were blessed by God, who had chosen them for Himself and given them the land of Canaan. When they entered the land, they found the people there committing horrible sins against God, even sacrificing their own children to idols. God told the Israelites to rid the land of these awful practices and to live in peace and righteousness, showing love and care to one another.

God, in His love and mercy, gave to Israel priests who would teach them His Word. If they would keep His Word and live it, they would have peace and be blessed. Unfortunately, the Israelites soon began to forget God and even the priests turned to lusting after the things of the flesh. God brought upon them severe judgment until they cried out to Him for deliverance. Time after time, God had to deal with Israel, but each time they cried out to Him, He forgave them and restored them.

Here, we see that Israel has once again sunk to the depths of idolatry and is suffering the judgment of God. Here again, God has sent them another prophet to tell them to return to Him. Again, God promises to forgive, heal, restore and revive Israel if they will call upon Him.

Direction for today: If you have ever been closer to the Lord than you are right now, return to Him!

Prayer for today: "Thank You, Lord, that You are our Father, ever welcoming us home."

Memory Verse

"Rejoice always, pray without ceasing, in everything give thanks; for this is the will of God in Christ Jesus for you." I Thessalonians 5:16-18 NKJV

November 2: Read Hosea 7,8

Key verse: *"And they do not consider in their hearts that I remember all their wickedess. Now their deeds are all around them; they are before My face" (Hosea 7:2 NAS).*

The greatest barrier to restoration is having an indifferent attitude towards God, leaving Him out of our thoughts, refusing to acknowledge our wrong. In verse one, God says, "When I would heal Israel, the iniquity of Ephraim is uncovered". God's desire is to heal the relationship between man and Himself. He wants to draw us — not reject us — but our sin and pride create a vast barrier that precludes reconciliation.

"I remember all their wickedness . . . their deeds are before My face", says God. This is the situation with rebellious, unregenerate man, but what a change takes place when we acknowledge our sin and repent of it! The Lord says, In Jeremiah 31:34, "I will forgive their iniquity, and their sin *I will remember no more*".

Before repentance, God remembers all our wickedness and our evil deeds are ever before His face. But all that we need to do is to turn from our sin and ask His forgiveness. He not only forgives us but *remembers our sin no more.*

Praise His precious Name!

Direction for today: If God can forgive and forget, so should we.

Prayer for today: "Thank You, Lord, for Your willingness to forgive my sin against You."

November 3: Read Hosea 9,10

Key verse: "Sow to yourselves in righteousness, reap in mercy, break up your fallow ground; for it is time to seek the Lord, till He come and rain righteousness upon you" (Hosea 10:12 KJV).

From the very beginning, Israel had great potential for fruitfulness. However, sin destroyed that influence, marred fellowship with God and almost destroyed the nation. They were sowing to themselves in sin, and they were reaping the harvest of that planting. Their crop was destruction and pain, and the ground had become hard and unable to bring forth good fruit, because the Lord had withheld the rain.

Hosea called the nation to begin to plant righteousness. They were to seek the Lord, do what was right, and then they would see the blessing of God poured out.

But the northern kingdom of Israel failed to do so, and they were conquered and destroyed because of their disobedient choices!

The same invitation, and the same warning, apply today. We are to sow in righteousness; then we will reap in the mercy of the Lord. "Whatsoever a man soweth, that shall he also reap" (Galatians 6:7).

Direction for today: We cannot earn our salvation through righteousness, but righteousness should be a by-product of our fellowship with God.

Prayer for today: "Father, may I grow in the righteousness of Jesus."

November 4: Read Hosea 11,12

Key verse: "They shall walk after the Lord: He shall roar like a lion: when He shall roar, then the children shall tremble from the west" (Hosea 11:10 NIV).

Once again, we see Israel pictured as the prodigal child. Though delivered out of bondage to Egypt, the prodigal continues in rebellion, totally oblivious to the tender hand of the father.

God is not one to drag us out, kicking and screaming, and push us in the proper direction. Rather, He lovingly leads us all the way. "As a man

213

would lead his favourite ox, so I led Israel with My ropes of love" (11:4 NIV).

As Israel appears bent on backsliding, the loving Father struggles with seemingly contradictory feelings of justice and love. He is angered by their sin, yet filled with compassion. To be true to Himself, a way had to be made to provide for both justice and love. A way *has* been made for us. Jesus, God's Lamb, was sent into the world so that, through His sacrifice, we might be redeemed from the curse of sin (Matthew 20:28).

One day, the Lion of Judah will roar, and His cubs will come bounding across the desert. He has gone to prepare a place for us so that we may be with Him! (John 14:3).

Doesn't that thrill you?

Direction for today: When the Lion of Judah roars, may it be to call you to Him, and not as a warning of judgment.

Prayer for today: "Thank You, Lord, that You lead me in love."

November 5: Read Hosea 13,14

Key verse: "I will heal their apostacy, I will love them freely, for My anger has turned away from them" (Hosea 14:4 NAS).

How infinite is the love and mercy of the Lord God!

Throughout this book, we have read of the terrible apostacy of the people of the northern kingdom of Israel. Despite their knowledge of all that the Lord God had done for His people from the time of the Exodus, Israel was unwilling to worship Him, and instead turned to the false gods of the former inhabitants of Canaan. They also suffered from the sin of pride. "Surely I have become rich, I have found wealth for myself" (Hosea 12:8), they say.

The sins of the people brought the wrath of God upon the nation. The prophet Hosea proclaims the forthcoming destruction of the nation, as God brings enemies upon His people. Yet, in the last chapter, we realize that God's punishment is not an end in itself. There is always His mercy, willing to grant forgiveness and restoration when His chastisement brings His people back to Himself. "I will heal their apostacy, I will love them freely" (Hosea 14:4).

The good news still holds today. No matter how far from God we may be, there is a way back — through faith in Jesus Christ. This will instantly bring us to a place of healing and love in the presence of God.

Direction for today: There is no sin or rebellion too big to disappear in the shadow of the cross.

Prayer for today: "Praise You, Father, that You 'love me freely'."

Joel

Hosea used the symbol of an unfaithful wife to show how God's people had been unfaithful to Him. Joel points to locust plagues as examples of God's judgment on His people.

We are not sure when Joel was written, and we know little about his personal history. The prophecy may have been spoken in the southern kingdom of Judah as early as 830 B.C., or the prophet may have ministered in the days following the return of the exiles, perhaps about 400 B.C.

The theme of the book is that the Day of the Lord is coming – a key point for God's relationship with His people. And, in Acts 2, we discover that Joel pointed prophetically to Pentecost as the inauguration of the new Day of the Lord. (Compare Joel 2:28:32 with Acts 2:17-21).

November 6: Read Joel 1

Key verse: "O Lord, to Thee will I cry . . ." (Joel 1:19 KJV).

Are you in a time of trouble, as you read this? Perhaps there are struggles in your family; it may be that you are in ill health; perhaps you have been hurt by a friend or someone in your church.

Whatever your need, the answer is the same: Jesus!

How often through the centuries have the people of God turned their faces heaven-ward and echoed the cry of Joel? "O Lord, to Thee will I cry!" Whatever our need, whatever our situation, if we call to the Lord from an open heart, He hears, and He answers!

Joel cried to the Lord, and received one of the greatest promises of the Old Testament, the promise of the outpouring of the Holy Spirit at Pentecost. Christians have cried out and found strength, healing, and inner peace.

It may be that your world seems to be crumbling around you. Remember, that world is nestled in the hand of God. Call out to Him, and He will answer you, and show you great and mighty things!

Direction for today: "Call unto Me, and I will answer thee, and shew thee good and mighty things, which thou knowest not" (Jeremiah 33:3).

Prayer for today: "Jesus, help me to remember to call unto You in every situation of life!"

November 7: Read Joel 2

Key verse: "Rend your heart and not your garments. Return to the Lord your God, for He is gracious and compassionate, slow to anger and abounding in love, and He relents from sending calamity" (Joel 2:13 NIV).

God is looking for those whose hearts are pure and contrite, who have humbled themselves before Him. The prophet Joel was making a strong plea for Israel to come back to God, to make their hearts right before Him.

"Rend your heart and not your garments." In Old Testament times it was a common practice to rend one's garments in repentance for sin. But God is saying He does not want the outer sign of repentance as much as He wants repentance from the heart.

In the times in which we live, it seems that everything is made easy: from disposable diapers to zip-lock sandwich bags. This is all very well, but the same attitude has at times made its way into the body of Christ. Salvation has been made to look *so* easy. The scriptures *do* say that everyone that calls on the name of the Lord will be saved (Joel 3:32), but Jesus Himself said, in Matthew 7, that not everyone who says "Lord, Lord" will enter into the eternal kingdom.

Where then is the balance? It is found in repentance.

God is looking for a people who will repent, turn away from the ways of the world and live for Him.

Direction for today: Is your heart broken and soft before the Lord?

Prayer for today: "Father, soften my heart and keep me a humble servant before You."

November 8: Read Joel 3

Key verse: "The Lord will be the hope of His people, and the strength of the children of Israel" (Joel 3:16b KJV).

War in the Middle East, sectarian violence in Northern Ireland, entire countries on the verge of bankruptcy, Russia and the U.S.A. building up their arsenals, acid rain and other forms of pollution destroying our environment. Is there no hope?

In the world today, this question is becoming more important and the answer is increasingly negative. As a people who know the Lord and know that Jesus is the only hope, the only light in the world that is becoming darker and darker, we must speak out.

This is not the time to hide our light under a bushel, or to look to pastors and fulltime evangelists to do the whole job for us. In a world whose standards and morals are based on the latest opinion poll rather than on the Word of God, we must stand firm on that Word.

As we take a stand for Jesus, He will be our strength and give us the words to speak.

Direction for today: Take a stand for Jesus, before your friends, co-workers and family.

Prayer for today: "Lord, if You give me the words to say, I will speak them."

Amos

Amos was a man of humble birth. He was a shepherd and an orchard worker, who lived and worked in Judah in the middle of the eighth century B.C. But this humble man was given two gifts from the Lord: he received visions from God, and he received a most difficult calling. Amos, a man of the southern kingdom in those days of political unrest, was sent by God to the northern state of Israel, there to proclaim a message of judgment from God.

He faithfully carried out this unenviable commission, publicly preaching harsh words of warning in the northern kingdom, and risking the results of extreme political unpopularity in order to obey his God.

Memory Verse

"The Lord is faithful, who will establish you and guard you from the evil one." 2 Thessalonians 3:4 NKJV

November 9: Read Amos 1,2

Key verse: "I will not revoke its punishment, because they rejected the law of the Lord and have not kept His statutes" (Amos 2:4 NAS).

God was about to bring judgment to the nations around Israel as well as Israel and Judah: His people, called by His name. But a proclaimer of judgment and punishment must have a shepherd's heart, so He called Amos the shepherd to be His instrument.

God judges justly. For very specific acts, actions and omissions He was going to punish each nation. His own people could not be excused because they were becoming like the nations around them. They were rejecting the Word of God.

I believe God is speaking to us today. We must reevaluate our Christian commitment. Are we truly God's people? Let us confess our sins, turn away from that which God abhors and truly exalt Jesus Christ in our lives.

Direction for today: The Lord is my shepherd, I shall not want.

Prayer for today: "Thank You, Lord, for supplying everything I need."

November 10: Read Amos 3,4

Key verse: "For behold, He who forms mountains and creates the wind and declares to man what are His thoughts, He who makes dawn into darkness and treads of the high places of the earth, the Lord God of hosts is His name" (Amos 4:13).

Oh, the majesty of this passage! The language of Amos is so rich in symbols and figures of speech. The magnificence of literary style seem only rivalled by some of the Psalms and portions of the book of Job.

Can't you feel the worship and adoration as Amos speaks of the power and glory of our Creator and Master? We need to remind ourselves of who this God is whom we serve.

Try beginning each time of prayer by praising God — not just saying "Praise you, Father; praise you, Jesus; praise you, Holy Spirit", but rather, speaking forth the reasons we have for praising Him. If you're not accustomed to doing this, you may be unable at first to think of much to say. But don't be discouraged, it will come, and you'll find that after a while you, too, will truly be filled with praise.

Direction for today: God is worthy of all praise.

Prayer for today: "Bless the Lord, O my Soul. Bless His holy name!"

November 11: Read Amos 5,6

Key verse: "For thus saith the Lord unto the house of Israel, See Me that you may live" (Amos 5:4 KJV).

God in His mercy so often grants individuals the opportunity of repentance, yet they do not return to Him. However, His mercy extends beyond human understanding. After pointing out Israel's continued state of rejection of Himself, the Lord continues in chapter five to make an appeal for these people to repent." "Seek ye Me and ye shall live" (vs. 4).

This is certainly a picture of God's love for today as well. We live in a world that rejects Him. We, as individuals, continue to go our many ways and reject God's love and yet He still says, "Seek ye Me and ye shall live."

In the wilderness, when the children of Israel were bitten by serpents, the Lord instructed Moses to raise a brass serpent and they would live. Jesus said to Nicodemus, in John 3:14, "And as Moses lifted up the serpent in the wilderness even so must the Son of Man be lifted up: That whoever believeth in Him should not perish, but have eternal life." Jesus was saying, "Seek Me and ye shall live."

To truly seek the Lord, we must surrender ourselves to Him in faith, accept His forgiveness, and serve Him daily. That can only be done as we repent of our sin and follow Him.

Direction for today: Life is found in following Jesus.

Prayer for today: "Lord, help me to seek after You today."

November 12: Read Amos 7,8

Key verse: "'Behold, the days are coming,' says the Lord God, 'when I will send a famine on the land; not a famine of bread, not a thirst for water, but of hearing the words of the Lord. They shall wander from sea to sea, and from north to east; they shall run to and fro, to seek the Word of the Lord, but they shall not find it" (Amos 8:11, 12 RSV).

After reading these words, I'm reminded of the time of King Josiah, when the law of the Lord was rediscovered after being hidden in the temple ruins. I also reflect on Psalm 137, in which is painted a picture of the people of Israel in exile. They're being taunted by their enemies as they sit and remember the days of glory in Judah. Both before the destruction of the temple and before the exile it's probably safe to say that the Israelites felt, "It'll never happen to us".

This is perhaps the way you also think. "A famine of hearing the Word of the Lord will never happen today", you say, "Not in our day!" Amos said that nowhere would the people be able to find the Word of the Lord. God forbid that should happen today!

Can we begin to appreciate what it would be like not to be able to hear the Word? What would it be like to live in a land in which the Word could not be found? A famine of the Word! "Never", we say, "not today." And yet?

God forbid we should ever take His Word for granted. Let us read and treasure it daily se we never have a famine and so it can always be found.

Direction for today: Think of all the reasons to praise God for His word.

Prayer for today: "Thank You, Lord, that I can always turn to Your Word. Help me to never take it for granted."

November 13: Read Amos 9

Key verse: *"In that day I will restore David's fallen tent. I will repair its broken places, restore its ruins and build it as it used to be"* (Amos 9:11 NIV).

The grace of God never ends. Amazing grace! Throughout the entire book of Amos, God is expressing His anger with the nation of Israel because of the pride of the people, their idol worship and their unfaithfulness.

And yet the Lord still offered restoration. He promised to restore, repair and rebuild. God said that He would do this for His people in spite of their sin.

We should thank the Lord continually for His continuing mercy. If He dealt with us as we deserve, none of us would be around to read these words! But despite our sins, failures and neglect, God is willing, ready and able to restore, repair and build our lives.

True confession and repentance will always result in God's gracious forgiveness — not because we are good, but because He is!

What a mighty God we serve. How unlimited is His patience, love and grace!

Direction for today: God can restore anything that is broken.

Prayer for today: "Lord, I bring to You a situation that needs to be restored by You (tell Him about that situation). I trust You to work a miracle."

November 14: Read II and III John

Key verse: *"Beloved, do not imitate what is evil, but what is good. The one who does good is of God; the one who does evil has not seen God" (III John 11 NAS).*

These short letters are quick glimpses into the life and doctrines of the early church.

The third letter of John deals with a problem that has been with the church from then until now — the presence, among belivers, of leaders with good motives and leaders with bad motives. Gaius, "beloved" of John (vs. 1), is a leader of this particular church, and he is commended (vs. 3). He is also a hospitable man, caring for the people of God as they travel in His service.

Diotrephes (vs. 9), is portrayed in sharp contrast to Gaius. Unlike Gaius, who served others with humility, Diotrephes "likes to put himself first", and refuses to allow travelling evangelists and leaders of the church to come into the congregation.

John leaves little doubt as to the seriousness of the proud and self-serving stand of this man . . . he is "imitating evil".

It is important to realize that both of these men are in the church of God — both are leaders of a particular congregation. We see, then, that our status in a church or Christian group indicates nothing about or relationship with God or our commitment to His work; all that matters, in the final analysis, is our standing before God.

Direction for today: Do everything to bring glory to God, and never to yourself.

Prayer for today: "Lord, help me to be like Gaius, a true and hospitable Christian."

Obadiah

We know very little about the author of this short book. His name means "Servant of the Lord", and thus may be a symbolic title. He preached a warning to the kingdom of Edom, proclaiming the wrath of God because of the country's enmity with the people of God. And he concluded his message with the familiar recounting of the coming day of the Lord and the restoration of Israel. Here again, we have loving evidence of God's assurances for His people, even in the worst times of the kingdoms of Israel.

November 15: Read Obadiah

Key Verse: *"The day of the Lord is near for all nations. As you have done, it will be done to you; your deeds will return upon your own head" (Obadiah 1:15 NIV).*

In this prophecy, Edom is denounced for her pride. Secure in their impregnable fortress (Petra), the Edomites felt that they were beyond the danger of invasion and conquest. Not only were they boastful, but they prided themselves on their wisdom. Although complacent in their belief that nothing could happen to them, divine humiliation was pending. Deceived by allies and friends, the Edomites would come to realize that neither their wisdom nor their might could save them (verses 1-9).

Is this judgment of Edom justified? The charges against her are clearly stated. In the day of Jerusalem's calamity, the Edomites had gloated and even surrendered fugitives to the enemy. They had been guilty of flagrant injustice (verse 10-14).

The day of the Lord will be a day of reckoning for all nations. Although it is the ultimate issue of history and is often spoken of as being imminent, its character, rather than its timing, is emphasized here.

Direction for today: The Day of the Lord is coming.

Prayer for today: "Lord, help me to be ready for the Day of the Lord; and may I do my part to prepare those around me for Your coming."

Jonah

Jonah is named for the main character of this book (see II Kings 14:25), who may not necessarily be its author. It is unlike the other minor prophets in that Jonah is essentially a narrative account.

The story of this book is unique, both in its detail about Jonah's flight from the Lord and subsequent stay in the belly of a great fish (see Matthew 12:38-41; 16:4), and in its account of a great turning to the Lord on the part of a heathen city, the great city of Nineveh.

We can learn from this book, much about the outcome of disobedience, and the fruits of repentance.

Memory Verse

"For there is one God and one Mediator between God and men, the man Christ Jesus, who gave Himself a ransom for all." I Timothy 2:5,6a NKJV

November 16: Read Jonah 1-4

Key Verse: *"So the people of Nineveh believed God, and proclaimed a fast, and put on sackcloth, from the greatest of them to the least of them" (Jonah 3:5 KJV).*

One of the terms used often in Christian circles is, "flowing in the Spirit." What does that really mean? Some believe this happens when a service is filled from one end to the other with supernatural works of healing and miracles. This *is* part of it, but it is much more basic than this.

Let's look at Jonah. Jonah was commanded by God to go to Nineveh and preach repentance. That didn't quite fit into his way of thinking, so Jonah went the other way. God judged him, he finally agreed to go, and a great revival swept through the city.

"Flowing in the Spirit" is meticulous obedience to God's written Word and to His direction in a believer's life. If Jonah had preached in Nineveh without God's direction, the revival would not have come. "Flowing in the Spirit" includes doing the works of God, but only as He directs.

Direction for today: Never try to hide from God; it is futile and foolish.

Prayer for today: "Thank You, Lord, that great revival and restoration can result from the preaching of Your Word."

Micah

The prophet Micah was a contemporary of Isaiah. His ministry, almost all of which was directed to the southern kingdom of Judah, may have covered a span of years as long as from 750-686 B.C. Micah railed against false and unspiritual leadership among the people of God. He prophetically attacked political leaders, economic oppressors and false prophets.

Micah had a clear vision of the relationship between the obedience of God's people and the threat of political enemies. He warned both the southern and northern kingdoms that their continued rebellion against God would result in political and military destruction.

November 17: Read Micah 1,2

Key verse: "Woe to them that devise iniquity and work evil upon their beds! When the morning is light, they practise it, because it is in the power of their hands" (Micah 2:1 KJV).

Micah is prophesying of the certain judgment that will come upon Israel because of evil practises. Israel was trusting, because of God's promises to their nation, that they could continue in evil and somehow be blessed. God never deceives the upright, but He will disappoint the hypocrites.

Psalm 1 tells us that the blessed man delights himself in the law of the Lord day and night. Instead of communing with God and recalling his Holy Word, there are those who lie awake scheming how they can defraud others for their own material gain. It is bad to do mischief upon a sudden thought, but much worse to devise it.

Some feel they are the "elect" and it gives them licence to continue in deliberate sin. James 1:22 says, "But be ye doers of the word and not hearers only, deceiving yourselves." Judgment is sure, but just as certainly with our repentance comes restoration by God.

Direction for today: "Woe" does not necessarily come upon people because God sends it; rather, they usually bring it directly upon themselves.

Prayer for today: "Lord, help me to keep my thoughts pure, so my life can be free from hypocrisy."

November 18: Read Micah 3-4

Key verse: "Come, and let us go up to the mountain of the Lord, and to the house of God of Jacob, that He may teach us about His ways and that we may walk in His paths" (Micah 4:2 NAS).

We live in a day of peace movements. "Ban the bomb", "stop war", people chant. We see pictures of men, women and children joining themselves into long chains of humanity to stop the increase of nuclear arms development; we read of others who go so far as to blow up factories which manufacture parts for nuclear weapons. Still others act as though they were really *for* war — committing acts of personal violence against those whose viewpoints differ.

What these peace activists don't realize is that their starting point for peace is all wrong. The prophet Micah would have us approach peace differently.

The Lord needs first to teach us His ways so we walk in His paths. It's only after we know the Lord's ways that we are able to walk in His paths. And it's only after people come to know the Lord that they have the desire to make instruments of peace out of tools of war.

If only we would do it the Lord's way! What a tremendous amount of energy we would save! What genuine peace there would be!

Direction for today: Know God, and you will know peace.

Prayer for today: "Thank You, Lord, for the peace that You give to Your children."

November 19: Read Micah 5-6

Key verse: "But thou, Beth-lehem Ephrathah, though thou be little among the thousands of Judah, yet out of thee shall come forth unto me that is to be ruler in Israel; whose goings forth have been from of old, from everlasting" (Micah 5:2 KJV).

The birthplace of our Saviour was foretold by Micah seven hundred years before Jesus was born. Micah was the only prophet who specifically said that Jesus would be born in Bethlehem.

Since nineteen of Judah's twenty kings had been born in the royal city of Jerusalem, it seemed unlikely that the Messiah-King would be born in Bethlehem.

All the circumstances surrounding the birth of Jesus seemed contrary to the fulfillment of this prophecy. Mary and Joseph were living in Nazareth, ninety miles from Bethlehem. But, because of a decree by Caesar Augustus of Rome concerning taxation, they had to travel to Bethlehem. And thus it was that the Saviour was born there.

The size of Bethlehem is also significant — "little among thousands of Judah". Christ is always born among the "little ones", in hearts humble enough to confess sin and acknowledge Him as Lord.

In the beatitudes we read, "Blessed are the poor in spirit: for theirs is the kingdom of heaven . . . Blessed are the meek: for they shall inherit the earth" (Matthew 5:3,5).

Direction for today: God will often use apparently insignificant things instead of the great or the impressive.

Prayer for today: "Lord, help me to be humble and simple enough that You can use me!"

November 20: Read Micah 7

Key verse: *"You will again have compassion on us; You will tread our sins underfoot and hurl all our iniquities into the depths of the sea" (Micah 7:19 NIV).*

Most of Micah's prophecies tell of troubles that will come on the world because of sin. These prophecies end with a summary that might have been written by one of our modern environmentalists: "The earth will become desolate because of its inhabitants, as the result of their deeds" (Micah 7:13 NIV).

But the book ends on a note of hope, because our God is still a God who pardons sin and forgives transgression, who does not stay angry forever, who delights in mercy (v. 18).

I may feel helpless and hopeless as I consider the magnitude and complexity of the world's troubles, but "it is better to light one candle than to curse the darkness". And I need to remember that, when Jesus comes into a life, the changes are usually gradual, rather than immediate.

If I will believe my sin is forgivable, that Jesus forgave me on the Cross, then with the help of His Holy Spirit I can see God straighten up the mess right around me, and trust Him to do the same for others.

Direction for today: The Lord "does not treat us as our sins deserve or repay us according to our iniquities" (Psalm 103:10).

Prayer for today: "Father, I praise You that my iniquities are dealt with and discarded at the cross of Jesus Christ."

Jude

> This short letter is the last of the "general epistles", that is, those sent to a general church audience instead of a particular church fellowship.
>
> The book is a strong warning against false teachers. Jude deals with the danger they present to the church, and to their own salvation! He also outlines the reaction true Christians should have, for we are called to faithfulness to Christ, mercy on the lost, and intense measures to "save others, snatching them out of the fire".

November 21: Read Jude

Key verse: "Now to Him who is able to keep you from falling, and to present you without blemish before the presence of His glory with rejoicing, to the only God, our Saviour, through Jesus Christ our Lord, be glory, majesty, dominion, and authority, before all time, and now and forever" (Jude 24,25 RSV).

In spite of all the rebellion, (verse 6) immorality, and unnatural lust (verse 7), rejection of authority and working of God (verse 8), contending with the devil (verse 9), greed and desire (verse 11), that goes on, Jude tells us how to stand clear of it all in order to escape "a punishment of eternal fire."

We can do that by building ourselves up in our most 'holy faith' . . . in other words, by reading God's Word, which produces faith, developing a personal relationship with Jesus and maintaining that relationship through prayer (verse 20). As we do so, God will keep us from falling and strengthen us to be the means of helping others.

Just think, you and I can, by listening to Jesus and being obedient to Him, be the means by which other people can be saved from eternal judgment.

Direction for today: Keep the faith.

Prayer for today: "Thank You, Lord, that You keep me from falling. Cleanse me of all my blemishes, and accept me into Your eternal kingdom!"

Nahum

While the dramatic account of the revival of Nineveh at the time of Jonah is undoubtedly true, in the book of Nahum we have evidence that the city returned to its wicked ways. This prophet, writing in the southern kingdom just before 612 B.C., predicts the downfall of Nineveh, a prophecy that was quickly fulfilled.

November 22: Read Nahum 1,2

Key verse: "The Lord is slow to anger and great in power" (Nahum 1:3 NIV).

If you were to go over this portion of scripture quickly, you could miss the message of love presented. Why? Because the main themes are judgment and destruction due to wickedness and idolatry in Nineveh.

This, of course, is not our first encounter with that city. In the book of Jonah we read of his reluctance to preach to the people of Nineveh and of their repentance when he finally did so. That was one hundred years prior to this time. The people had obviously returned to sinning against God, yet the Lord has been patient with them. Now He begins to reveal His power in justice.

We need to take courage today, however, as we are reminded that He is patient and slow to anger. Verse seven of chapter one also encourages us, for it states, "The Lord is good, a refuge in times of trouble. He cares for those who trust in Him" (NIV). The key is *trust*. As we trust in Him, He will not forsake us but will be our Strength and Protector.

God desires a people who will repent and live for Him. He keeps reaching out to us, calling us unto Himself. Have you responded to His call? If not, won't you do so right now?

Direction for today: God's desire is to deal with us through repentance, not judgment.

Prayer for today: "Lord, I pray that our country would turn to You in repentance and avoid Your hand of judgment."

"For God has not given us a spirit of fear, but of power and of love and of a sound mind." 2 Timothy 1:7 NKJV

November 23: Read Nahum 3

Key verse: *"O King of Assyria, your shepherds slumber; your nobles lie down to rest. Your people are scattered on the mountains with no one to gather them" (Nahum 3:18 NIV).*

Today's chapter is aimed especially at leaders in the churches of our land. Notice the terrible result whenever the leaders abdicate their responsibility: the people are scattered and the land is destroyed.

In the past few decades, a number of churches have gone through astounding changes. Some have abandoned many of the truths taught in the scriptures; others have rejected the miracle-working power of God. It is not surprising, although very sad, that the people of these churches often find themselves under attack, scattered and frightened. Why does this kind of thing happen? It is because the shepherds and the rulers went to sleep!

If you are a leader, be sure to remain awake, with your eyes fixed on Jesus and the Word of God. Allow the Holy Spirit to work in you in whatever way He will; do not quench the Spirit.

If you are a Christian in a church where the leaders have slipped into slumber, pray for them fervently. God can still restore your chuch, and win people to Jesus through it.

Direction for today: Shepherds, awake! Sheep, keep together and pray for your shepherd.

Prayer for today: "Lord, revive those churches which have fallen from the truth of the gospel."

Habakkuk

The date and biographical information concerning this book and its author are subjects of conjecture. No one is sure when Habakkuk lived or who he was, but one thing is clear – this prophet had received powerful inspiration from the Lord!

Habakkuk outlined the punishment of God's people for their disobedience in the first two chapters, but finished on a great note of triumph as the Lord delivers His people. Habakkuk was able to proclaim: "The Lord is my strength!"

November 24: Read Habakkuk 1,2

Key verse: *"How long, O Lord, will I call for help, and Thou wilt not hear? I cry out unto Thee, 'Violence!' yet Thou dost not save" (Habakkuk 1:2 NAS).*

Because of sympathy for his fellowmen, Habakkuk cried to the Lord as though he himself was in need of help. He asked 'Why, Lord, are the righteous oppressed while the evil prosper. Am I helpless to stop it?'

Surely thousands of Christians who have been wrongly accused, tortured, or put to death must have asked the same question: "Why?"

One of the greatest lessons of this book is to follow the example of Habakkuk. When he received no answer, he said, "I will stand on my guardpost and will keep watch to see what He will speak to me" (2:1).

In the midst of a Chaldean invasion, the prophet Habakkuk declared, "The righteous man shall live by faith" (Romans 1:7,17). And this message is still being proclaimed by Christians in every part of the world.

Direction for today: Remember your oppressed Christian brothers and sisters as though you were suffering with them.

Prayer for today: "Lord, rescue those Christians who are suffering under persecution."

November 25: Read Habakkuk 3

Key verse: *"Though the fig tree does not bud and there are no grapes on the vines, though the olive crop fails and the fields produce no food, though there are no sheep in the pen and no cattle in the stalls, yet I will rejoice in the Lord, I will be joyful in God my Saviour" (Habakkuk 3:17,18 NIV).*

This is truly the perspective of the believer. So often we get so caught upon in mundane concerns of the day-to-day world that we forget the larger picture.

God is the victor. Christians will spend all of eternity in heaven with Him. Our reward is sure; our Saviour reigns on high! Jesus has gone ahead to prepare places in heaven for us. We will live in resurrection bodies without pain or tears.

In the light of such realizations, a broken refrigerator, a car that isn't working, or a difficult exam at school somehow seem much less important.

That is what Habakkuk thought. In fact, he declared that even in the face of famine, drought and poverty, he would still rejoice in the Lord. Actually, he was only making sense — eternal sense!

Direction for today: Whatever my circumstances, I will rejoice in the Lord.

Prayer for today: "Father, I simply rejoice in You!"

Zephaniah

The prophet Zephaniah ministered in the southern kingdom after the fall of the north, during the reign of King Josiah (640-609 B.C.) Zephaniah was probably a relative of Josiah, a descendant of King David.

In the days of Josiah, spiritual reform was instituted, but it was not sufficiently wide-spread. Zephaniah looked ahead and saw that the people were not truly faithful, and that this would bring judgment from the Lord. But beyond that, he saw the restoration of a faithful remnant of God's people.

November 26: Read Zephaniah 1

Key verse: *"Those who have turned back from following the Lord, and have not sought the Lord, nor inquired of Him" (Zephaniah 1:6 NKJV).*

Our reading today does not paint a pleasant picture of which we would like to be a part. But perhaps God wants to give us lots of warning. He does not desire that anyone would perish but that all would come to repentance. Thank God that He has been patient with us, giving lots of opportunities to turn from our sins and unto Him. God's mercy is ever reaching out to draw us unto Himself. But, for many, all the opportunities in the world do not make any difference: they refuse to have anything to do with God.

Our key verse refers to many who once followed the Lord. As in the parable of the sower, perhaps Satan stole the word out of their hearts; perhaps they were offended by tribulations and persecutions; perhaps the cares of this life choked out God's Word. Whatever the reason for their turning away from Him, the Lord reminds such people that they are included in those to be judged. But, if they will repent and call on Him, they will be delivered from judgment.

Direction for today: God's abundant mercy gives us living hope.

Prayer for today: "Lord, give me the opportunity to restore to You a brother or sister who has fallen from faith."

November 27: Read Zephaniah 2

Key verse: *"Seek ye the Lord, all ye meek of the earth, which have wrought His judgment; seek righteousness, seek meekness: it may be ye shall be hid in the day of the Lord's anger" (Zephaniah 2:3 KJV).*

Pride is a destructive force. Solomon said, "Pride goeth before destruction, and a haughty spirit before a fall" (Proverbs 16:18).

Here Zephaniah prophesies the utter destruction of Nineveh, the capital city and crown jewel of the Assyrian empire.

Assyria was one of Judah's greatest and cruelest enemies. They had suffered under her domination. Nineveh was by far the largest of all the ancient cities. Protected by an inner wall 10 stories high and 50 feet thick, with towers 20 stories high, Nineveh seemed indestructible. The inner wall was protected by a moat 150 feet wide and a series of outer walls extending about half a mile outward. It is not surprising that the residents possessed a vaunted sense of their own superiority. They "dwelt carelessly" and flaunted their strength.

History reveals, however, that this once mighty city was completely obliterated within 50 years of her climax in power. How ironic that her destruction was so complete that, until the 19th century, her existence was thought, by many who did not believe the Bible, to be a myth.

As believers, we must be humble before God. We cannot afford to harbour pride in our hearts . . . spiritual or otherwise. Pride brings trouble (Proverbs 13:10), hardens our heart (Daniel 5:20), causes spiritual decay (Hosea 7:9,10), hinders our progress (Proverbs 26:12) and ultimately leads to destruction.

Direction for today: Pride goes before destruction.

Prayer for today: "Help me, Lord to walk humbly before You so that I may be lifted up to heavenly places in Christ."

November 28: Read Zephaniah 3

Key verse: "The Lord your God is with you, He is mighty to save. He will take great delight in you, He will quiet you with His love, He will rejoice over you with singing" (Zephaniah 3:17 NIV).

What wonderful promises! Our God is with us. If we live in that knowledge, our lives will involve constant communion with our Lord. Imagine that He walks beside you wherever you go; and then realize that it is true!

Not only is He there, but He is there to rescue you. He is mighty to save! There is no situation where God is not with you; there is no situation too difficult for Him. What a reason for complete trust! This is why we can be quiet in His love. Our rest in the Lord is the child-like rest of complete assurance. We rest in the Lord with no doubts concerning our safety, or our peace.

And did you know that God delights in you? When you live according to His will, He is delighted. We rejoice in God, but God also rejoices in us. Your obedient, joyful life brings joy to the Creator of the Universe!

Direction for today: Live to bring joy to the Lord.

Prayer for today: "Thank You, Lord, that I can rest in Your love."

Haggai

Haggai is a prophet of the post-exilic period; that is, he lived after the days of Ezekiel and Daniel, who were exiled in Babylon. Haggai returned from the captivity to minister to those who had come back to Israel to begin to rebuild the country. He is mentioned in the book of Ezra (5:1 and 6:14). In this book, we find the prophet involved in rebuilding the temple, which had been destroyed when the Babylonians sacked Jerusalem.

November 29: Read Haggai 1,2

Key verse: *"Thus speaketh the Lord of hosts, saying 'This people say, "The time is not come, the time that the Lord's house should be built"... 'Is it time for you, O ye, to dwell in your ceiled houses, and this house lie waste?'" (Haggai 1:2,4 KJV).*

Fourteen years had passed since the work had ceased on the Temple (Ezra 4:24). The people in Haggai's time could give many reason why it was not the time to renew their efforts: the opposition of the Samaritans, their own poverty, the losses they had sustained from bad harvests, the many long hours they had to work in the fields.

Disregarding all possible excuses, Haggai said, "Consider your ways". How can you expect to enjoy the comfort of your own house while the house of God remains in ruins? "Consider your ways"—think about what has happened to you! Why is it that you reap a bad harvest? Why is it that you are never satisfied? Why is it that your wages are not meeting your needs? Why is it that you look for much and get so little?

"But seek ye first the kingdom of God, and His righteousness; and all these things shall be added unto you" (Matthew 6:33).

Direction for today: Are your priorities God's priorities?

Prayer for today: "Father, may I always put Your priorities first."

Memory Verse

"We should live soberly, righteously and godly in the present age, looking for the blessed hope and glorious appearing of our great God and Saviour Jesus Christ." Titus 2:12b,13 NKJV

November 30: Read Zechariah 1-3

Key verse: *"'For I,' declares the Lord, 'will be a wall of fire around her, and I will be the glory in her midst'" (Zechariah 2:5 NAS).*

It is a beautiful promise of God that He will be our protection against the attacks and temptations of the world.

In our society today, we are encouraged, directly and indirectly, to build walls around ourselves and to "take care of number one". We are perfectly safe behind our walls because if no one knows who we really are then no one can hurt us.

When we come to the Lord we must, by an act of our own will, be willing to knock down those walls we have so carefully built up, day by day and month by month. This is not so that He can see in, for He knew us even before we were formed in our mother's wombs, but as an act of surrender. It is a way of saying to the Lord, and to the world, "I trust in the Lord to protect me, to be my wall of fire and the glory in my midst".

Direction for today: You can take care of the Lord's business, because He is taking care of yours.

Prayer for today: "Lord, help me build bridges instead of walls."

12

The Peace of Christmas

*It begins in November. "Christmas is coming,"
we are reminded by displays set up way ahead of
time in most stores. It seems we just can't wait
to start preparations for the festive season.
Coloured lights frame frost-tinted windows,
wreaths hang from our doors and
pine cones decorate our mantles.*

*Over on the coffee table, or perhaps on the
mantlepiece, piano or by the window, a group of
miniature shepherds and wise men have
gathered. Some stand silently, others kneel
beside the small child who sleeps soundly,
despite the tiny animals who curiously crowd in
around Him. Jesus, the Christ of Christmas,
born to bring peace to the world His Father
loved so much, lies quietly in a manger.*

*"Buy now – don't leave things until the last
moment this year!" Thus the advertisements
shout at us. So we listen and get busy doing all
we can to make **this** Christmas a "success".
Every day becomes important. Our calendars are
carefully marked and unlike most months
of the year, we have something planned
for every weekend. The closer we get to
Christmas day, the more frazzled we feel.
Isn't it ironic that the Prince of Peace should
find so little peace on His birthday?*

*This Christmas, let us allow the Lord to take us
back to the peace of that special Holy night. Put
away the whirl of Christmas this year and find
the stable. It was there that God reached out
to a world lost in sin and gave us Jesus,
the Christ, who has **never** stopped
reaching out to us!*

– Karen Fawcett Shepherd

233

Zechariah

Zechariah shared the mission of Haggai. Together, they urged the returned exiles to rebuild the temple, the spiritual symbol that God was the central figure of all Hebrew life. He ministered around the year 520 B.C., at the beginning of the return from Babylon.

His concern was for the immediate restoration of the nation, but the Spirit of God brought him a message far beyond his time on the earth. Zechariah prophesied a great deal concerning the coming Messianic age as well.

December 1: Read Zechariah 4-6

Key verse: "This is the word of the Lord to Zerubbabel: 'Not by might nor by power, but by my Spirit,' says the Lord Almighty" (Zechariah 4:6 NIV).

That is God's battle plan. It is His direction for the lives of individual Christians, for the spread of the gospel, and for the building of the church.

At times in history, countries which believed themselves to be "Christian" tried to use the might of armies to win converts to Christianity. It was folly. There have been occasions when a family has tried to force a son, daughter or husband to accept Christ. This, too, was futile.

The kingdom of God will be built by His Spirit. The might or the power of man is nothing beside the power and authority of the Holy Spirit. When the Spirit moves, things happen that could never take place through all the efforts of human beings.

We need to learn to step aside, abandon our own carnal efforts, and allow the Spirit to work, in us and through us. There is the true source of power — power to change the world!

Direction for today: Forget might and power and allow the Holy Spirit work.

Prayer for today: "Lord, work in me, and through me, by Your Holy Spirit."

December 2: Read Zechariah 7,8

Key verse: "Let us go with you, because we have heard that God is with you" (Zechariah 8:23b NIV).

In its context, this is a prophetic pronouncement about the nation of Israel. But it should also apply to the Christians in our day.

We often believe that no one in our society is interested in the gospel. But the truth is that we are surrounded by people who are spiritually starving. If that were not true, the counselling telephones at 100 Huntley Street would be silent, and they never are.

People want to know the answers to life. They long to know if there is real meaning to their existence; if there is any way the emptiness in their lives can be filled.

Often, they have tried many other solutions, only to find that none of them work.

Christian, be brave. Be willing to put your testimony on the line. When people hear that you know God, some may run, and some may mock — but others will come to learn of Him from you.

Direction for today: There is really no such thing as a "silent witness".

Prayer for today: "Lord, may it be said of me, 'We have heard (or seen) that God is with you'."

December 3: Read Zechariah 9,10

Key verse: "Rejoice greatly, O daughter of Zion; shout, O daughter of Jerusalem: behold, thy King cometh unto thee: He is just, and having salvation; lowly, and riding upon an ass, and upon a colt, the foal of an ass" (Zechariah 9:9 KJV).

Zechariah's message was to the returned exiles, far more than words of comfort and encouragement. It was a message of hope, foretelling the coming King of Kings.

This prophecy was fulfilled in part when Jesus entered Jerusalem, "riding upon an ass" (Matthew 21:2-5).

But the cires of "Hosanna" were soon changed to, "Crucify Him!" The King was rejected and betrayed for only thirty pieces of silver (Matthew 26:15; compare Zechariah 11:12; also compare Matthew 27:3-5; Zechariah 11:13).

But Zechariah foretold of a time when the King would return and His will would be done "in earth, as it is in heaven" (Matthew 6:10). All evil will be removed, and His people shall reign with Him. "and the Lord shall be king over all the earth . . ." (Zechariah 14:9), and a spirit of "HOLINESS UNTO THE LORD" (14:20) will prevail.

We have the wonderful privilege of living after fulfillment of our Lord's earthly ministry and in the expectation of His soon return.

Direction for today: Rejoice, because the King has come to you personally!

Prayer for today: "Hosanna; the King reigns!"

December 4: Read Zechariah 11,12

Key verse: "And it shall come to pass in that day, that I will seek to destroy all the nations that come against Jerusalem" (Zechariah 12:9 KJV).

The phrase that appears about seven times in this chapter is "in that day". A specific time is in focus for the events pictured in these chapters. In chapter 11, there is the prophecy regarding the price that would be

235

paid for the betrayal of the Lord Jesus Christ. Following this is the reference to the false shepherd, who would come in specific relationship to the nation of Israel.

The restoration of Israel as a nation, which took place in our generation, was essential for the fulfillment of the prophecies of chapter 12 to be realized. The complete occupation of the city of Jerusalem by the children of Israel was another essential ingredient in this all important event.

The attitude held by many nations regarding present day Israel is significant. Zechariah talks about Jerusalem being a burdensome stone to all nations. Many today have their eyes on this strategic city but are being held in check. Others look upon Israel with apprehension, keenly aware that the events in the entire Middle East are centred around that small nation.

The time referred to in our key verse, "in that day", could very well be near at hand. The prophetic time clock has already been set, but only the Omniscient God knows when the hour will strike. How thankful we should be that our God is still in charge of the affairs of our universe!

Direction for today: Although we do not know what the future holds, we do know who holds the future.

Prayer for today: "Lord Jesus, may I be ready when You return."

December 5: Read Zechariah 13,14

Key verse: "And I will put this third into the fire, and refine them as are refiner's of silver, and test them as gold is tested. They will call on My name, and I will answer them. I will say, 'They are My people' and they will say, 'The Lord is my God'" (Zechariah 13:9 RSV).

It's probably true to say that none of us, if we had the choice, would choose to be refined in fire. But if the alternative to being refined is to be cut off and to perish (13:8), I'd choose to have the Lord refine me.

In the natural, refining is done to bring out impurities. Heat is applied and the dross is boiled out. What's impure has to come out because of the heat that's applied.

In the same way, the Lord uses refining processes on us to produce purity within us. He applies various forms of "heat" to bring out the impurities in us, not because He enjoys seeing us "boil".

Our gracious Father applies heat to us so we may be those who are His people; that's why we are refined and tested.

Direction for today: If God is your God, then you are one of His people.

Prayer for today: "Lord, refine me and test me, that I might be pure."

Malachi

Malachi is one of the latest books of the Old Testament, possibly the last to be written. He probably ministered in the period after the temple had been rebuilt by the returned exiles.

His message is one of love and warning: he declares God's love for His people, but warns against falling back into the sinful patterns that led to His severe punishment of them.

December 6: Read Malachi 1-4

Key verse: *"For I the Lord, do not change; therefore you, O sons of Jacob, are not consumed" (Malachi 3:6 RSV).*

This is perhaps the most important truth in the scriptures: *God does not change* In a world in which values and apparent morals change week by week; in lives in which our emotions can swing from one end of the pendulum to the other; in relationships which change from day to day; in circumstances which take surprising turns, we can turn to this one foundational truth: *God does not change!*

On this focal statement hangs the basis for our faith. The same God who created the world brand new, from out of nothing, is the God who promises to create in us a new heart (See Genesis 1:1; Psalm 51:10). The same God who expressed His love for His people in the earliest days of Israel (Deuteronomy 7:13) also expressed His love in the ultimate Way, through Jesus Christ His Son (John 3:16). This love continues unchanged, available to each one of us. *God does not change!*

As we have read these books of the prophets, we have learned much about our Lord and God. He is a God of justice and truth, of righteousness and holiness; a God who will judge wickedness but will always deal in mercy and love with those who will repent of sin and turn to Him. This God, proclaimed by Malachi and Nahum and Joel and Ezekiel, is the same God of justice and mercy. *God does not change!*

Almost every other religion in the history of the world has included capricious gods — imaginary or diabolical deities who changed with their own whims, who were capable of good or evil, who were made in the image of fallen man. But our God is not at all like that. *God does not change!*

On this eternal truth rests the faith of all true believers. Praise our everlasting Lord!

Direction for today: The Lord does not change; He will always be the protector of His people.

Prayer for today: "Lord, may my love for You also be unchanging."

The Revelation to John

This complex and fascinating final book of the Bible is usually enti-
tled, "The Revelation to John", but perhaps the best title is found in the
first words of the book: "The Revelation of Jesus Christ".

John, probably Jesus' best friend among the disciples, is given a
new Revelation of the Lord. Jesus is seen as the final Judge, the conquering holy Warrior. The book sweeps across thousands of years of
human history, as the writer first conveys messages from Christ to
seven churches of Asia Minor, and then proceeds to record visions
and revelations that reach to the end of time, and the beginnings of the
new heaven and the new earth.

There is no Biblical book that has engendered more contention; this
is because of the interpretation of these often cryptic revelations. Yet
there is no book that contains clearer promises of victory in the Lord
Jesus Christ.

Memory Verse

*"I thank my God, making mention of you always in my prayers, hear-
ing of your love and faith which you have toward the Lord Jesus and toward all saints." Philemon 4,5 NKJV*

December 7: Read Revelation 1

**Key verse: "I am He who lives, and was dead, and behold, I am
alive forevermore. Amen. And I have the keys of Hades and of
Death" (Revelation 1:18 NKJV).**

One need not look much further to discover a great many basic truths
about the gospel of Jesus Christ. Here, as the Lord identifies Himself to
John in the first chapter of this wonderful Revelation, He makes it very
clear who He is.

Someone once wrote: "Born — lived — died/An all-purpose epitaph
for every man." Those three words will be true of all of us, if things unfold
as they have since creation. But they are not true of Jesus. He was born,
He did live, and He did die. But more: He is *not dead*, for He is risen and is
"alive forevermore".

And, wonderful news, we can share in that "life forevermore", because
when Jesus rose from the dead, He returned with the keys of death and
hell (Hades — the place of the dead). He has unlocked the bars of that
great eternal prison house, opened wide the gates, and invited to us to
spend eternity with Him!

And so the epitaph, for those who are followers of Christ Jesus, changes to "Born — lived — born again — living forevermore with Jesus"!

Direction for today: As we are excited about the return of Jesus, let us also remember to pray for the salvation of those who have still not received Him as their Saviour.

Prayer for today: "Lord, bring many unbelievers into the kingdom."

December 8: Read Revelation 2

Key verse: "I have this against you, that you have left your first love. Remember, therefore, from where you have fallen, and repent and do the deeds you did at first" (Revelation 2:4,5 NAS).

The message to the church at Ephesus was directed specifically to those particular members of the body of Christ. But that message might also be the overall purpose of the entire book of Revelation: to remind Christians of the scope and magnitude of the spiritual battle between Christ and the enemy, and to call us all to "front-line" involvement.

Each of us would do well to examine ourselves, asking if we, too, may have cooled from our first love. It is important to remember that these Ephesian Christians had much about their Christian stance to commend them — Jesus spoke of their patient endurance and their rejection of false prophets. Yet their love for Him had dimmed, and despite their continuing works they were in danger of being "removed" from a place of service.

Direction for today: If I am not as close to Jesus as I once was, it is not Jesus who has pulled away!

Prayer for today: "Lord, may I love You with the same intensity and commitment as when You first saved me."

December 9: Read Revelation 3

Key verse: "Remember therefore how thou has received and heard, and hold fast, and repent. If therefore thou shalt not watch, I will come on thee as a thief, and thou shalt not know what hour I will come upon thee" (Revelation 3:3 KJV).

Today's reading covers the letters to the churches of Sardis, Philadelphia, and Laodicea. Scholars see a different period of dispensation represented in each church, so these three churches today represent three different periods in history, each with its spiritual condition.

The church at Sardis is a dead church (Revelation 3:1 KJV). The church needs a revival, a new start in the walk of holiness. There are a few, nonetheless, in Sardis who "have not defiled their garments; and they shall walk with me in white: for they are worthy" (verse 4). An invitation is extended for all to awake and overcome this state of spiritual paralysis. "He that overcometh, the same shall be clothed in white raiment; and I will not blot out his name out of the book of life, but I will confess his name before My Father, and before His angels" (3:5 KJV).

The church of Philadelphia is one of the two that received no rebuke from the Lord (the other was Smyrna). Verse 8 says, "I know thy works: behold, I have set before thee an open door and no man can shut it: for thou hast a little strength", and we believers should not rest, satisfied in little, but should strive to grow in grace, to be strong in faith, giving glory to God. To this church Christ says, "I have set before thee an open door, and no man can shut it". Some scholars see the church of Philadelphia in the period of the great missions of the last century, in which more missionary work was done than any period before.

The church of Laodicea has been suggested to be the picture of the church of the 20th century: the lukewarm church, self-centred and self-satisfied. The Lord's rebuke to this church is harsh, "I know thy works, . . . thou art wretched, and miserable, and poor, and blind, and naked" — but in verses 20 and 21, He turns His reproach into a message of love. "Behold, I stand at the door and knock: if any man hear My voice, and open the door, I will come into him and will sup with him, and he with Me" (Revelation 3:20 KJV).

Direction for today: Hold fast to the faith that has saved you.

Prayer for today: "Lord, help me to endure in faithfulness to You."

December 10: Read Revelation 4-5

Key verse: "Worthy are Thou, our Lord and our God, to receive glory and honour and power; for Thou didst create all things, and because of Thy will they existed and were created" (Revelation 4:11 NAS).

Chapter four records what must have been a most dazzling view of the glory of God and the reaction of those around Him. Then a scroll appears, into which everyone wants to look. But they are unable to do so because of the seals which no one is worthy to break; no one, except the Lamb. When it is announced that the Lamb, Jesus, is able to break the seals because of His conquering life, all heaven seems to burst out in spontaneous praise and worship and singing.

And thus it should be! For no one but this same Jesus is able to break the seals on our lives, and set us free to worship and to know Him!

Direction for today: Let him that glories, glory in the Lord!

Prayer for today: "Worthy art Thou, O Lord. Worthy art Thou."

December 11: Read Revelation 6,7

Key verse: "They are before the throne of God and serve Him day and night in His temple; and He who sits on the throne shall spread His tabernacle over them. They shall hunger no more neither thirst anymore, neither shall the sun beat down on them, nor any heat; for the Lamb in the centre of the throne shall be their Shepherd, and shall guide them to springs of the water of life. And God will wipe every tear from their eyes" (Revelation 7:15-17).

The sixth chapter of Revelation introduces the most awesome period of time the world has ever known. This was decreed by God for the primary purpose of shaking man loose from a false sense of security. The first of the three chronological judgments — seals, trumpets and vials - is set forth in chapter 6. The seal judgments cover approximately the first quarter of the Tribulation, or the first twenty-two months. The four horsemen present the picture of man's inhumanity to man. They seem to be a divine prediction of the affairs of man which will cause much human suffering.

Chapter 7 tells us that at the beginning of the Tribulation there is a great soul harvest throughout the world. The opening of this fifth seal teaches that, after this harvest has begun, there will be a time of great personal persecution for the children of God. These, then, are the Tribulation saints. When the sixth seal is opened, the earth is violently shaken by a giant earthquake, indicating that it is a great day of God's wrath. It indicates His displeasure following the persecution of His saints.

A great revival is yet to come. It will not occur within the Church Age, but during the Tribulation period. This coming worldwide revival is prophetically described in the seventh chapter of the book of Revelation, appearing right after the seal judgments to indicate that it takes place during the first twenty-one months of the Tribulation. The primary converts will be Jews from all the tribes, and Jews will also be evangelists.

Direction for today: Look forward to that day when God will wipe every tear from your eyes.

Prayer for today: "Lord, thank You for the place You are preparing for me!"

December 12: Read Revelation 8,9

Key verse: *"And in those days men will seek death and will not find it; and they will long to die and death flees from them" (Revelation 9:6 NAS).*

Chapter 7 had offered us a respite from the recounting of fierce judgment. In today's reading, however, we return to vivid descriptions of the results of the justice of God being meted out:

"peals of thunder and sounds and flashes of lightening and an earthquake" (8:5).

"there came hail and fire, mixed with blood . . . and a third of the earth was burned up, and a third of the trees were burned up, and all the green grass was burned up" (8:7).

"Something like a great mountain burning with fire was thrown into the sea; and a third of the sea became blood" (8:8).

"a third of the creatures, which were in the sea died and a third of the ships were destroyed" (8:9).

"a third of the sun and third of the moon and a third of the stars were smitten" (8:12).

"the bottomless pit was opened; and smoke went up out of the pit, like the smoke of a great furnace; and the sun and the air were darkened by the smoke" (9:2).

Locusts were loosed upon the earth and permitted to torment the people for five months; "and their torment was like the torment of a scorpion when it stings a man" (9:5).

Little wonder that men would seek death. And Chapter nine goes on to tell of frightening scenes of death and destruction. But what amazed me upon first reading this passage is found in verses 20 and 21: "And the rest of mankind . . . did not repent of the works of their hands, so as not to worship demons and the idols . . . and they did not repent of their murders . . . sorceries . . . immorality nor of their thefts".

How, we ask, can men be so rebellious and stupid? How could their 'understanding become so darkened'?

Direction for today: You stand at the brink of hell, to prevent as many as you can from leaping in. Do not despair. Do not give up.

Prayer for today: "Lord, turn my unsaved friends and relatives to Yourself."

December 13: Read Revelation 10,11

Key verse: *"The kingdom of the world has become the kingdom of our Lord and of His Christ, and He shall reign for ever and ever" (Revelation 11:15 RSV).*

This climactic announcement, familiar the world over through Handel's magnificent "Hallelujah Chorus" in the "Messiah", is the ultimate answer for political turmoil. Eventually, the complexities and confusion of man's rule of man will end, the injustice and self-interest of our political systems will be no more, and Jesus will rule on the throne of the universe, finally acknowledged as King of kings and Lord of lords. And He shall reign for ever and ever!

That is good news to everyone who now acknowledges Jesus as King and Lord. But, as we read in the accompanying verses in these chapters, it will be very bad news to all who set themselves in opposition to the plan of God.

The coming of the Kingdom of Peace ruled by Christ will be preceded by the judgments wreaked upon the millions of rebels against God.

Jesus *will* rule over all things. We can welcome this Lordship, now, individually, or we can suffer as traitors and rebels when His kingdom is established, overriding all opposition. The choice is clear!

Direction for today: Jesus, who now reigns in Your heart, will one day reign over a new heaven and a new earth.

Prayer for today: "Hallelujah — the victory is Yours, oh Lord!"

"God, who at various times and in different ways spoke in time past to the fathers by the prophets, has in these last days spoken to us by His Son." Hebrews 1:1,2a NKJV

December 14: Read Revelation 12,13

Key verse: *"And they overcame Him by the blood of the Lamb, and by the word of their testimony; and they loved not their lives unto the death" (Revelation 12:11 KJV).*

Those who overcame the great "accuser" did so in three ways. First and foremost by the blood of the Lamb - Jesus Christ. We are justified freely by the blood of Christ (Romans 3:24). Through the atoning blood of Jesus, who was the *final* sacrifice, we have the victory! Our Lord's victory at Calvary avails for those who follow Him!

Secondly, they overcame by the "word of their testimony". This was a witness borne on behalf of the matchless power of God! The redeemed bear witness of their Redeemer. Overcomers stand up for Jesus. Overcomers are undaunted by seeminly insurmountable circumstances and stand firm upon the promises of God. The enemy cannot stand up against the testimony of the saints.

Lastly, they "loved not their lives unto death." Although John had the martyrs in mind, it is clear that this same quality of devotion is expected from all followers of Jesus. Paul said: "None of these things move me, neither count I my life dear unto myself, so that I might finish my course with joy and the ministry, which I have received of the Lord Jesus, to testify the gospel of the grace of God" (Acts 20-24).

Your struggles are not to be shrugged off as insignificant, for they are part of a great conflict between good and evil. Satan has opposed Christ from the beginning and continues to oppose His followers. Though the enemy's power is very real, he is *not* victorious. He knows he has already been beaten and has little time left. He is powerless against the redeemed of God!

Direction for today: Greater is He that is in you than he that is in the world. Believe that!

Prayer for today: "Thank You, Jesus, that You are the Overcomer!"

December 15: Read Revelation 14

Key verse: *"Here is a call for the endurance of the saints, those who keep the commandments of God and the faith of Jesus" (Revelation 14:12 RSV).*

There is much of importance in this chapter of the Lord's message to John: The picture of the Lamb and the 144,000 on Mount Zion; the voice of the Lamb and the new song of the saints; the angels and their ministries, and the call for endurance.

We rejoice over each of these, but today we need to consider endurance. If the devil can't get us to sin deliberately and overtly, he can tempt us to become discouraged and to give up.

The dictionary defines endurance as, "the power to last, to withstand hard wear . . . the power to stand something without giving up; holding out; bearing up." Christians need to develop the ability to "hang in there". Countless circumstances can discourage us and cause us to give up, but our Lord wants us to endure.

From this verse, it would apper that endurance comes by way of obedience to God's commands and continuing in the faith. This is the same faith which Abraham possessed, the same faith of the three men in the fiery furnance, and it is our faith. It's the faith which knows that our God *WILL* . . . And because God *WILL*, we can endure.

Direction for today: True believers are believers who endure.

Prayer for today: "Father, give me grace to endure."

December 16: Read Revelation 15,16

Key verse: "And they sang the song of Moses the bond-servant of God and the song of the Lamb, saying, 'Great and marvellous are Thy works, O Lord God, the Almighty; righteous and true are Thy ways, Thou King of the nations" (Revelation 15:3 NAS).

This song was sung by those who had confessed Christ, defied the beast and had been victorious. Their song is reminiscent of the triumphant song of the Israelites after they had crossed the Red Sea (Exodus 15).

The scene of rejoicing and praise comes in the midst of the destruction of the sinful, and the pouring out of the wrath of God. So it is that we are able to be calm and peaceful — even joyous — in the midst of turmoil and havoc, so long as we have the assurance of the love and forgiveness of God. *Nothing* can compare with the peace this brings.

Direction for today: Those who endure, triumph!

Prayer for today: "Righteous and true are Thy ways, Thou King of the nations."

December 17: Read Revelation 17

Key verse: "These will make war with the Lamb, and the Lamb will overcome them, for He is Lord of lords and King of kings; and those who are with Him are called, chosen, and faithful" (Revelation 17:14 NKJV).

"The Lamb will overcome!" What a triumphant statement! Jesus Christ, "the Lamb of God who takes away the sins of the world" (John 1:29) will overcome! Jesus, the sacrifical Lamb who took our place so that our just penalty might pass over us, to Him, will overcome!

Although this is a statement that refers to the final, ultimate triumph over the enemies of God, it is equally true today. For Jesus has already, surely, won the victory. If He had not, these prophecies in the book of Revelation would be speculation, not truth! The victory now belongs to Jesus, the Lamb.

Perhaps, in your life today, you need a taste of that victory. Come to the Lamb of God, and spiritual peace and victory will be yours. Perhaps you feel defeated by temptation, sin, or circumstances. Look up, for the Lamb has aready won your victory!

You have been chosen; be faithful, and you will be a conqueror!

Direction for today: "In the world you have tribulation, but take courage; I have overcome the world" (John 16:33 NAS).

Prayer for today: "Father, give me the strength to be an overcomer in Christ."

December 18: Read Revelation 18

Key verse: "In one hour such great wealth has been brought to ruin!" (Revelation 18:17 NIV).

Many empires and kingdoms have been built. The irony of the situation is that kingdoms and empires take years to build but God can destroy them in less than an hour.

God's judgment edifies the saints and destroys the sinners. He has total control over all situations. An example of this was when the Roman Empire fell. It took years and years of wars, construction, and rules to build such an empire. People were baffled by its fall. Saint Augustine wasn't mystified at all. He pointed out that all great things can be destroyed through God.

Whether it takes a second or an hour, or many years, God will build up His work and destroy evil.

The great thing about today is that Jesus Christ wants to build you up. He wants to edify you by adding His character to your life. Love, Joy, Peace are only a few attributes He wants in your life. In one hour, great wealth can be brought to ruin; but Jesus Christ's wealth lasts forever.

Direction for today: Build in Christ; it will last forever.

Prayer for today: "Lord, may I never put my trust in material security."

December 19: Read Revelation 19

Key verse: "Hallelujah! For our Lord God Almighty reigns. Let us rejoice and be glad and give him glory!" (Revelation 19:6-7 NIV).

What a spectacular scene we see portrayed in Revelation chapter 19! God is seated upon His throne. From the throne John hears, "what sounded like the roar of a great multitude in heaven" and "what sounded like . . . the roar of rushing waters and like loud peals of thunder" (Revela-

tion 19:1 and 6). This is John's description of the praises that were offered to God around His throne in heaven.

These praises were of jubilant adoration, exaltation and thanksgiving. God was, indeed, who He said He was and had done what He said He would do. The 24 elders and the four living creatures could do nothing but fall down before the throne and join their worship and praise, proclaiming God as "King of kings and Lord of lords".

One need not wait for the "great day" spoken of here in John's revelation, to approach God's throne and enter into praise such as is described in this chapter. The majestic worship of God can be experienced today by surrendering the occupancy of the throne of our lives to Him. When God is acknowledged as Lord, His love causes our praise to become joyous, filled with thanksgiving for His continuous blessings.

Direction for today: Praise and bless God, and He will in turn bless you.

Prayer for today: "Hallelujah; for the Lord our God the Almighty reigns!"

December 20: Read Revelation 20

Key verse: "Blessed and holy are those who have part in the first resurrection. The second death hath no power over them, but they will be priests of God and of Christ and will reign with Him for a thousand years" (Revelation 10:6 NIV).

In reading this chapter, our conclusion can only be that God has everything in control. That should be a comfort as we face the frustrations of

246

daily life. It would seem, at times, that everything is out of control and Satan is having his way. To some degree that is true, as Satan does seek out those whom he can destroy and he does influence lives.

On the other hand, it must be remembered that, although we have a free choice and Satan can tempt us, the final outcome depends on our response to the Lord.

Our God is a powerful God who is in control. We can put our trust and confidence in Him and know that He has the final say.

Direction for today: Remember that, whatever the weaknesses and ills of your present body, you will spend eternity in a new resurrection body!

Prayer for today: "Thank You, Lord, that I shall reign with You."

Memory Verse

"Confess your trespasses to one another, and pray for one another, that you may be healed. The effective, fervent prayer of a righteous man avails much." James 5:16 NKJV

December 21: Read Revelation 21

Key verse: *"And I heard a loud voice from the throne saying, 'Now the dwelling of God is with men, and He will live with them. They will be His people, and God Himself will be with them and be their God'" (Revelation 21:3 NIV).*

Almost all of the history of man has been spent in waiting — waiting which was necessitated only by our foolish and evil sin. God originally established His dwelling place with man, in the Garden of Eden. But Adam and Eve foolishly decided that that was not good enough. They sinned, broke fellowship, and were banished from the Garden.

And the waiting started. Mankind has been waiting for the re-establishment of God's dwelling with them.

For a short while, God dwelt among us in Jesus. That was the first stage of the great reconciliation. The waiting was almost over. Within a few weeks of Jesus' return to heaven, the Holy Spirit came to dwell within every believer. That was stage two of God's plan. But still, the world is clogged with sin, and plagued with death.

Finally, God will call history to an end, and we will see Him, face to face. The dwelling of God will again be with men, and it will be sinless, perfect and eternal.

Direction for today: When God dwells with mankind, be there!

Prayer for today: "Lord, thank You that You love us enough to give all of mankind a second chance to live with You for eternity!"

December 22: Read Revelation 22

Key verse: "Come, Lord Jesus" (Revelation 22:20).

If only all Christians were sincerely and constantly breathing that prayer, what a difference it would make in the lives of individuals, and in the life of the world.

"Come, Lord Jesus." As we prayed this, we would be declaring Jesus as our Lord, and we would be longing for the day when that Lordship was finally completed, and we will, physically and literally, dwell with Him.

"Come, Lord Jesus." We would be constantly aware that history will some day come to an end, and that everything we have done that pertains only to this world will be swept away. Would we not then focus more on the eternal things?

"Come, Lord Jesus." We would also remind one another that, when history ends, so will the opportunity of the lost to be saved. And our prayer should give impetus to our desire to bring many many more into the family of God before the final culmination of all things (Revelation 21:8).

"Come, Lord Jesus." As we come into His presence in this prayer, we will be more and more aware of the sweetness of a life lived close to Jesus. Our lives will change; we will be more and more like Him.

Let us pray: "Come, Lord Jesus!"

Direction for today: As the Bible ends with an invitation, our mission as people of God begins: we are to extend this invitation to come to the Lord.

Prayer for today: "Come, Lord Jesus."

December 23: Read John 1:1-23

Key verse: "The Word became flesh and lived for a while among us. We have seen His glory, the glory of the one and only Son, who came from the Father, full of grace and truth" (John 1:14 NIV).

Matthew and Luke begin their gospels with the miracle of the birth of the Son of God. John looks at the greatest miracle from an even wider perspective. He makes it very clear who this man, Jesus, really is: the Word, who became flesh, was truly and completely God.

John's term, "the Word", is a marvellous description of Jesus' mission on earth. Jesus came to earth to bring us the glorious message that God loves us. God loves us so much that He was willing to live among us, and to die for us!

The One who created all things, was born in a manger and died on a cross, carrying your sin and mine.

Jesus walked this earth to carry the message of love; He came to bring "light" to a world that had stumbled in darkness for centuries. And although many in the world preferred the darkness, some responded to the light. And those that responded and believed the Word became children of God.

What a message! What a miracle!

Direction for today: When God speaks through His Son or through His word, it only makes sense to listen!

Prayer for today: "Praise You, Jesus, that You chose to live among us. Praise You that You live in my heart right now!"

December 24: Read John 1:1-23

Key verse: "'I am the Lord's servant,' Mary answered. 'May it be to me as you have said'" (Luke 1:38 NIV).

Has anyone ever been given a more difficult task? Mary was a young girl, and a virgin. She was betrothed to a respectable businessman, and was eagerly expecting her wedding.

And then her life was thrown upside down. She must have thought she was dreaming when an angel appeared to her. The dream took on even more bizarre overtones when the visitor announced that she was going to have a child.

She protested that she was a virgin, but Gabriel insisted that God would bring this miracle to pass. All of the implications must have rushed through Mary's mind: the scandal, the questions, the impact this would have on her marriage plans. But Mary was well chosen; she was a true servant of God.

She simply said, "I am the Lord's servant." This was an answer of immense faith, and unquestioning obedience. She did not know how this would all work out, but she trusted God.

Mary is a wonderful example to all who seek to serve the Lord.

Direction for today: When God speaks, obey.

Prayer for today: "Father, I am Your obedient servant."

December 25: Read Luke 2:1-20

Key verse: "And she gave birth to her firstborn, a son. She wrapped Him in strips of cloth and placed Him in a manger, because there was no room for them in the inn" (Luke 2:7 NIV).

This is where it all begins: a healthy baby boy born in a stable, and cradled in a manger. Close by are a young mother, and a faithful foster father.

John said that Jesus "became flesh". Luke shows us that He did so in the most humble manner imaginable. This baby was to grow through childhood, and to spend His early manhood as a simple carpenter. When the word tells us He is able to identify with our temptations and troubles as human beings, it speaks the full truth. Jesus lived as a boy and man; God in flesh, God living a simple life in a small country in the Middle East.

Who would have guessed that the humble birth was the greatest miracle in the history of the world? Who would have guessed that this baby in a manger would transform history, and change the lives of millions of people who have learned to worship this Jesus Christ.

And who would have guessed that a small baby in a manger would defeat Satan, death and hell to rule over all creation, for all eternity. But, praise God, it is true, the truth that sets all believers free!

Direction for today: On this Christmas Day, give thanks for the greatest gift imaginable.

Prayer for today: "Lord Jesus, I worship You."

December 26: Read Matthew 2:1-12

Key verse: "Where is the one who has been born King of the Jews? We saw His star in the east and have come to worship Him" (Matthew 2:2 NIV).

Very few people near Bethlehem knew what had taken place in their village. Almost no one else was aware of the birth of the King. Herod, the tyrannical ruler of the land, was greatly surprised to hear of another king in his country.

But while most of the residents of planet earth missed the significance of the greatest moment in history, the rest of the universe was hushed with anticipation. Heaven was watching intently, and angels appeared on several occasions to announce the great event. On the night of Jesus's birth, angels startled a group of simple shepherds with cosmic harmony soaring through the heavens.

Even the stars and planets seemed to sense the great moment. And one certain star was ablaze with the news — news that wise men interpreted correctly. Praise God, that He has allowed us to share in the celebration!

Direction for today: Like that star, Christians should shine with the great news we have to share!

Prayer for today: "Praise You, Lord of the Universe!"

December 27: Read Matthew 3

Key verse: "I baptize you with water for repentance. But after me will come one who is more powerful than I, whose sandals I am not fit to carry. He will baptize you with the Holy Spirit and with fire" (Matthew 3:11 NIV).

Like Mary, John the Baptist had an unenviable task. He was called by God to risk his life, and his work eventually caused his execution! He was to awaken the attention of the people of Israel. Then, when everyone was following him, John knew he must deflect all of the attention to a man who he knew both as his cousin, and as the Lamb of God, the Baptizer in the Holy Spirit.

He put all of his own ambitions and desires to one side, and obediently served the Lord. He prepared the way for Jesus and announced the mission of the Son of God.

Jesus, said John, had come to initiate an entirely new way of knowing God. Jesus would baptize His followers in the Holy Spirit.

Until then, the people had known God from afar. When Jesus sent the Holy Spirit, God came to dwell in the hearts of His people. God's power was suddenly at work in individual lives. John's humble obedience properly prepared the way for all of the miracles to follow.

Direction for today: Be obedient to the Lord.

Prayer for today: "Lord, I submit to the complete control of Your Holy Spirit."

Memory Verse

"Therefore humble yourselves under the mighty hand of God, that He may exalt you in due time, casting all your care upon Him, for He cares for you." I Peter 5:6,7 NKJV

December 28: Read Matthew 13:1-23

Key verse: "But what was sown on good soil is the man who hears the word and understands it. He produces a crop, yielding a hundred, sixty or thirty times what was sown" (Matthew 13:23 NIV).

How is your heart? It is often good for believers to take what might be called a spiritual ECG — an examination of the condition of your inner being.

This well-known parable of the soils is often applied only to unbelievers, as an explanation of why some people respond to the gospel, and others turn away. But Christians can have heart problems, too, and can find their hearts have become hard.

Look at the results of the sowing in the story. Has your heart become rocky, so that you don't hear God's voice anymore? Or have you remained a shallow, baby Christian ever since you first met Jesus? Perhaps your life has become crowded with material concerns which are choking out your faith.

It is not too late. Allow the Lord to soften your heart, and receive the good seed of the Word of God.

Direction for today: Keep your heart soft, ready to receive the word of the Lord.

Prayer for today: "Lord, help me to produce fruit unto righteousness."

December 29: Read Luke 6:20-38

Key verse: "Be merciful, just as your Father is merciful" (Luke 6:36 NIV).

These are great words with which to enter a new year. In this pointed teaching by Jesus, we learn much about God's expectations for us as we live out the life of a believer.

The key to this teaching is mercy: God has been so merciful to each of us, and He expects us to show mercy to others with whom we share our lives.

The warnings to the rich are clear statements of how our lives should *not* be lived. We are to show active love to those who mourn. If you live out your faith this coming year, your life will include people who you may have never encountered before.

Perhaps the most difficult command is to love our enemies. This love is not supposed to be merely verbal declarations: we are to do good to those who hate us, bless those who curse us, and pray for those who would mistreat us.

Obedience to these commands will significantly alter the lifestyle of most Christians. But to disobey would be to rebel against God.

Direction for today: Show the love of Christ to everyone you encounter.

Prayer for today: "Lord, help me to love with the love of Jesus."

December 30: Read John 3:1-21

Key verse: "For God so loved the world that He gave His one and only Son, that whoever believes in Him shall not perish but have eternal life" (John 3:16 NIV).

It is no accident that this is the best known verse in the Bible. This is the gospel in a nutshell; it tells the whole story.

We have read half of the Bible in the past twelve months. If is good to focus, today, on the essential, and to apply it to ourselves individually.

Here is the truth: God sent Jesus to live, and to die, because He loved *you*! You are an object of the love of God. He has lavished the most precious thing in the universe on you — His love.

But He did not stop there. Not only has He given you His love, He has also given you the gift of eternal lfie. You need not spend eternity where each of us should rightfully be: in the eternal death of hell. You need not perish for God has offered the gift of eternal life.

Direction for today: If you have received God's wonderful gifts, praise Him! If not — why not?

Prayer for today: "Thank You, Lord, for Your great gifts."

December 31: Read John 10:1-18

Key verse: "I am the good shepherd; I know My sheep and My sheep know Me" (John 10:14 NIV).

At midnight tonight, we enter a new year. In our troubled world, that may not seem like good news.

It is true that there seem to be many reasons to fear the future: there is danger of war, of violence in our cities, of families falling apart.

So isn't it wonderful to know that Jesus, our Good Shepherd, will lead us step by step, each day of this year and the rest of our lives. Our Shepherd protects us; He guides us; He provides all of our needs.

When we recognize our Good Shepherd, we realize that we have nothing to fear. We can rest safely in His fold. Stay close to the Good Shepherd, today, tonight, and in all the days to come, and you will have peace and joy all the days of your life. And you will dwell in the house of the Lord forever!

Direction for today: A wise sheep stays close to the Shepherd.

Prayer for today: "Jesus, I thank You that You will be with me through each day of the coming year."

Notes

Notes

Notes